# The Social Psychology of Groups

*The Social Psychology*

*of Groups*

# JOHN W. THIBAUT
*University of North Carolina*

# HAROLD H. KELLEY
*University of Minnesota*

NEW YORK · JOHN WILEY & SONS, INC

LONDON · CHAPMAN & HALL, LTD

# The Social Psychology
# of Groups

LIBRARY OF CONGRESS CATALOG CARD NUMBER  59–11813

PRINTED IN THE UNITED STATES OF AMERICA

# *Preface*

In the summer of 1953, upon finishing an earlier work (Kelley
and Thibaut, 1954), we agreed that for our next joint project
the order of authorship would be reversed  The continuation of this
agreement is indicated by the order in which our names appear on the
title page of this book  The order of authorship shown there does not
signify any difference in our respective contributions to the thought or
writing. It is highly unlikely that either of us could have written this
book alone, and we assume equal responsibility for its strength and
weaknesses

On that earlier occasion we resolved that if ever given an appropriate opportunity we would write a textbook for the small group field
Such an opportunity presented itself when both of us were able during
the year 1956–1957 to accept appointments as Fellows at the Center
for Advanced Study in the Behavioral Sciences, Stanford, California
The unusually favorable circumstances at the Center encouraged us—
even inspired us—before beginning to write to take a long and fresh
look at the basic theoretical problems of the small group field. As a
result, we devoted most of the first half year to the luxury of developing and following out the implications of what we believe to be a
rather new approach to the old problems of interdependence, attraction to the group, power and control, status evaluations, social norms,
etc. When the goal of producing a book finally reasserted itself, it was
clear that our textbook had also to be a presentation of this theoretical
viewpoint

Despite the attempt to be systematic and cumulative, it must be
admitted that this end product of our efforts has a very eclectic appearance  We have borrowed freely, as we saw fit and needed to

borrow, from conceptions originating in such areas as economics, learning theory, and sociology. Ideas have been used that best fit the demands of clear understanding and internal consistency without concern for their disciplinary origins. The selection of concepts and
assumptions was not guided by any explicit a priori conception of what
a theory of interpersonal relations should be. They were selected
(and we would justify them) only on the grounds that they seem to
"work" (i.e., they fit or "explain" the data) and they "feel" right (i.e.,
they seem internally consistent and do not violate our intuitions) We
claim no innovations in regard to basic ideas We have merely selected
and revamped for our purposes a number of notions that are already
part of the intellectual equipment of most social psychologists

The refurbishing of old ideas for new purposes inevitably creates
problems of disagreement about meanings In numerous instances
we have tried to give rather delimited conceptual definitions to such
familiar notions as "power," "attraction to the group," "status," and
"group goal"—definitions related to our basic assumptions and more
or less consistent with one another Once a concept had been defined,
we tried to adhere to the prescribed meaning and not to attach to it
any connotations from prior usage. We must ask the reader to do the
same—to avoid bringing to these terms any of the additional meanings
they may have for him. This problem might have been avoided by
the use of neologisms, but this, in our estimation, creates other and
more serious problems. In some instances an attempt has been made
to show how our definition or usage relates to existing ones, but a
thorough practice of this procedure would have cluttered the text
needlessly and overtaxed our capacities for scholarship.

The approach presented here does not flow from our own research
efforts (although the reverse process is already in effect) but from our
familiarity with the research literature of the field and a strong desire
to keep theory and data as intimately related as possible. Of course, a
theory written now inevitably poses questions that past research cannot answer, so we have often resorted to anecdotes and authoritative
statements in lieu of better evidence. On occasions, when the point
seemed important enough, speculation has even been permitted to slip
the leash of evidence entirely. We hope the text provides enough
cues to the quality of various pieces of evidence that even the unwary
reader can distinguish the more from the lesser proven assertions.

It is with some reservations that we have used the designation
"theory" for what we present. The reader will not find here a deduc-
tive system that poses questions for research and also proposes, in the

form of research hypotheses, the answers  He will find an attempt
to analyze a variety of important phenomena in the same limited set
of simple terms and to show the interrelatedness of phenotypically
diverse research findings  The main value of our work, we believe,
is to highlight interconnections and to point out important research
areas without necessarily suggesting the answers to be found there.
Perhaps what we present is better described as a "point of view" or
"framework" rather than a theory.  In the first two chapters there is
a number of comments about the nature of this approach and its relation to existing theories  These are offered very tentatively, in full
awareness of the limitations of our own perspective as a basis for judging and classifying our own work.  In the final accounting the reader
must make these judgments for himself.

JOHN W. THIBAUT
HAROLD H. KELLEY

*Chapel Hill, North Carolina*
*Minneapolis, Minnesota*
*June 1959*

# *Acknowledgments*

It would be difficult to exaggerate our indebtedness to the center for Advanced Study in the Behavioral Sciences The opportunity there provided for intensive thought and study without the interference of interruptions or the pressures of deadlines is to be found in none of the other situations open to the contemporary social scientist These special circumstances enabled us to set a much higher goal for our work than otherwise would have been possible and to adopt a time perspective suited to its attainment To the staff of the Center and their total devotion to the welfare and freedom of the Fellows we shall always be indebted The stimulating input from our colleagues at the Center must also be mentioned prominently among its facilitative features. Kenneth Arrow, A. H. Halsey, William Lambert, Theodore Newcomb, Richard Savage, Harrison White, and John Whiting contributed in various and important ways to our work.

Our most sincere thanks are extended to Kurt Back, Nicholas Demerath, Leon Festinger, Edward Jones, Harold McCurdy, Lloyd Strickland, Edmund Volkart, and Ben Willerman for their comments and criticisms made after reading preliminary versions of the manuscript. They are not, of course, to be held responsible for errors or deficiences appearing in the final version

We are much indebted to Fred Heinzelmann, David Mechanic, and Roland Radloff for their careful and skillful library assistance. The preparation of the manuscript in its various revisions was provided by Jill Geer Ballesteros, Patricia Berger, Joanne Landau, and Diana Thompson, and to them we are very grateful.

Our "home" universities provided support for this book in many direct and indirect ways We here acknowledge the consistent support of the Institute for Research in Social Science of the University of North Carolina and the Laboratory for Research in Social Relations of the University of Minnesota

Acknowledgment should certainly be made of the various persons who have contributed to our intellectual orientation to group psychology Although their specific concepts do not figure prominently in our present approach to this field, the attitudes toward research and theory expressed by Kurt Lewin and others of the original Research Center for Group Dynamics at the Massachusetts Institute of Technology form a central and enduring part of our outlook

Last, but certainly not least, to our wives and children, who uncomplainingly withstood the uprooting moves and periods of neglect associated with the preparation of this book, we lovingly dedicate any rewards therefrom.

J W. T.<br>H H. K

We wish to thank the following publishers for permission to reprint excerpts from the indicated works Addison-Wesley Publishing Company for G W Allport, *The Nature of Prejudice*, and material by H H Kelley and J W Thibaut in G Lindzey (Ed ), *Handbook of Social Psychology*, The American Psychological Association and the respective authors for materials by T M Newcomb in *American Psychologist*, by L. Berkowitz, B Bettelheim, C Bondy, and A. J. Spector in *Journal of Abnormal and Social Psychology*, by J W Atkinson in *Journal of Experimental Psychology*, by R. S. Lazarus, J Deese, and Sonia F Osler in *Psychological Bulletin*, and by Helen L Koch in *Psychological Monographs*, The American Sociological Society and the respective authors for portions of articles in the *American Sociological Review* by E. Benoit-Smullyan, N S. Hayner and E Ash, W E Vinacke and A. Arkoff, and R F Winch, T Ktsanes and Virginia Ktsanes, Appleton-Century-Crofts for E. R. Hilgard, *Theories of Learning;* and E A. Ross, *Principles of Sociology;* Richard Christie for material from *An Experimental Study of Modifications in Factors Influencing Recruits' Adjustment to the Army*, Duke University Press for material by K. Lewin from *Character and Personality*, reprinted in Gertrud Lewin (Ed ), *Resolving Social Conflicts* (Harper and Brothers), and material by C D Smock in *Journal of Personality; Educational and Psychological Measurement* for material from an article by W. E. Martin, J G Darley and N Gross; The Free Press for A. W. Gouldner, *Patterns of Industrial Bureaucracy*, T Parsons and

R F. Bales, *Family, Socialization and Interaction Process;* and H L. Wilensky, *Intellectuals in Labor Unions,* Harcourt, Brace and Company for H I Hogbin, *Law and Order in Polynesia;* and G. C. Homans, *The Human Group;* Harper and Brothers for L Festinger, S Schachter and K Back, *Social Pressures in Informal Groups,* E T. Hiller, *Social Relations and Structures,* Gertrud Lewin (Ed), *Resolving Social Conflicts,* M Sherif, *The Psychology of Social Norms,* M. Sherif and Carolyn Sherif, *An Outline of Social Psychology,* and G. E. Simpson and J M Yinger, *Racial and Cultural Minorities An Analysis of Prejudice and Discrimination,* Henry Holt and Company for material by A. Davis, B B Gardner and Mary Gardner in G. E. Swanson, T M. Newcomb and E L Hartley (Eds), *Readings in Social Psychology,* material by K Lewin, from G. Watson (Ed), *Civilian Morale,* reprinted in Gertrud Lewin (Ed), *Resolving Social Conflicts* (Harper and Brothers), S. Potter, *The Theory and Practice of Gamesmanship,* and *One-upmanship,* R F. Winch, *The Modern Family,* and W. W. Waller and R. Hill, *The Family* (originally published by the Dryden Press), Houghton-Mifflin Company for F. H. Allport, *Social Psychology,* Longmans, Green and Co for Helen H Jennings, *Leadership and Isolation,* McGraw-Hill Book Company for A W Green, *Sociology An Analysis of Life in a Modern Society,* W W Norton and Co, for E. A. Cohen, *Human Behavior in the Concentration Camp,* and H S Sullivan, *The Interpersonal Theory of Psychiatry,* Princeton University Press for S A. Stouffer, E A. Suchman, L C DeVinney, Shirley A Star and R M Williams, *The American Soldier· Vol I Adjustment during Army Life,* and material by E Stein and Suzanne Keller in *Public Opinion Quarterly,* Rinehart and Co, for R. M MacIver and C H Page, *Society An Introductory Analysis, Scientific American* for material by W Heron, State University of Iowa for material by M L Farber in the *University of Iowa Studies in Child Welfare,* Tavistock Publications, Ltd, and the respective authors for portions of articles in *Human Relations* by Pamela Bradney, F Merei, B H Raven and J. Rietsema, and R. C Ziller, *Time* for material reprinted in M Sherif and Carolyn Sherif, *An Outline of Social Psychology* (Harper and Brothers); University of Illinois Press for F E Fiedler, *Leader Attitudes and Group Effectiveness;* The University of Liverpool Press for W H. Scott, J A. Banks, A. H. Halsey, and T Lupton, *Technical Change and Industrial Relations,* University of Minnesota Press for R Rommetveit, *Social Norms and Roles* (copyright by Akademisk forlag, Oslo), The William Alanson White Psychiatric Foundation for portions of articles in *Psychiatry* by R. J. Lifton, and E H Schein, John Wiley and Sons for A Chapanis, W. R. Garner and C T Morgan *Applied Experimental Psychology Human Factors in Engineering Design,* J. K Folsom, *The Family and Democratic Society;* A B Hollingshead, *Elmtown's Youth,* Williams and Wilkins Company for R. L Dickinson and L. Beam, *A Thousand Marriages,* and for portions of articles in *Social Forces* by S Adams, F L Bates, and R. K Merton.

# *Contents*

# 1.

## *Introduction*

In this book is presented a theory of interpersonal relations and group functioning. The major motivation that governed this effort was a desire to give cumulative treatment to a discussion of some persistent problems in social psychology and to answer for ourselves the question how do the data of the field look when they are arranged by their relevance to a conceptual structure that begins with relatively simple assumptions and adds further ones only as they become necessary? If it is not entirely idiosyncratic, any success along these lines might be expected to be useful both as a guide to research and in contributing some order and simplification to an increasingly bewildering congeries of fact

What kind of theory should one construct for this purpose? From the very first books with *social psychology* explicitly in the title, quite different answers to this question have been suggested  The book by the psychologist William McDougall (1908) was mainly an attempt to identify and classify the various social motives  In the same year the sociologist Edward A Ross initiated a contrasting tradition for social psychology by defining its distinctive mission as the analysis of social interaction  In the years since 1908 many writers on social psychology have implicitly accepted the injunction of Ross to concern themselves with social interaction  To mention merely a few of these, we might point to Dashiell's (1935) comments on the social situation as a "reciprocal affair" in which each person is "stimulable and reactive," Cottrell's (1942) reinforcement analysis of the "interact pattern," Lewin's (1947) interpretation of dyadic interaction as a "three-stage process," Bales's (1950) extensive discussions of interaction in small decision-making groups, and Sears's (1951) S-R references to "double

*1*

contingency" in the "social episode" It is in the tradition of social psychology represented by these works that the present book is written

Some of the implications of Ross's injunction, to begin with social interaction, may be seen by considering the distinctive aspects of social interaction that are revealed when it is compared with the simpler situation with which individual psychology has traditionally dealt In the typical experiment in psychology the subject is in some manner under the management of the experimenter, who controls the presentation of stimuli, the opportunities for behavior available to the subject, and, most importantly, the provision of diverse incentives and rewards for behavior In general, by these various means, the experimenter exerts control over the behavior of the subject, and the procedures by which he does so constitute the independent variables of the experiment The behaviors that the subject actually emits constitute, of course, the dependent variables.

In these experiments it is usually assumed that the subject has no counter-control over the experimenter What the subject does makes no difference to the investigator (at least if he is thoroughly in his scientific role of impartial seeker of truth), and even if it does make a difference it cannot be permitted to cause him to deviate from his pre-arranged schedule of activities This assumption must be valid if the two sets of variables are to have the status of *independent* and *dependent*, in which the former can be viewed as antecedent to the latter in causal efficacy

The situation is sharply different when social interaction is considered. The simplest situation is that in which two subjects interact in response to a task set by the experimenter The possibility is now introduced that each subject will exercise control over the other We attempt to develop some of the substantive implications of this kind of reciprocal control in the subsequent chapters of the book We now merely note that methodologically the complexity that is added by reciprocal control may be denoted by the loss of a clear separation between independent and dependent variables Each subject's behavior is at the same time a response to a past behavior of the other and a stimulus to a future behavior of the other, each behavior is in part dependent variable and in part independent variable, in no clear sense is it properly either of them.

If it is true that free social interaction leads to an ambiguity about what is dependent and what is independent, and since social psychology is traditionally committed to the use of experimental methods as at least an important part of its technical repertoire, how has investigation proceeded? The answer seems to be that the problem has been largely bypassed. This will be seen more clearly in a brief description of some of the main types of social-psychological research. In all of these some degree of experimental control has been maintained

One of the most commonly used procedures in social psychology involves the presentation to an individual subject of a social stimulus fixed by the experimenter. For example, the subject may be required to make judgments of emotions from photographs of facial expressions, to respond to the various items of an attitude questionnaire, or to indicate his most likely response to (verbal descriptions of) hypothetical situations. Similar in principle is the use of a "live" or a tape-recorded *stimulus person* in research on social perception and of preinstructed experimental accomplices in certain types of experiments

Social research of the sort outlined in the preceding paragraph need not be different, at least in degree of experimental control, from standard experimental work with individual subjects. Social interaction per se is not studied and the experimenter controls the task presented to the (individual) subjects. There does exist, though, a type of research in which social interaction clearly occurs but is not the explicit or main object of study. These are investigations in which a group or collectivity of persons replaces the individual subject and which focus on the effects of variations in aspects of the group's environment (e g, the task or external threat) or properties of the group (e g., leadership style or composition of membership) as they bear on the performance (or morale) of the group. These studies are basically similar to those with individual subjects described above, except that some processes exist in the group studies (social interaction) which do not exist in the individual studies. The interaction itself is not usually studied. When he is primarily interested in discovering predictable regularities between properties of the group's environment (or of the group itself) and rates of group performance, the investigator may choose to ignore (or to describe only casually in passing) the processes of social interaction that intervene between the independent and dependent variables. The investigator's choice may be very wise if he can safely assume that the intervening processes will contribute only a random variability that is small in relation to the potency of his independent variable and the sensitivity of his dependent one. That so many studies of this sort have been successful in discovering these over-all regularities and uniformities is surely some evidence that this assumption is frequently valid. Nevertheless, social interaction is a worthy object of study in its own right. In the chapters which follow we attempt to develop an approach to the study of interaction that permits at the same time a consideration of the more traditional research of social psychology

The approach to be proposed takes as its independent variables the possibilities for reciprocal control possessed by the members of a collectivity. Only that control mediated by the ability to affect another person's outcomes (such as rewards, payoffs, reinforcements, and utilities) is considered, although for reasons given in Chapter 2 this limitation is not felt to be very restrictive  Thus the analysis begins with a description of the way in which two or more individuals are interdependent in achieving favorable outcomes  The dependent variables are the various aspects of a relationship that can be viewed as outgrowths of the particular pattern of interdependence present there  These include properties of the interaction process, norms, and roles.

In other words, we start with a description of the problem that confronts a number of people if a continuing relationship among them is to be viable  This problem is defined in terms of the possibilities the participants have for contributing to or detracting from each other's outcomes  Our theory, then, is in large part a set of hypotheses about the important dimensions of this problem—that is, about the significant variations in the patterning of their interdependency  The description of the relations of objective interdependency that characterize a designated set of persons dominates the discussion throughout the book and gives it whatever unity and cumulative character it may have.

Once their objective interdependency has been described, it becomes possible to determine what the members of the collectivity *should do* if their relationship is to be viable, stable, and optimally satisfactory  But the actual course of the interaction and its products can be congruent with the expectations the theory sets for them only if it is assumed that the actors have accurate understanding of their problems of interdependency and have the necessary insight into the required social solutions or the opportunity to develop such solutions by some learning process or transfer of training from similar situations. In dealing with this transition from the objective interdependency to interactive behavior, our interest is clearly psychological. Just as the student of perception concerns himself with discrepancies between objective phenomena and subjective representations of them, our focus is upon the perception and understanding of objective interdependency and factors affecting the veridicality of these perceptions. But let it be emphasized that these problems are meaningful only if means exist of describing the "stimulus"—the objective structure of interdependent relations. Distortions and inaccuracies of cognition are revealed by comparing actual social processes with those predicted from the objective potentialities mentioned above.

Rather simple psychological assumptions are made to account for discrepancies between the objective situation and the actual social behavior (or, for that matter, for correspondence between these two) We accept as a basic premise that most socially significant behavior will not be repeated unless it is reinforced, rewarded in some way  No stand has been taken as to the range of events that may constitute rewards for the individual This we believe is a matter for empirical research Some of the events reported to have reward value in studies of interpersonal relations are discussed in Chapter 3 At times we have been tempted to invoke certain special social motives (e g , a need for power or status) to explain specific phenomena That we resisted this temptation is not to deny the existence of such motives nor to deny the importance for social psychology of a careful analysis of them (in the manner of McClelland, et al , 1953, for example) However, since the list of such motives is still an open-ended matter and an indefinite number of plausible ones may be added, the appeal to a motive to explain any given social phenomenon seems both too "easy" and too unparsimonious A genetic learning approach seems rather unsatisfactory at present for the same reasons As long as the early conditions of learning are not known in complete detail, one may too easily refer to plausible learned drives or acquired reinforcements as the need arises

The theory that we propose seems on balance to be primarily a  functionalistic one. The central concern is with the solutions that must be found to problems created by interdependency These solutions are implicitly evaluated against standards set by the conditions necessary for group viability. Thus the focus is first of all upon what is functional from the point of view of the group or social relationship However, an equally strong interest in the adaptations of the individual follows immediately Because the existence of the group is based solely upon the participation and satisfaction of the individuals comprising it, the group functionalism becomes an individual functionalism The ultimate analysis then is in terms of the vicissitudes of individuals as they try out various adaptations to the problems confronting them The adaptations of interest to social psychology are necessarily carried on jointly because the common problems of interdependency impinge upon all of the members, though in somewhat different ways The adjustment one individual makes affects the adjustments the others must make, which in turn require readjustment of the first, and so on   Nevertheless, whatever the social processes by which individual adaptations are coordinated and reconciled, the implications of the adaptations for the collectivity are constantly in the forefront of the theoretical purview.

In the analysis that follows we begin with the two-person relationship, the dyad   We so begin in order first to attempt to understand the simplest of social phenomena by endeavoring to be as clear and as explicit as we can about the conditions necessary for the formation of a dyadic relationship and about the interpersonal relations manifested there   Our bias on this point is apparent   we assume that if we can achieve a clear understanding of the dyad we can subsequently extend our understanding to encompass the problems of larger and more complex social relationships   Hence we devote what may appear to some readers as a disproportionate amount of space to the problem of the functioning of the dyad: most of the nine chapters that make up Part I of the book   The basic concepts that we use throughout the book are introduced, defined, and illustrated in our analysis of the dyad.   It is our conviction that these concepts have general applicability beyond the dyad   We attempt later on to document this conviction in our discussion of complex relationships in Part II.

# PART I

*Dyadic Relationships*

# 2.

# *Analysis and Concepts*

In this chapter are presented the basic elements of a theory of small groups. Since these elements are used in analyzing and developing the topics covered in all later chapters, an understanding of the present chapter is a prerequisite for reading the later ones

The building of any theory of social behavior requires making a great many simplifying assumptions  The phenomena considered are entirely too complex to be dealt with in their raw form  Many of the nuances and variations in social behavior must be disregarded if the human observer with all of his limitations is to detect any recurrent patterns. We have tried to be as explicit as possible in introducing our assumptions  However, in this very explicitness it may strike the reader that we have *overly* simplified complex and important matters He is likely to find that we have ignored or diminished the importance of events or principles that he has always regarded as the essence of social interaction  To this it can only be said that our simplifications have led to a formulation that we have found to be useful in understanding and ordering the subject matter of group psychology  To evaluate the validity of this testimony, the reader must be willing to endure the hardships of learning the concepts presented in this chapter and to assess for himself whether any clarification is thereby brought to the subsequent topics  We would be the last to deny that other sets of assumptions and concepts are valuable in group psychology, nor would we deny that other and more ingenious approaches could be imagined  To put it simply, we could not find the time to consider what the list of sufficiently plausible theoretical systems might include nor even to evaluate thoroughly the alternative systems that have presented themselves to us at the various points in this undertaking

Our conceptualization of the dyad, a two-person relationship, begins with an analysis of interaction and of its consequences for the two individuals concerned   The major analytic technique used throughout the book is a matrix formed by taking account of all the behaviors the two individuals might enact together   Each cell in this matrix represents one of the possible parts of the interaction between the two and summarizes the consequences for each person of that possible event   Although consequences can be analyzed and measured in many ways, we have found it desirable to distinguish positive components (*rewards*) from negative components (*costs*).  The many factors affecting the rewards and costs associated with each position of the matrix are described and note is taken of certain sequential effects that are not handled systematically in the present scheme.

The actual course of interaction between two individuals is viewed as only partially predictable from the matrix   Initial interactions in a forming relationship are viewed as explorations which sample only a few of the many possibilities   Interaction is continued only if the experienced consequences are found to meet the standards of acceptability that both individuals develop by virtue of their experience with other relationships   Several such standards that an individual may apply are identified, and these are related to such phenomena as attraction, dependence, and status   These concepts then set the stage for the more intensive analysis carried forward in subsequent chapters

To clarify the ways in which the matrix of outcomes may be used in the prediction of behavior, we conclude the chapter by discussing in some detail the conditions under which it may be so used and anticipating briefly some of the further applications of the matrix to problems developed later in the book

## 2 1   ANALYSIS OF INTERACTION

The essence of any interpersonal relationship is *interaction*   Two individuals may be said to have formed a relationship when on repeated occasions they are observed to interact   By interaction it is meant that they emit behavior in each other's presence, they create products for each other, or they communicate with each other.  In every case we would identify as an instance of interaction there is at least the possibility that the actions of each person affect the other

There are many things that an individual can do in interaction with another person   It might be said that each person has a vast repertoire of possible behaviors, any one of which he might produce in an interaction. There are many different ways of describing and analyzing the items in this repertoire   For example, a boy and girl are observed in their first conversation   The observer may list the specific bodily movements and verbal statements each makes, or he may simply describe the general "progress" that each makes with the other—what each attempts to accomplish in the interaction and the extent to which this is achieved   Although the exact choice depends somewhat upon the problem considered, for most purposes we have chosen to employ a unit of analysis that is intermediate between these extremes   In the example we would note that the boy first tells about his recent activities on the football field   He then, perhaps with considerable embarrassment and in a back-handed way, compliments the girl on her appearance.   He finally helps her with an algebra problem.   The girl's behavior would be described in similar terms.

Our unit for the analysis of behavior is referred to as the *behavior sequence* or *set*.   Each unit to be identified consists of a number of specific motor and verbal acts that exhibit some degree of sequential organization directed toward the attainment of some immediate goal or end state.   Typically, a sequence of this sort consists of some responses that are mainly instrumental in moving the person toward the final state   Other responses—perceptual, interpretive, consummatory in nature—can usually be identified as affording appreciation or enjoyment of the goal state.   If enough observations were at hand, the elements of a given sequence could be identified on the basis of certain statistical regularities·   the elements would be found to occur together repeatedly and to be performed in certain sequential arrangements   Transitions from one sequence to another would be observed as points at which serial dependency is low, actions at the end of a sequence providing relatively little basis for predicting what actions will follow

The organization apparent in behavior sequences suggests that the person maintains a more or less constant orientation or intention throughout the sequence   We refer to this aspect of the behavior sequence as *set*, although loosely we use set and behavior sequence interchangeably   When a behavior sequence is observed, we may say that the individual has assumed a certain set.   The probabilities of occurrence of the instrumental and appreciative behaviors comprising the sequence are heightened when the appropriate set is aroused   However, a set may be aroused without the corresponding behavior sequence being enacted   Thus the concept of set is useful in considering situations in which there is a tendency to produce a given sequence but in which this tendency does not, for various reasons, result

in overt performance of the sequence    In this case we may still deduce
the existence of a set if certain other manifestations (evidence of conflict or tension) are present    The specific set or sets aroused at any
given time depend upon instigations, both from within the person
(e g , need or drive states) and from outside (incentives, problem
situations or tasks confronting him, experimental instructions), and the
reinforcement previously associated with enactment of the set    The
stability of a set depends upon the temporal persistence of the stimuli
that serve to instigate it.

Each person's repertoire of behaviors consists of all possible sets
he may enact (or behavior sequences he may perform) and all possible combinations of these sets    Any portion of the stream of interaction between two persons can be described in terms of the items they
*actually produce* from their respective repertoires.

### 2.1 1    THE CONSEQUENCES OF INTERACTION

When the interactions of a number of persons are observed, it
usually becomes quite apparent that interaction is a highly selective
matter, both with respect to who interacts with whom and with respect to what any pair of persons interacts about    Not all possible
pairs of individuals are observed to enter into interaction, and any
given pair enacts only certain of the many behaviors they are capable
of.    Although there are several different ways of accounting for this
selectivity, we assume that in part it indicates that different interactions in different relationships have different consequences for the
individual    Some relationships are more satisfactory than others, and
the same is true of some interactions within a given relationship    The
selectivity observed in interaction reflects the tendency for more satisfactory interactions to recur and for less satisfactory ones to disappear

The consequences of interaction can be described in many different
terms, but we have found it useful to distinguish only between the
rewards a person receives and the costs he incurs.

By rewards, we refer to the pleasures, satisfactions, and gratifications the person enjoys    The provision of a means whereby a drive
is reduced or a need fulfilled constitutes a reward    We assume that
the amount of reward provided by any such experience can be measured and that the reward values of different modalities of gratification
are reducible to a single psychological scale

By costs, we refer to any factors that operate to inhibit or deter the
performance of a sequence of behavior.    The greater the deterrence to
performing a given act—the greater the inhibition the individual has
to overcome—the greater the cost of the act    Thus cost is high when

great physical or mental effort is required, when embarrassment or anxiety accompany the action, or when there are conflicting forces or competing response tendencies of any sort   Costs derived from these different factors are also assumed to be measurable on a common psychological scale, and costs of different sorts, to be additive in their effect

The consequences or *outcomes* for an individual participant of any interaction or series of interactions can be stated, then, in terms of the rewards received and the costs incurred, these values depending upon the behavioral items which the two persons produce in the course of their interaction   For some purposes it is desirable to treat rewards and costs separately, for other purposes it is assumed that they can be combined into a single scale of "goodness" of outcome, with states of high reward and low cost being given high-scale values and states of low reward and high cost, low-scale values   Admittedly, such a scaling operation would be a very ambitious enterprise and would present a number of technical difficulties   However, the present interest is in the theoretical consequences of such an operation (real or imaginary) rather than in its technical properties or even its feasibility

### 2.1.2   THE MATRIX OF POSSIBLE INTERACTIONS AND OUTCOMES

All portions of the interaction between two persons, A and B, can be represented by the matrix shown in Table 2-1.  Along the horizontal axis of this matrix are placed all the items in A's behavior repertoire and along the vertical axis, the items in B's repertoire   The cells of the matrix represent all possible events that may occur in the interaction between A and B, since at each moment the interaction may be described in terms of the items (consisting of one or more sets) that each one is *enacting*   (This assumes that each person is always in some set, even if only in a passive set in which he merely makes the responses necessary to observe, interpret, or appreciate what the other person is doing )  Although Table 2-1 presents the matrix in its most general form, for many purposes a much simpler matrix will provide an adequate description of the possibilities.  This will be true, for example, when an experimenter restricts his subjects to a limited number of responses or when an observer partitions his subjects' behavioral repertoires into a small number of mutually exclusive and exhaustive classes

Entered in each cell of the matrix are the outcomes, in terms of rewards gained and costs incurred, to each person of that particular portion of the interaction   If rewards and costs are combined into a

# The Social Psychology of Groups

## TABLE 2-1

### MATRIX OF POSSIBLE INTERACTIONS AND OUTCOMES

|  |  | A's repertoire |  |  |  |  |  |  |  |
|---|---|---|---|---|---|---|---|---|---|
|  |  | $a_1$ | $a_2$ | ... | $a_n$ | $a_1a_2$ | $a_1a_3$ | ... | $a_1a_2\cdots a_n$ |
|  | $b_1$ | $r_A,c_A$ / $r_B,c_B$ | etc. | ... |  |  |  |  |  |
|  | $b_2$ | etc. |  |  |  |  |  |  |  |
|  | : | : |  |  |  |  |  |  |  |
| B's repertoire | $b_n$ |  |  |  |  |  |  |  |  |
|  | $b_1b_2$ |  |  |  |  |  |  |  |  |
|  | $b_1b_3$ |  |  |  |  |  |  |  |  |
|  | : |  |  |  |  |  |  |  |  |
|  | $b_1b_2\cdots b_n$ |  |  |  |  |  |  |  |  |

single scale of goodness of outcome, the matrix can be simplified as in Table 2-2.

## 2.2 EXOGENOUS DETERMINANTS OF REWARDS AND COSTS

The reward and cost values entered in the matrix in Table 2-1 depend in the first place upon factors that are more or less external *to the relationship*. Each individual carries his values, needs, skills, tools, and predispositions to anxiety with him as he moves among the various relationships in which he participates. Hence we refer to them as *exogenous* factors.

The magnitude of rewards to be gained by the two members from the various elements will depend upon their individual needs and values and the congruency of the behaviors or behavioral products with these needs and values. Each person's rewards may be derived (1) directly from his own behavior and/or (2) from the other's behavior. The former consist of rewards the individual could produce for himself if he were alone. Any rewards he receives that depend in any way upon the other individual, even if only upon the presence of the other, will be considered as depending upon the other's behavior. For example, A obtains satisfaction from doing things for

B. We can interpret this to mean that B can produce rewards for A (probably at very low cost) by simply assuming a passive set in which he receives A's contributions and, perhaps, acknowledges receipt in some way.

In what might be characterized as a true trading relationship all of each person's rewards are derived from the other's efforts. More typical, perhaps, is the case in which each one's rewards depend in part upon his own behaviors and in part upon the other's behaviors.

When A produces an item from his repertoire, his costs depend on

TABLE 2–2

MATRIX OF POSSIBLE OUTCOMES, SCALED ACCORDING TO OVER-ALL
GOODNESS OF OUTCOMES

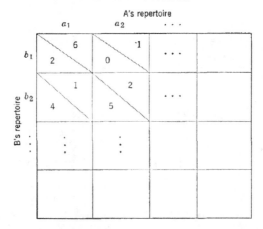

his skills and on the availability to him of efficient tools or instruments as well as on the degree to which anxiety or discomfort is associated with producing the various elements. Where A's actions are concerned, B's costs depend on the degree to which any of A's behaviors are punishing to him, whether by arousing anxiety or embarrassment or by causing physical harm.

## 2.3 ENDOGENOUS DETERMINANTS OF REWARDS AND COSTS

The second class of determinants of rewards and costs includes those intrinsic to the interaction itself, referred to as *endogenous* factors. The central point is that the specific values associated with a given item in A's repertoire depend upon the particular item in B's repertoire with which, in the course of the interaction, it is paired

As noted in the discussion of sets, the performance of a set requires making a series of responses, some of which are primarily instrumental in nature and others, primarily consummatory Even the enjoyment of one person's performance by another requires that the latter make some responses of an attentive and consummatory type For all responses of which a person is capable there are other responses that are more or less incompatible with them. By incompatibility is meant that these responses tend to interfere with the performance of one another. The performance of one response serves as a distraction or disturbance to the performance of the other.

One consequence of this interference is to raise the costs required to produce one or both responses In the extreme case one or both responses may be completely inhibited by the other There is also the likelihood that under conditions of interference one or both responses will be performed less well (i e., less strongly, less rapidly, or less accurately) In this regard, however, there is the possibility that, for simple, easy-to-perform, overlearned, highly integrated responses, interference may not affect or may even improve the quality of performance.

Response interference may exist, of course, whenever a person is enacting two or more sets at the same time If A produces the item $a_1a_3$ from his repertoire and if set $a_1$ includes responses incompatible with those in $a_3$, then the total costs involved are likely to be greater than if he had on one occasion enacted $a_1$ and on another, $a_3$ Furthermore, the total rewards might very well have been greater in the latter case. The reward and cost values associated with the item $a_1a_3$ in A's repertoire will reflect any such interference effects that may exist

Interference may also be created by a set which, though partially aroused, is not overtly enacted For example, A may be producing set $a_1$ at the same time that there are weak instigations to set $a_3$. The latter behavior sequence may not be enacted but response *tendencies* may be aroused which interfere with the optimal production of $a_1$ The partial arousal of sets is important in interaction because, as noted earlier, the behaviors of other persons often act as instigators of sets. So interaction affords many opportunities for response interference to arise

Consider the implications of response interference for the effects of interaction upon rewards and costs Assume that A produces set $a_1$ from his repertoire The cost of producing the responses subsumed under this set will be minimal (where the minimum depends on such relatively stable exogenous factors as his tools and skills) only if no tendencies to make incompatible responses exist at the same time   If while A is performing $a_1$, B is also enacting set $b_2$ and this action partially arouses set $a_3$ in A, a set which is incompatible with $a_1$, then A's costs of producing $a_1$ are likely to be heightened and the quality of his behavior to be decreased   If the reward value of $a_1$, either to A himself or to B, depends upon the quality of A's performance, this will also suffer

If $b_2$ interferes with $a_1$, then $a_1$ is likely also to interfere with $b_2$ (Here we assume that interference is frequently a symmetrical relation.)   One consequence of this interference is that A's enjoyment of $b_2$ may be attenuated by virtue of its being presented while he is in set $a_1$   His costs of making the necessary consummatory responses are likely to be raised   He will have to work harder to "receive" and "process" the content of $b_2$   His rewards may also be reduced because of his not being able to give the necessary attention or consideration to B's performance of $b_2$   The same situation may, of course, be considered from the point of view of B's costs and rewards.

In general, response interference raises the cost of making responses, whether these are the instrumental responses essential to the enactment of a set or the attentive, interpretive, and appreciative responses essential to its consummation.   Interference may also operate to lower rewards by producing a deterioration in the quality of responses made.   This deterioration of quality may not occur, however, for activities that are well learned and performed more or less automatically   In the presence of an incompatible set such responses may even be enacted with greater intensity, frequency, or accuracy than usual, which might be expected to result in the availability of more or better rewards and, possibly, in an intensification of the pleasures derived from appreciating or consuming them

The foregoing statements about the effects on reward-cost outcomes of the simultaneous arousal of incompatible sets may be represented in the simplified form of Table 2–3   This table shows the outcomes to A when we consider a simple situation in which each member has only two sets in his repertoire   Note that the hypothetical numbers entered in the table have been arranged to show a statistical interaction effect, that is, the size of A's outcome depends on the particular combination of one of his own sets with one of B's sets   The patterning of outcomes to A might conceivably have occurred in the following way.

If $b_1$ partially arouses some responses (or set) incompatible with $a_1$ and if $b_2$ is similarly incompatible with $a_2$, then interference either in

B's production of the behavior or in A's attending to, interpreting, or consuming the rewards would reduce A's outcomes, in this case from 4 units to 2 units.

This example is merely illustrative and should be taken only to suggest a way in which a statistical interaction of outcomes may be derived from the effects of interference or facilitation.

### 2.3.1   SEQUENTIAL EFFECTS — *C₁ dɛɛɛɾ ɛ ⌃⌄*

Another type of endogenous determinant of rewards and costs in the dyad has to do with the time-patterning of the various items of a repertoire. The rewards and costs derived from the enactment of an item in a repertoire will be affected by the prior items enacted. More specifically, as the same behaviors are repeated over and over, the reward value of each unit of behavior may decrease over time. This is

TABLE 2–3

POSSIBLE OUTCOMES TO A WHERE EACH MEMBER'S REPERTOIRE
HAS ONLY TWO SETS

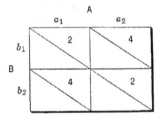

the commonly observed tendency of a need state to *satiate.* A parallel effect would be expected on the cost side. As the same behavior is repeated, the production of the behavior will become gradually more costly as *fatigue* sets in.

Because of these two effects of immediate repetition, the successive arousal of the same set would require increasingly strong instigations to overcome fatigue, and at the same time the recipient of the behavior would become less and less likely, as satiation develops, to instigate the producer to repeat his behavior. Hence the likelihood of immediate re-arousal of a set usually will be less than the likelihood of initial arousal of that set. As a direct consequence, in order to keep rewards up and costs down, both members of a dyad are likely to shift, over time, from one item to another in their repertoires with very little immediate repetition of the same items.

Although there will be a tendency to avoid such situations, sometimes there will be overridingly strong instigations from the task requirements or from outside the dyad to repeat the same sets Relationships in which such instigations are chronic or in which repertones include too few alternatives to permit nonrepetition will either be dissolved or become intermittent

Although these sequential effects are undoubtedly important, we will disregard them in entering numbers in the reward-cost matrices This does not imply any disparagement of the significance of such sequential effects but only that they must be studied by means other than those of such reward-cost matrices as are described here Nor does this mean that the numbers entered to describe reward-cost outcomes are totally free from satiation and fatigue effects The psychologically scaled rewards and costs of individual items of a repertoire would be expected to include any experienced fatigue (as cost increase) or satiation (as reward decrease), insofar as these effects occur within a single item) However, satiation and fatigue will not be reflected in a matrix as an accumulation over a sequence of identical or similar items) The numbers entered in a matrix represent instead the maximum rewards and minimum costs on the assumption that there is no transfer of satiation or fatigue from item to item. )

## 2.4 THE ACTUAL COURSE OF INTERACTION

The matrix formed by A's and B's behavioral repertoires taken jointly defines all the different things they might possibly do in interaction with each other. The reward-cost values in the matrix represent the outcomes each person would experience for each of the manifold interaction possibilities. In a sense, the facts summarized in this matrix set the limits within which their actual interaction must occur The actual course of their interaction cannot, however, be predicted merely from a knowledge of this matrix Whether or not interaction will be begun, what course it will actually take, and what reward-cost positions each individual will actually achieve—these all depend upon a number of factors only some of which are related to the matrix of possible outcomes

Interaction may begin for quite different reasons One or both persons may know something about the other and, on the basis of this information, may (anticipate that interaction would yield good outcomes ) This would result in a deliberate decision to seek out the other person and interact with him Under other circumstances the two persons may be thrown together by the operation of factors beyond their control Their jobs may bring them together, common friends may introduce them, or residence in the same neighborhood may result in a chance meeting  In these instances interaction is begun in response to the immediate situation without any necessary anticipation of the possible consequences by either participant

Whether or not interaction continues. once begun, depends upon similar considerations  If (good outcomes are experienced in initial contacts) or if (these contacts lead the persons to anticipate good outcomes in the future,) the interaction is likely to be repeated, and, of course, the (external influences of work, friends, and neighborhood) may continue to make interaction necessary

According to the view expressed above, the early (exploratory inter-action) actions are very important in determining the further fate of the potential relationship . The interaction occurring during this period may be conceived as a sampling process in which the pair of individuals, by virtue of the items each selects from his behavioral repertoire, experience a sample of the possible interactions and outcomes represented by their joint matrix.  The sampling analogy suggests a number of generalizations  For example, the greater the proportion of good outcomes in the matrix, the more likely they are to be experienced during early contacts.  Similarly, the larger the sample drawn (that is, the more different interactions in the first encounter), the greater the likelihood the two individuals will experience the better of the outcomes potentially available to them  Of course, the interactions sampled are unlikely to be representative of the entire universe of possibilities  The situation in which first contact occurs may favor the arousal of certain sets to the exclusion of others  For example. only certain kinds of behaviors are appropriate when two men meet in the course of their work  There are general cultural mores which deal with the correct things to do and say when first introduced to another person  Even in the absence of external instigations to certain sets, the individual may draw selectively from his behavioral repertoire  In new relationships in which the ultimate payoff is uncertain individuals are unlikely to produce items of high cost to themselves  For example, A may completely avoid mentioning a certain esoteric interest if this has evoked contempt in other relationships  If this happens to be an interest B shares and enjoys discussing, one of the best outcomes potentially available in the A–B relationship may be completely overlooked

Whatever the nature of the early exchanges between A and B, they will voluntarily continue their association only if the experienced outcomes (or inferred but as yet unexperienced outcomes) are found to be adequate. This raises the problem, to which we next turn, of the criteria against which experienced or anticipated outcomes are evaluated.

## 2.5 EVALUATION OF OUTCOMES: COMPARISON LEVELS

In evaluating the adequacy of the sampled and anticipated outcomes of a relationship, the members of a dyad will have need for some kind of standard or criterion of the acceptability of outcomes. At least two important kinds of standard for such an evaluation can be identified. To try to make the distinction between these two standards as intuitively clear as possible, we may begin by saying that the first of these, called the *comparison level* (or CL), is the standard against which the member evaluates the "attractiveness" of the relationship or how satisfactory it is. The second, called the *comparison level for alternatives* (or CL$_{alt}$), is the standard the member uses in deciding whether to remain in or to leave the relationship. The two standards are distinguished in recognition of the fact that circumstances may require a person to remain in a relationship that he regards as unsatisfactory. Although these standards are described and illustrated in some detail in Chapters 6, 7, and 10, a bit of elaboration is probably called for.

CL is a standard by which the person evaluates the rewards and costs of a given relationship in terms of what he feels he "deserves." Relationships the outcomes of which fall above CL would be relatively "satisfying" and attractive to the member; those entailing outcomes that fall below CL would be relatively "unsatisfying" and unattractive. The location of CL on the person's scale of outcomes will be influenced by all of the outcomes known to the member, either by direct experience or symbolically. It may be taken to be some modal or average value of all known outcomes, each outcome weighted by its "salience," or strength of instigation, which depends, for example, upon the recency of experiencing the outcome and the occurrence of stimuli which serve as reminders of the outcome. Because these factors are likely to be absent or weak in the case of relationships and interactions that are unattainable, the latter will ordinarily have little weight in determining the location of CL.

CL$_{alt}$ can be defined informally as the lowest level of outcomes a member will accept in the light of available alternative opportunities. It follows from this definition that as soon as outcomes drop below CL$_{alt}$ the member will leave the relationship. The height of the CL$_{alt}$

will depend mainly on the quality of the best of the member's available alternatives, that is, the reward-cost positions experienced or believed to exist in the most satisfactory of the other available relationships

As in the case of CL, the outcomes that determine the location of $CL_{alt}$ will be weighted by their *salience* (how strongly they are instigated) Unlikely outcomes in the alternative relationship will usually have little weight in fixing the location of $CL_{alt}$ because, again, the salience of such outcomes will ordinarily be rather low.

The alternative relationships with which the present one is compared in evolving the $CL_{alt}$ may include other dyads, more complex relationships, or even the alternative of joining no group, of working or being alone From this last alternative it appears that a member's $CL_{alt}$ will usually be heightened to the degree that he is independently able to produce rewards for himself at competitive costs More precisely, the $CL_{alt}$ will be heightened by any favorable reward-cost positions that a member can regularly attain by virtue of his ability to carry self-produced rewards with him from relationship to relationship Since such rewards are portable, the attractiveness of all alternatives is increased by an amount equal to these rewards

From the foregoing comments it is plain that if a relationship is to form and survive positions above $CL_{alt}$ must exist and positions below $CL_{alt}$ must be eliminated from the relationship What may not be quite so obvious is that the $CL_{alt}$ may also eliminate some of the best positions in the reward-cost space. Specifically, A's good outcomes will be eliminated from the relationship if these outcomes are attainable only when B's costs of producing them are so high that B's corresponding outcomes are below his $CL_{alt}$. An increasing proportion of A's best outcomes can be attained in the relationship (1) the lower is B's $CL_{alt}$ and (2) the greater the degree to which the goodness of A's and B's outcomes are positively associated; that is, both have high rewards and/or low costs in some cells of the matrix (Table 2-1) and low rewards and/or high costs in other cells. These two conditions mean that a given dyad can make possible the attainment of better reward and cost values than are available in other relationships only if, to some degree, each member's behavior in the dyad contributes to the other's rewards without a corresponding excessive increase in his own costs. (In short, a prerequisite for the existence of the dyad is a dependence of the rewards of each upon the other's behavior, that is, a condition of interdependence)

To summarize the main points developed so far, the formation of a relationship depends largely upon

(1) the matrix of the possible outcomes of interaction;

(2) the process of exploring or sampling the possibilities; and *ultimately*

(3) whether or not the *jointly* experienced outcomes are above each member's CL$_{alt}$.

### 2.5.1 ATTRACTION AND DEPENDENCE IN THE DYAD

We have asserted that whether or not an individual attains (or at least expects to attain) reward-cost positions above his CL$_{alt}$ determines whether or not he will remain in a given dyadic relationship. It is but a small step to the further assumption that the degree to which his attained positions exceed his CL$_{alt}$ determines how greatly he depends on the dyad for favorable outcomes. Accordingly, the numbers entered in the cells of the simplified matrix of possible outcomes (Table 2–2) will usually be scaled from CL$_{alt}$ as the zero point. The entries in such a matrix indicate the degree to which each person is dependent upon the dyad, and the pattern of entries shows the manner in which the two persons are interdependent.

However, the individual may be greatly dependent on the dyad without its being "attractive" to him to a commensurate degree—without his being satisfied with the relationship. In other words, a member's dependency on the group (hence, as we will see in Chapter 7, its power over him) is not necessarily highly correlated with his attraction to the group, his "morale" or satisfaction from belonging to it.

It is to afford a way of dealing with this possible discrepancy between dependency and attraction that CL$_{alt}$ is distinguished from CL, where, to repeat, the former's relevance is to dependency and the latter's relevance is to attraction. In any viable relationship the individual's outcomes will be located above his CL$_{alt}$; but his CL may have several different positions in relation to his outcomes and CL$_{alt}$. First, it may be below both. In this case the individual may be expected to be highly satisfied with the relationship. It affords him outcomes superior to his CL, and at the same time he is provided with only slightly less favorable outcomes in his available alternative relationships. The relationship may be highly attractive without his necessarily being greatly dependent on it.

Second, his CL may be below his outcomes but above his CL$_{alt}$. In this instance he will find the relationship satisfactory, but his dependence upon it will exceed his attraction to it.

Finally, there is the very important class of *nonvoluntary* relationships in which the CL exceeds the individual's outcomes (and, of course, his CL$_{alt}$). Any relationship has a nonvoluntary component, to the degree that salient outcomes, unavailable in the relationship, are superior to those that exist in the relationship. In this respect, relationships will vary only in degree. However, we rather arbitrarily define a nonvoluntary relationship as one in which the individual's outcomes in the relationship fall below his CL. Here he would be expected to be dissatisfied with the relationship. In extreme cases, as in prisons and concentration camps, the outcomes in the relationship may be so poor that hardly any still poorer alternatives are available. This type of relationship is described in Chapter 10.

A person's attraction to a dyad depends upon his evaluation of his outcomes in relation to his CL, where the CL reflects the entire population of outcomes known to the person. An important subclass of such outcomes is that which includes the outcomes perceived to be attained by one's partner in the relationship, hence one's own outcomes may come to be evaluated in relation to a standard based on such perceived outcomes. A consideration of these evaluations permits us to introduce the concept of *status*, further discussion of which is deferred to Chapter 12.

## 2 6   THE NATURE AND UTILITY OF THE OUTCOME MATRIX

As used here, the matrix is a device for representing the joint outcomes from social interaction accruing to the members of a dyad. In subsequent chapters we attempt to extend the application of the matrix in two ways: (1) to aid in assessing the viability of a group, the satisfactions and patterns of interdependence of its members, and the processes through which the members influence and control one another, and (2) to permit an analysis of behavior in groups larger than the dyad. In view of its pervasive utilization in the remainder of the book, it seems advisable to be as clear as possible about its nature and functions.

The matrix closely resembles the payoff matrices used in game theory (Luce and Raiffa, 1957). Our matrix would describe a non-zero-sum game, inasmuch as A does not necessarily achieve his payoffs at B's expense or vice versa. However, in important ways our assumptions about this matrix differ from game theoretic assumptions. First, we do not assume that the values in the matrix are fixed, even over short time spans. Because of satiation and fatigue, if the combination of actions represented by a particular cell is repeated, on successive occasions the reward values are likely to decline and the costs to increase. One important consequence is that interaction is not ordinarily the mere repetition of one combination of best items.

Interaction is not usually a game in which there is a single best or *dominant* solution Rather, it often consists of successive movements from one cell of the matrix to another

Second, we do not assume that the persons begin the game with complete knowledge of the entire matrix and the payoffs contained therein. These facts are discovered through a process of exploration, partly trial and error in nature and partly governed by prediction, extrapolation, etc The reward-cost matrix is the matrix of *objectively* available outcomes. However, for some purposes we shall assume that the matrix describes the *subjective* understandings and anticipations of the possible interactions and outcomes, however inadequately these may represent the actual universe of possibilities.

The use of the matrix in this book may also be compared with that, of Deutsch (1957) in his investigations of interpersonal trust. There are many different sources of the rewards and costs that we summarize in each cell For example, in an experimental situation the experimenter might award points or dollars in a way that depends on the joint decisions of the two subjects. But the subjects might also gain satisfaction from other sources, as, for example, from helping each other or from competing with each other. We assume that *all* of the outcomes to the individual resulting from a given joint action are indicated by his payoff numbers in the various cells In contrast, Deutsch has followed the convention of using the matrix to represent only the payoffs delivered formally by the experimenter Other sources of variations in rewards are introduced by experimental instructions (e g, giving the subjects a cooperative versus a competitive "orientation"), but these are treated outside the game matrix The matrices seem, for Deutsch, to be largely a means of depicting the formal structure of experimental situations His theoretical orientation is not primarily a game theoretic one but consists instead of a logical and phenomenological analysis of various interpersonal constructs We raise this point of comparison not as an adequate characterization of Deutsch's approach but to emphasize the fact that our analysis always assumes that *all of the relevant variations in costs and rewards are represented by the matrix values*

Since matrices of the type proposed here have not been widely used in social psychology, it is perhaps not too serious a digression to consider the possible utility of this device, particularly in the prediction of behavior The reward-cost matrix, as we have previously said, is an "objective" statement of the possible outcomes, given the behavior repertoires of the two persons This matrix is only a description of the *consequences* of behaviors and strictly speaking cannot be used to predict the behaviors themselves. Only under certain conditions does it seem possible to predict behavior from such a matrix

Consider the use of A's outcomes to predict his behavior. Suppose that B enacts a given behavior and further suppose that the reward-cost matrix is such that the outcomes to A vary, depending upon what he does in turn Suppose we actually observe A's behavior in a large number of such instances and then place in each cell of the matrix, alongside the reward-cost values, the proportion of the observed instances (given each of B's several behaviors) in which A manifests each of his behaviors We refer to these proportions as *probabilities* of each of A's behaviors, understanding each one to indicate the likelihood that A will perform a certain act, given the fact that B has performed a certain one

If there are no major discrepancies between these probabilities and the corresponding reward-cost values, then the reward-cost values could be used to predict behavior If there are major discrepancies, the values cannot be so used and merely indicate consequences of behavior

In this book we limit ourselves to the use of reward-cost matrices on the grounds that in ordinary social relationships the two sets of values ultimately tend to correspond fairly well We will now attempt to defend this view. In order to do so, we must comment briefly upon the determinants of behavior and their contributions to discrepancies between the consequences of an act and the probability that it will occur We have chosen to use a very simple behavior theory which we believe to be largely compatible with more sophisticated models and precise enough for present purposes We assume that the probability of any one of A's behaviors being elicited is a function of two factors (1) the strength of instigation to it (from either external or internal stimuli) and (2) previously experienced reinforcement resulting from it Probability of occurrence reflects both of these factors, whereas the objective reward-cost matrix reflects only the reinforcement consequent on the act

We can, then, identify two classes of situations in which there may be discrepancies between the probability of elicitation and the outcome.

(1) When responses are so dependably under the control of a stimulus that they can be elicited even when the consequences are unfavorable.

(2) When the objective reinforcements have not yet been experienced.

The first class of situations includes a variety of behaviors which depend for their elicitation mainly upon strong instigation or which are so "ready" to be elicited that little instigation is necessary. One such class would be reflexive behavior, such as elimination responses in the infant and startle responses. Another class would include the highly overlearned habits or routines that occur dependably whenever appropriate cues set them off. Routines would include those learned through special training and drill and social-role practice. Phenomenally, these are the instances in which a person acts without taking account of consequences. (For example, soldiers, firemen, and policemen are trained to react automatically in danger situations without regard to reward-cost outcomes.) Time pressure or urgency of action may be viewed as heightening the effects of instigations. This is illustrated by the children's game "Simon says." The readiness to behave imitatively, probably even initially a powerful factor, is established by practice trials during which imitation is appropriate. Then, under the necessity of acting quickly, children imitate the action of the leader even when it constitutes an error (presumably a negative outcome for the child).

The second class of situations includes those in which the contingencies between specific behaviors and particular objective reinforcements have not been experienced enough to have been learned. These would consist often of situations that are objectively novel, whether recognized as such or not. Phenomenally, the person does not yet have sufficient information about the objective consequences to take account of them accurately, even though, being under no strong instigations or time pressure, he may have time to do so. Time pressure and powerful instigations may act not only to prevent the use of information about consequences (as indicated earlier) but may also prevent the acquisition of accurate and adequate information in the first place. A person's exploration and sampling of the matrix may be severely limited and biased by these factors. The processes of acquiring information about the matrix of consequences are a major concern in discussing the formation and development of social relationships.

Under other conditions there is high correspondence between the probability of behavior elicitation and the reward-cost outcomes. This is true when (1) instigations are in line with outcomes or (2) when instigations are weak and outcomes are known in advance.

Is it defensible to believe that, as we have already asserted, situations of noncorrespondence tend over time to generate the conditions for correspondence, hence enabling a matrix of outcomes to form the basis for a useful theory of interaction? We think so for the reasons that follow.

A person does learn the consequences of his actions if given the opportunity (time, exposure) and if he has the talents. Moreover, when a person enters a relationship in which there are powerful instigations to behaviors with unfavorable consequences, some sort of change is very probable. either he leaves, or the instigations are somehow eliminated or made more appropriate  If they come from inappropriate habits he has carried into the relationship, he may relearn more suitable ones  If the instigations are provided by others' behavior, they may change their behavioral output in order to insure survival of the relationship (assuming it matters to them). The socialization of reflexive and other kinds of "primitive" behavior consists largely of selective adaptations by which the individual learns to seek favorable (or at least nonpunishing) occasions for discharging urgently instigated behavior and the social environment tends to provide accommodating occasions  (Adult Western males generally urinate in the toilets provided for them rather than in the streets ) In brief, by selectivity and relearning on the part of the individual and by a kind of accommodation to him on the part of social arrangements, there tends to develop an approximate correspondence between instigations to behaviors and the consequences of behavior  Discrepancy between instigation and outcome perhaps mainly characterizes unstable and transient relationships or the early stages of relationships that later stabilize

For these reasons we believe there will typically be in any given relationship increasing correspondence between the antecedent determinants of behavior and the reward-cost consequences of behavior  Therefore, the reward-cost matrix becomes increasingly useful in predicting behavior as relationships become stable  It should be emphasized, however, that this does not mean that such behavior is governed by anticipations of consequences, covert calculation of the relative merits of different actions, or the deliberate attempt to maximize outcomes  Quite the contrary. Precisely because instigations do correspond increasingly well with outcomes, the individual may, with impunity, act more and more automatically (in response to habits, routines, or role prescriptions) and give less and less attention to the surveillance of his environment, the discernment of response alternatives, and the weighing of consequences  When the matrix is stable, an adaptive solution (in terms of cost minimization) is provided by routines that obviate these complex cognitive activities and automatize the procedures for gaining adequate outcomes  After sufficient experience in a stable situation (after the person has surveyed it thoroughly, rehearsed his repertoire of responses, and formed an adequate conception of the interdependency pattern), he can often formulate rules for the moment-to-moment choice of behaviors Rules that other persons have found successful in similar relationships are frequently available to him in the form of role prescriptions taught by exhortation or example

When following these routines, behavioral choices may provide good and even (perhaps) maximal outcomes However, to repeat, adaptive performance need not be construed as evidence of a continuing, deliberate, purposive hedonism

Only when these routines break down—when a changed situation begins to provide instigations to behaviors having poor outcomes—need the individual return to a consideration of consequences At these points of discontinuity old routines may be maladaptive and no appropriate alternative routines may be available. At these critical junctures the person may become deliberate and thoughtful as to consequences—when he enters a new relationship, undertakes a new task, acquires new items in his response repertoire, or learns to make new discriminations as to the states of the external world If he is not coerced by strong instigations, he may lengthen his time perspective and attempt to guide his behavior by an assessment of the long-term consequences At these decision points, if the person has the ability and means of acquiring accurate information and of rehearsing his response alternatives, the matrix describing the objective consequences of each action becomes especially pertinent to the prediction of behavior

In short, when the situation is relatively stable, behavioral routines that operate as though they have taken account of the outcome matrix tend to become adaptive solutions When the situation changes, reflecting its change in a new outcome matrix, the new matrix will also have utility in predicting behavior if certain conditions are met

Finally, over and above the advantages of the outcome matrix that have been noted, there is an important additional class of reasons, given our present aim, for using such a matrix rather than a matrix of probabilities In dealing with many kinds of social events it is important not only to be able to assess the probability of various behaviors but also (and especially) to be able to describe and perchance to predict some psychological states of the person. his attraction to the group, his subjective status, his satisfaction with a social role, and the impact on him of types of power which control his fate For this purpose it appears to be necessary to employ a concept having to do with the psychological consequences of interaction, whether the concept is called reward-cost outcome, valence, utility, or reinforcement. The reader who is interested in a further ramification of this thesis is referred to Chapter 9, where some of the power implications of analyses by response probabilities and by reward-cost outcomes are compared.

# 3.

# *Rewards and Costs*

In the next four chapters we return to the main topics of the preceding analysis, with the aims of exploring some of the relevant theoretical issues and of documenting with data as many as possible of the generalizations made in Chapter 2. In the present chapter we attempt to describe some of the main determinants of *rewards and costs* to the members of a dyad. Chapter 4 deals in some detail with several of the possible mechanisms and consequences of behavioral *interference* in dyadic relationships. In Chapter 5 we discuss some aspects of the *formation* of a dyad, and finally in Chapter 6, the processes by which the two members *evaluate their outcomes* in it.

The preceding development can be summarized as follows the reward-cost positions the members of a dyad may achieve in the relationship will be better (1) the more rewarding to the other is the behavior each can produce and (2) the lower the cost at which such behavior can be produced. If both persons are able to produce their maximum rewards for the other at minimum cost to themselves, the relationship will not only provide each with excellent reward-cost positions but will have the additional advantage that both persons will be able to achieve their best reward-cost positions at the same time. Neither will be likely to drop even temporarily below his $CL_{alt}$ in producing optimal outcomes for the other, nor will it be necessary for the members to take turns achieving the best outcomes possible under the relationship

To illustrate this general point, let us take a very simple example from a study of cooperation in rats (Daniel, 1942). Pairs of hungry white rats were put in a box with a grid floor through which passed

31

a mild electric current   Near the center of the box was a food crock, and at the far end of the box was a platform which, when depressed, cut off the electric current in the grid floor   The electric current was sufficiently "unpleasant" to deter the animals from feeding, yet the platform which turned off the current was located far enough from the food crock so that no animal could, at the same time, both feed and cut off the current   For either rat to feed the other had to learn to depress the platform for him, and an interchange of this kind of cooperative behavior was indeed learned by a high proportion of the pairs

In a second experiment Daniel (1943) varied the procedure by installing over the food crock a cover which was open only as long as the platform was depressed.  He also gradually reduced the electric current during the cooperative trials   In other respects the procedure and apparatus remained the same   With shock-avoidance totally eliminated from the situation, the cooperation between the animals was found to break down

At the risk of being anthropomorphic, let us translate Daniel's findings into our terms   In the first experiment by depressing the platform any animal could cut his own costs (avoid shock) and at the same time enable the other animal to be rewarded (feed at food crock)   At costs which were low compared with those incurred when the shock was experienced, each animal could provide high rewards to the other.  In the second experiment, when shock-avoidance was eliminated, providing rewards to the other actually increased each animal's costs somewhat (the effort required to move the platform)   Thus rewards could not be provided at low cost (i e , while cutting one's own costs) as in the first experiment   Hence the likelihood of "formation and persistence of the dyad" was greater in the first case than in the second

In the realm of human relationships the major evidence bearing on the foregoing generalizations about rewards and costs comes from two major sources  sociometric research and investigations of dating and engagements   Sociometry is a method originated and developed by Moreno (1934) for determining the patterns of friendship and interpersonal choice for various activities (e g , to work with, play with, or room with)   A sociometric choice made by A of individual B may be taken as an indication of A's desire to form a relationship with B, at least under the circumstances specified in the criteria given for making the choice   When this choice is reciprocated (i e , when B also chooses A) or when the friendship is found, by observation or question, actually to exist, we may assume that the necessary conditions for dyad formation have been fulfilled

Similarly, if they may be assumed to be voluntary, male-female pairs who repeatedly go on "dates" or are "engaged" constitute dyads in which both individuals apparently are desirous of continuing the relationship. Evidence from marriages must be interpreted a bit more cautiously. Since marriage is viewed as a more permanent relationship than most other dyads, it is more likely to reflect outside pressures and influences (legal, familial, etc) both with regard to its establishment and its continuation Certainly there are enough difficulties involved in breaking up a marriage that not all marriages may be properly regarded as voluntary relationships

## 3 1 EXAMPLES OF REWARDS AND COSTS

Let us begin with some examples in order to illustrate what is meant by rewards and costs in friendship relations These illustrations are drawn largely from Jennings (1950) who used Moreno's sociometric method to study the friendship choices of some 400 adolescent girls living in the New York State Training School for Girls

### 3.1.1 SOCIOMETRIC CHOICE AND REWARDS

A number of Jennings' examples show how those persons chosen most to work with or live with do things for the other girls that the less frequently chosen fail to do For example, visits to the psychology office in behalf of another individual are reported to have been made by none of the less frequently chosen girls but by thirty-five per cent of those frequently chosen Similarly, encouraging and helping a new girl was reported for five per cent of the infrequently chosen but by some ninety per cent of the frequently chosen.

In some instances the rewards provided seem to be based upon *similarities* between two persons. In explaining her choice of another girl to spend leisure time with, one of the girls says, "You'll think this is a crazy reason but it's the truth She likes noise like I like noise I'm always holding myself in in the house, don't yell around or nothing Susan and I race all over the place in our free time—from the store to the ravines—we get some use of our energy . . Most people are just too quiet or too dead to suit us, not enough fun" [p 260]

In explaining her reasons for choosing Jean, Catherine says in a similar vein, ". The same things disgust us and the same things delight us We get a lot of comfort from each other" [p 197]

In other cases the rewards provided each other seem to be based on *differences* For example, here are Doris' reasons for choosing Jacqueline. 'She is buoyant and picks you up and she's dramatic and when she tells about something she almost lives it. . She has great ideals and she fills you with ambition      She gives you advice in a way that makes you think for yourself, not that she thinks it's right just because she says it   And just to see her breezing along sort of breezes you along with her. . . She used to sit by the hour and let me stream my sob-stories out to her and she could sort of add a word here and there so you'd scarcely know it until you got to see her point of view and not your own anymore. . . . Jacqueline can lead and not make the girls feel they are being overpowered but rather that they are doing things of their own accord" [pp 191–193, italics omitted]   The opposite side of this complementary relationship is revealed in Jacqueline's reasons for choosing Doris. "Doris brings all her troubles to me and calls me sister and I would do the same only I feel I have to act different like I was older, though I am younger She'd never tell the other girls what goes on in her mind, only to me" [p 194]

To promote a friendship, a person must not only be *able* to provide rewards for others but must also be *willing* This willingness may stem from the fact that the person derives direct satisfaction from the behaviors which are rewarding to others   Jennings says this of the frequently chosen girls "Each appears to possess to a greater or less degree unusual capacity to identify with others to the extent of feeling solicitude for them or to act in their behalf" [p 204]   Thus the most chosen girls often have altruistic motivation in contrast to the infrequently chosen girls who appear relatively self-bound and egocentric

### 3 1.2  SOCIOMETRIC CHOICE AND COSTS

Some of Jennings' examples also bear on cost considerations.  For example, Doris and Jacqueline describe each other's tendencies to avoid creating depression or anxiety among other girls  Doris says of Jacqueline, "She acts more sure of herself than she really is and is under a terrible strain and then you can sense that she is tired out and goes to her room to be alone. When she is angry she'll go to her room and cry it out and not produce the anger in public like some girls" [p 193, italics omitted].

And Jacqueline says of Doris, "Nothing ever ruffles her and if she does have anything wrong with her, she'll go to her room and not make the other girls feel bad too, although she has a temperament and you have to be careful how you treat her" [p 194]

On this point, Jennings comments, ". . each leader appears to succeed in controlling her own moods at least to the extent of not inflicting negative feelings of depression or anxiety upon others Each appears to hold her own counsel and not to confide her personal worries except to a selected friend or two . . " [p 203]

A girl may even be liked primarily because she reduces another's costs For example, one girl says of Janet, "Y-y-you see, it's like this —I st-st-stutter and she-she thinks it's cute I can be myself with her Lots of people in my house try to help me over st-stuttering but Janet says, 'don't bother, it's cute the way you talk' I'm always glad to see her, especially when I've been in the house all day, like Sundays— they keep at it so much it makes me feel they won't think much of me if I don't get over it" [p. 261].

### 3.1.3 REJECTION

Persons may be chosen infrequently because they raise costs or because they provide little in the way of reward For example, Jessie is described in terms of raising other's costs and refusing to provide them with reward. One girl says of Jessie, "She likes to do things the opposite what others like to do whether it's right or wrong She's stubborn and she has an awful rotten disposition She's always flying around in tantrums" A second girl says, "She goes around with a look on that makes you feel that you have done something She's always on the outs about things, antagonistic-like, acts as if other girls were against her when it's herself who is against everybody" A third girl says of Jessie, "She has a fierce temper She's terribly nervous She stands in front of you and sways back and forth or bites her hands, the knuckles" [p 173] It is well known that stutterers (Rosenberg and Curtiss, 1954) and persons with similar mannerisms heighten the discomfort of people with whom they interact.

One of the girls is described in terms that suggests that she has little potentiality to reward others One acquaintance says of her, "She gets along with people but they tease her because she doesn't fight back She's so quiet that if I talk with her, it's mainly a conversation with myself, I wouldn't get anything out of being associated with her." A second girl says, "There's nothing definite about her. She never takes sides on issues that come up She's slow and sort of not interesting. There's nothing against but nothing in her favor much either You don't feel she's around hardly" [p. 168].

Research by Jones and deCharms (1957) suggests that persons who have the ability but lack the motivation to reward others tend to be rejected more strongly by their colleagues than persons who merely lack the ability. In Jennings' protocols Vera seems to have the ability but not the motivation. One girl says of her, "She's quite bright in school and she gets along good but when she gets around someone, it seems as though she is asking dumb questions or arguing on points that don't matter—like how a thing should be said. . . What interests the rest interests me, but she figures very few things are interesting and mostly only her own ideas.  Sometimes she isn't tactful and shows she hasn't much respect for people who can do only little tasks and then of course when she wants them to cooperate with her on a project they refuse and are mean about it" [p 181]. Another girl says of Vera, "She antagonizes a person to such an extent that hardly anyone will congratulate her when she deserves it, she's so painful to cooperate with" [p. 182].

More often than the frequently chosen girl, the less popular one attempts forcibly to extract rewards for herself. For example, twenty-nine per cent of the infrequently chosen girls but only five per cent of the frequently chosen were described as showing aggressive and dominant behavior, getting another individual to do things for them or to obey them.  Attention-demanding behavior was more frequent among the less popular (twenty-seven per cent versus two per cent), as was praise-seeking behavior (twenty-four per cent versus five per cent).  Similar results are presented by Bonney (1947).

Jennings summarizes her findings in the following terms

> Study of the behavior attributes accompanying high and low choice-status gives a view of individuals who differ respectively in capacity to contribute to the needs of others to interact with mutual appreciation and benefit [p 216]
>
> In the work and living groups, the motivations given for the choice structure almost invariably reflect some degree of helpfulness, improvement, or aspiration, *in addition to* whatever element of enjoyment is suggested.  In brief, there is implied an *altering* of how the individual now sees himself, to be achieved by his associating with the chosen person because he can "gain" thereby or because the chosen person assumedly has "qualities" he would like to have, and, to some degree also, out of sheer appeal as "someone *I* could help" [p 260]

As a final example of rewards in dyadic relationships, consider the relationships referred to as "dates" in the American youth culture. We quote Hollingshead (1949):

> Girls learn from older girls and from the boys that they are expected to be submissive to physical advances after the boy has made the proper

overtures by bestowing material favors such as a show, a ride, food, candy, perhaps some small gift. Both boys and girls know that there has to be an exchange of favors or the game is not being played to the mutual satisfaction of the players [p. 419]

This view of the dating relationship has been presented by many observers of adolescents, particularly Waller (Waller and Hill, 1951) Perhaps it seems overly cynical, placing too much emphasis on the short-term bargaining or trading nature of some of these relationships and overlooking some of the longer term satisfactions they often provide and the more subtle aspects of the interaction process necessary for the relationship to be satisfactory to both participants The point should be made, however, that whatever the gratifications achieved in dyads, however lofty or fine the motives satisfied may be, the relationship may be viewed as a trading or bargaining one . The basic assumption running throughout our analysis is that every individual voluntarily enters and stays in any relationship only as long as it is adequately satisfactory in terms of his rewards and costs To adopt this assumption requires no prejudgment as to the nature of the trading process or about the kinds of needs satisfied in relationships.

## 3.2 ABILITIES

Some of the foregoing examples suggest that persons preferred by others as partners in dyadic relationships often possess abilities not possessed by the nonpreferred From his survey of the literature on traits related to popularity, Bonney (1947) finds several factors that seem to imply the existence of abilities to reward others. physical health and vigor and being a source of new experience to others Other factors suggest skills in interaction that operate to keep costs down: emotional stability and control, adaptability and tolerance, and an attitude of good will toward others In general, better liked persons are rated high on "good" traits. for example, generosity, enthusiasm, sociability, punctuality, fairmindedness, sense of humor, and dependability However, because these ratings are usually made by their friends rather than by objective observers, we may wonder what contribution the "halo" effect makes to these results

In a study by Gilchrist (1952) there is evidence that perceived ability is related, under specifiable conditions, to sociometric choice. Sets of four (college-student) subjects, working individually, took a test of verbal reasoning ability and then were formed into pairs to work on a modified Vigotsky block-sorting test. By a prearranged design, half of the subjects on each task (or pairs, on the second task) were scored

as failing, whatever then actual scores were, and half as succeeding
Sociometric information was obtained between the two tasks and
after the tasks were finished   In general, there was a marked tendency
for the subject perceived to be successful on both tasks to receive a
disproportionate number of choices as the most desirable partner for
activities of the kind represented by the experimental tasks.  However,
other data from this and a further experiment (Shaw and Gilchrist,
1955) suggest that a person will discontinue choosing to work with a
successful person if it becomes apparent that that person does not
reciprocate the choice.  Thus the high costs and low affiliative rewards
anticipated from working with someone who doesn't desire the relationship may outweigh the high rewards anticipated by virtue of his
ability   In a similar vein French (1956) presents evidence that the
preference for competent persons as work partners may be outweighed
by affiliative rewards, depending upon the individual's motivation
Subjects high in achievement motivation tended predominantly to
choose as workmates persons of demonstrated ability, whereas subjects
high in affiliation motivation tended to choose from among their
friends, even though the friends had poor performance records

One question regarding ability is whether there are general abilities
promotive of dyad formation or whether the revelant abilities are
pretty much specific to the special needs and problems of each pair of
persons   For example, is intelligence important in interpersonal relationships?  The evidence indicates that intelligence as measured by
current tests has some relation to sociometric status, so it may have
some general value in most interpersonal relationships   Other skills
relevant to such things as putting people at ease and being sensitive to
their internal states, though perhaps unmeasurable at present, are also
probably of general value

On the other hand, there seem to be many abilities the value of
which depends upon the specific persons and circumstances   Jennings
emphasizes this "specificity" view of abilities   From her detailed
studies, she comes to the conclusion that there are no general qualities
or personality traits related to being chosen often as an associate.
Rather, there are specific abilities to meet the specific needs of other
persons in specific problem situations.  Being liked or chosen requires
that the individual be able to recognize and respond to the needs of
the chooser

Admittedly, we would be hard put to isolate the general abilities,
and more so to catalogue all of the specific abilities, that contribute to
satisfactory reward-cost outcomes for the participants   However, it
is clear that whatever these abilities turn out to be in any given rela-

tionship they will function to create in proportion to their degree, a product that is both rewarding and uncostly  Thus a skillful member's low costs of production enable him to afford high rewards to the other without at the same time falling below his own $CL_{alt}$.

## 3 3 PROPINQUITY

Some *contact* or acquaintance between a pair of people is, of course, an essential precondition for the formation of a relationship between them  Evidence from Festinger, Schachter, and Back (1950) documents the obvious fact that the less the physical distance between people and the more in the course of their daily activities their required paths cross, the more likely they are to develop social visiting relationships  Presumably this is so because contacts between people depend upon the ecological factors of distance and pathways  Similarly, Powell (1952) found that the differential proximity of houses in two Costa Rican villages was associated with the frequency of visiting between families  In a village where the houses are all grouped closely together fifty-three per cent of the visiting was reported to be on a daily basis, whereas in an open-country type of settlement where the houses are spread out over a considerable distance only thirty-four per cent of the visiting was on a daily basis  Gullahorn (1952) explicitly investigated rate of interaction as a function of proximity in an office of thirty-seven people in a large corporation.  After two and one half months of observation and interviewing, he concluded that distance was the most important factor in determining rate of interaction.

In short, physical factors place limits upon the set of persons who are available for an individual to establish relationships with.  That this set of available persons may broaden somewhat with time is suggested by Newcomb's (1956) finding from his study of friendship development in a student rooming house, described more fully later in this chapter.  Early in the period of investigation greater liking was reported among pairs of men living on the same floor than among those on different floors  This effect had disappeared by the end of a semester

Propinquity is also likely to be associated with *similarity* of attitudes and values, a variable to be discussed in the next section  For example, there are many communities in which persons from different religious and ethnic backgrounds live in special sections—in a Little Italy or a Polish district  Under these conditions, persons who live near each other will be more similar than persons from different parts of town with regard to such factors as race, religion, educational level, social class, and all the attitudinal and value correlates of these factors Thus, as others have pointed out, propinquity tends not only to limit the field of persons from which an individual can select but also often narrows down this field to a set of persons similar to him in many respects   This raises questions about the interpretation of the vast amount of data indicating that friends, dating or engaged couples, and married people are similar with regard to such things as religious affiliation, occupation, ethnic background, or amount of education (Burgess and Wallin, 1953)   Specifically, we may wonder whether the observed similarity is an artifact of the tendency for relationships to be governed by considerations of propinquity or whether similarity acts as a determining factor even within the "field of eligibles," to borrow Winch's term (Winch, 1952)   Almost certainly both are true Some evidence that similarity per se is important will be presented shortly

Contrariwise, because of the typical confounding of propinquity and similarity, it may be asked whether propinquity has any effect if similarity is held constant   In both the studies by Festinger, Schachter, and Back (1950) and by Gullahorn (1952) situations existed in which the population was relatively homogeneous and in which people were distributed pretty much at random through the physical space. Thus the effects of proximity in these studies cannot be explained on the basis that people who are close are also similar or, for other reasons, have special reasons for preferring each other.

Beyond its relation to the likelihood of contact and to similarity, does spatial distance play any role in dyad formation?  Our analysis suggests the further possibility that distance might contribute to the costs of a relationship. It seems reasonable to assume that providing rewards for each other over large distances would involve greater costs (effort expenditure, expenses of traveling or communicating) than over small distances   Various forms of the general principle that organisms will tend to act in such a way as to minimize energy expenditure have been summarized by Hilgard (1948) under the heading of the law of least action or the law of least effort   "Rats in mazes, other things equal, do tend to take the shorter of two paths to a goal, and to choose the confinement compartment which means less delay toward the goal" [p. 247].  In a series of experiments with children Wright (1937) reports a similar tendency to select that means to a goal that is easiest or least time-consuming

From the law of least action, we would expect propinquity to have a positive effect on relationship formation even under circumstances in which it bears no relation to degree of similarity or likelihood of contact The best way to check this would be on the persistence of relationships after the participants have been physically separated by some distance, this separation occurring for reasons not related to their similarity Thus we could assume adequate contact has already occurred in all pairs and further that those removed from each other are no less similar than those remaining close to each other. Data on this point do not exist, but our everyday observations of the dissolution of dating, "going steady," and engagement relationships with separation would suggest the validity of the hypothesis Even when continuation of the relationship is possible, the effort and expense required to continue it often becomes too great in the light of the rewards received

If the physical distance separating the members of a dyad is greatly increased and if this adds to their cost of maintaining their relationship, then it would follow that a relationship voluntarily maintained over great distances would have to provide some sort of compensation for the high cost. Thus we might expect that the cost would be lower in other respects or that the reward provided would be higher, as compared with relationships maintained over short distances If we assume that similarity with regard to values operates to reduce cost and/or heighten reward, then relationships maintained over great distances would be expected to show relatively high value similarity

This hypothesis has been stated in substantially the same terms by Williams, et al (1956), and survey evidence has been produced in its support. Residents in a suburban housing development were interviewed as to their best friends within the development and their best friends outside it, in the larger neighboring community The original respondents and the persons they named as friends were also questioned with regard to their attitudes on such matters as educational policies, use of leisure time, religious participation, and political issues A count was then made of the number of items on which the members of each respondent-friend pair expressed value agreement Consistent with the hypothesis, it was found that respondents showed far greater agreement with the friends residing outside their immediate community than with those friends residing in the same area Although this result is consistent with the hypothesis, we may not regard it as proven for the reason that in this particular case we cannot be sure that out-of-area friends are similar to within-area friends in all relevant respects other than value similarity and proximity. For example, the out-of-area friends may have been more similar in their occupations, so that ease of contact on the job may have more than made up for difficulty of contact in the residential areas.

Powell (1952) also presents evidence that may be taken as supporting the hypothesis that high costs must be compensated for by high rewards    Villagers in Costa Rica indicated with whom they would be most likely to interact on various occasions    Events of greater importance or special significance (a fiesta or a sick call) were more likely to involve interactions with persons outside the immediate community than events of low importance (a mere visit or going to borrow something)

### 3 4    SIMILARITY OF ATTITUDE

We have already noted that persons who do become friends may be more similar than people paired at random because contact may be limited to a homogeneous "field of eligibles"    This provides one explanation of why the members of various dyads have been found to come from similar religious and ethnic backgrounds, to have similar social attitudes, etc   We may now ask whether, within a set of persons all of whom have the same opportunity for contact with one another, those with similar attitudes tend to become friends and to associate with each other    A number of studies have shown that friends tend to resemble each other in their attitudes and values (Lindzey and Borgatta, 1954, Lazarsfeld and Merton, 1954)    However, to obtain a true answer to this question requires information about individual attitudes *prior* to contact, since, as we know, opinions tend to become similar with interaction and friendship.    Therefore, any similarity observed at later stages may be an outcome of the relationship rather than a factor contributing to its initial formation

Newcomb designed a study precisely to answer this question (1956)    Strangers (male college students) were measured with regard to their attitude similarity before meeting each other    They were then placed together in a rooming house and assigned to rooms so that propinquity was not related to degree of similarity    Then they were periodically asked questions about how favorably they felt toward one another and who associated with whom    (The answers to these questions may be regarded as indications of willingness to enter relationships with each other )    The number of objects about which there was a given degree of attitudinal similarity, as determined before interaction, was found to predict later interpersonal attractions    The individuals most similar in their attitudes were most likely to associate with each other after having had an opportunity to get acquainted

Why is value similarity an important factor in friendship development?    The answer may be stated in terms both of *ability to reward*

each other and the *cost of providing this reward* If we assume that in
many value areas an individual is in need of social support for his opinions and attitudes then another person's agreeing with him will constitute a reward for him In other words, provision of opinion support
may be considered as having learned reinforcement value * Thus
two people with similar values may provide rewards for each other
simply by expressing their values This may also be considered as a
low-cost operation, since it is easy for a person to express the values
he really feels, particularly when that expression is to a person found
to be more or less receptive to his opinions

This explanation asserts, it may be noted, that value similarity
promotes dyad formation only if there is a need for social support on
the values concerned and if the values are expressed Proof of the
latter must, of course, come from examining situations in which similarity exists but is never expressed It seems obvious that this would
not promote friendship any more than unexpressed dissimilarity

This analysis can be viewed as a variant of Newcomb's thesis that
" . . interpersonal attraction varies with perceived similarity in regard
to objects of importance and of common relevance . ." [p 579] To
be perceived, similarity must be expressed in some way The factors
of "importance and common relevance" probably specify the principal,
if not the only, conditions under which social support for one's attitudes is rewarding

Many persons are uncertain about how to regard themselves they
are not certain of their abilities, their social stimulus value, or their
worth For these persons, their self-evaluations constitute opinions
about which they are concerned and in need of social support Accordingly, we would expect to find the formation of interpersonal relationships to be facilitated when two individuals hold opinions of each
other that are similar to their respective self-evaluations. This creates
a situation in which each can reward the other by expressing opinions
that validate the accuracy of the other's self-image Further, assuming
that people generally have predominantly positive attitudes about
themselves, relationship formation would be facilitated by their having positive evaluations of each other Put in everyday terms, this

---

* The reinforcement value of agreement with opinions is suggested by Verplanck
(1955) who found that, if person A agrees with the opinion statements of person
B, B will increase his rate of making such statements Verplanck's data do not
reveal whether there is an increase in the expression of *certain* opinions or in the
general class of behavior "stating an opinion," or both, but much other research on
social influence would lead one to expect considerable increase of the former type
Verplanck's data may also be interpreted as indicating that agreement reduces the
restraints (costs) often associated with voicing opinions

assertion is that a friendship is made more likely if the two persons can honestly say nice things about each other   In the strategies of how to "win friends and influence people" this suggests the importance of praise and flattery.

This general line of thinking has been stated most clearly by New-comb who also provides confirmatory evidence from the study de-scribed above.   The students were found to express greater liking for their fellows who express high liking for them than for colleagues who expressed little liking   This tendency for the individual's rating of others to reflect their ratings of him was almost as strong on the fourth day in the life of the group as at the end of their fourth month to-gether   Even more closely related to the individual's attraction to various others was found to be his perception of their relative likings for him [p 581]   The typical subject was also found to like others who he believed would describe him in pretty much the same way he described himself, this being especially marked if the others were be-lieved to agree with the favorable aspects of his self-image [p 582]

Perceiving that another person likes you, then, is an important con-tribution to wanting to associate with that person   In addition to Newcomb's evidence, Taguri (1952) had previously found that socio-metric choices tend to be directed toward those perceived as liking the chooser.   The reader will also recall the evidence from Shaw and Gilchrist (1955), cited earlier, which indicated the withdrawal of choice from a person who fails to reciprocate it.

The detrimental effects on relationship formation of negative inter-personal evaluations has been verified in experimental situations (Kel-ley and Shapiro, 1954, Dittes and Kelley, 1956)   Incidental to investi-gating another problem, each subject was given fictitious information about how other subjects evaluated the desirability of his continued presence in the group   This information was not related in any way to how he was actually evaluated.   The effect upon his desire to con-tinue further association with his colleagues was very striking   When told the others evaluated him poorly the typical subject exhibited large losses in his desire to remain in the group and in his liking for work with the other members

Eng (1954) has found some evidence that the importance of others' evaluations of oneself varies with the intimacy of the situation in which the relationship exists   His data indicate that acceptance of oneself was considered more important by college fraternity men in selecting a man with whom to go on a double date or camping trip than in select-ing one to represent the fraternity at an important meeting   From her research, Jennings (1950) came to a very similar conclusion   If we assume that perception of others' acceptance is veridical, we are able to derive that mutual choices will be more frequent when the criterion for choice involves a more personal situation   Both Jennings and Eng found this to be true.

## 3 5   COMPLEMENTARY NEEDS

Our generalization, stated earlier, is that dyad formation is facilitated by the members being able, at low cost to themselves, to provide their partners with high rewards   This implies that each person can do something for the other one which that person cannot do for (or by) himself   Thus we should find formation probable not only when pairs of people share values and attitudes but also when they have different talents, possessions, etc , and when the differences are such that each person can provide something the other one needs   For example, one boy has a car, the other, a gasoline credit card, and both want to take a trip

The hypothesis that differences which permit a symbiosis between the pair are promotive of relationship formation has been stated by Winch (1952) as the theory of *complementary needs.* ". .   Each individual seeks within his or her field of eligibles for that person who gives the greatest promise of providing him or her with maximum need gratification" [p. 406, italics omitted]   It is hypothesized that maximum need gratification occurs when two people have different and complementary need patterns rather than similar ones

Winch has applied this theory to the analysis of marriage-mate selection, under conditions in which, as in America, the marriage relationship is viewed as an important source of need gratification, it is entered into voluntarily by both partners, and opportunities are provided (by dating and courtship practices) for mutual assessment of the gratification potentialities in the relationship   Winch gives as examples the following.

> If A is highly ascendent, we should expect A to be more attracted maritally to B who is submissive than to C who, like A, is ascendent   If A is somewhat sadistic, we should expect A to be more attracted maritally to B who is somewhat masochistic than to C who is sadistic   If A is a succorant person, we should expect A to be attracted to nurturant B rather than to succorant C   And in each of these cases B should be reciprocally attracted to A (Winch, Ktsanes, and Ktsanes, 1954, p 242)

Winch and his co-workers (Winch, 1955*b*) have tested this hypothesis by detailed analysis of records of twenty-five married couples At least one member of each couple was a college undergraduate at the time, and the sample was fairly homogeneous with respect to race, age, and socioeconomic background  In order to study couples as close as possible to the time of the formation of their relationship, only those who had been married two years or less were used  On the basis of interviews and the TAT, the needs of each of the fifty individuals, including such variables as need abasement, need dominance, and need succorance, were measured  Following the reasoning suggested in the examples given above it was hypothesized that complementarity would manifest itself in two ways: (1) the correlation between husbands and wives on the same variable (e g , nurturance) would be negative, and (2) the correlation between husbands and wives on different variables (e g , nurturance and succorance) would be positive  Although the evidence from the TAT and case-history interview are not consistent with the hypothesis, neither are they consistent with the similarity (homogamy) hypothesis.  On the other hand, the results from a special interview designed to elicit evidence on needs and from ratings made by a five-man conference using all the data are in line with the hypothesis.  [Two other analyses, too complex to be reported here, also support the hypothesis (Winch, 1955a, Ktsanes, 1955)  Both are also based upon the need interview data, so they essentially add nothing to the simpler analysis ]

Other investigators. employing different personality-assessment procedures, have failed to find evidence consistent with the hypothesis of complementary needs  Bowerman and Day (1956) gave an objective personality schedule, designed in part to measure personality needs, to sixty college couples who were engaged or considered themselves regular dating partners  The results show consistent support for neither the complementary need hypothesis nor the similarity hypothesis  Evidence slightly favoring emotional similarity has been presented by Burgess and Wallin (1953).  By analyzing self-ratings made by engaged persons, they found similarity in the degree of daydreaming, loneliness, feelings easily hurt, and touchiness.  For example, individuals who characterize themselves as having their feelings easily hurt or as being touchy on various subjects will tend, more than would be expected by chance, to become engaged to other individuals who admit possessing these same traits  Similarity between friends in introversion-extraversion and steadiness of emotional response has also been reported by Flemming (1935).

The results from these and other studies of personality characteristics seem to yield inconsistent results  In view of examples and anecdotal evidence presented by Jennings, Burgess and Wallin, and others, the existence of complementarity phenomena can hardly be denied  However, systematic investigations so far do not yield strong support for the theory  Whether this is due to inadequacies in methodology (e.g , failure to measure needs and abilities at the appropriate level) or to the fact that complementarity is not very important in mate selection remains to be decided by future research

In general, it seems likely that similarity and complementarity both contribute to the rewards persons obtain from interactions  Some relationships may be based largely on similarity and others, largely on complementarity  Gross (1956) found both kinds of relationships in an investigation of informal groupings at an Air Force base.  The groups he describes as "consensual" were comprised of men who found one another congenial by virtue of having made similar decisions or holding similar opinions (e g , two men who are dissatisfied with the air base)  Other groups which Gross describes as "symbiotic" tended to be composed of men of dissimilar or contrasting characteristics which enabled them to provide different sorts of rewards for each other: for example, a married man provides a single man with a "home away from home" and in so doing satisfies his own need to be nurturant  It appears, then, that within the set of persons available for interaction (where *availability* refers to the costs determined by physical, social, and cultural factors) an individual may find it especially rewarding to interact with certain other persons for a variety of different reasons  In some cases the rewards depend on similarity (as in the case of value support), and in others the rewards depend on differences which are in some manner complementary.  The prediction of interpersonal relationships should, in our opinion always take account of reward and cost considerations, although it seems likely that dependable but fairly complex generalizations linking similarities and differences to interpersonal attraction will eventually be possible.

In the preceding discussion we have not touched upon the many sociometric studies made of similarity with respect to such personal characteristics as physique and intelligence, as, for example, the studies summarized by Lindzey and Borgatta (1954).  These show little consistency and, therefore, provide little basis for making generalizations  It may be true that the complementarity hypothesis holds for some characteristics (as in Winch's data) and the similarity hypothesis for others  As Newcomb has suggested, personal characteristics may provide a basis for similarity of attitudes by virtue of their being observable and reacted to evaluatively by those who observe them

## 3 6  POWER AND STATUS

A number of studies have dealt with the relation between socioeconomic status and direction of sociometric choice in elementary
school classes, college student groups, and small communities (Lindzey and Borgatta, 1954)   In general, the results show that individuals
(make their choices primarily within their own status level or in adjacent levels.  This may be explained partly in terms of opportunities
for contact and having similar values, but there may also be a question
of cost involved   For example, Hollingshead (1949) says of the
adolescent youths in his sample, "These people, like the typical member of each class, want to associate with people similar to themselves,)
Here they feel comfortable, for they are 'among my kind of people'
This appeared to be an important principle in the organization of the
leisure time activities of each class" [p  100].

In addition, the data indicate that (when choices are made outside
one's own level they are directed more often toward higher status levels
than toward lower ones.)  This indicates that association with people
of higher status yields certain kinds of rewards not available from
people of lower status   As to the basis and nature of these rewards we
may only guess.  One possibility is that people at higher status levels
are intrinsically different in those personality traits and skills)revelant
to rewarding others   Another more likely possibility is that the higher
status people have(greater extrinsic means (economic resources or possessions) for rewarding others)  W F Whyte's (1943) analysis of a
street-corner gang suggests that one source of the high-status person's
ability to provide rewards is his social contacts and friends in other
groups

A third explanation may be the "rubbing off" effect.  It has been
observed that the prestige of a person tends to be conferred on those
who associate with him   By such association, a low-status person may
also(participate vicariously in the privileges and satisfactions )enjoyed
by the higher status person   And, of course, the(lower person may
actually gain some status in the eyes of other people )  Folsom (1943)
describes how in college dating the rewards a person receives from
other groups are affected by the status of persons he dates

> The fraternities and sororities apply considerable social pressure to the
> "dating" of their members   One gets merits, whether formally recorded
> or not, for dating with a coed of a high-ranking sorority, demerits for
> association with an "independent."  The net result of this competition
> might seem to be to match each person with one of fairly equal rank, as
> happens in society in general   But there is another result   It is to dis-
> courage pairing altogether among the lower ranks.  The fire of competi-

tive dating burns hot at the top, smoulders at the bottom. The low-ranking student often has more to gain by abstaining altogether than from dating with a person of his own rank [p. 532].

## SUMMARY

We have reviewed a number of studies on the determinants of friendships and other more or less stable pair relationships. The general assumption is made that for a dyadic relationship to be viable it must provide rewards and/or economies in costs which compare favorably with those in other competing relationships or activities available to the two individuals. With this as a starting point, the comparison of successful and unsuccessful relationships provides a basis for drawing inferences about the factors that contribute to rewards and costs. Considered in the present chapter are those factors we have termed *exogenous.* These are the personal characteristics, situational factors, physical objects, and so forth, which, in the sense that they constitute "givens" or "boundary conditions" for the relationship, are external to it. (The next chapter deals with the reward and cost determinants we have labeled *endogenous.*)

Anecdotal and systematic evidence from sociometric studies generally bears out the major assumption of our analysis: persons are chosen as friends or workmates if they are able and willing to help others in various ways and if others are able to act with a minimum of tension and restraint in their presence. On the other hand, persons are rejected if they fail to provide help to others (particularly if they are able but refuse to do so) or if they raise others' costs by inducing anxiety or discomfort. (Abilities enter into this picture insofar as they enable one person, at low cost, to help another.

The factor of propinquity (proximity in physical space) has been shown to play an important facilitative role in friendship, engagement, and dating relations, but various theoretical interpretations may be made of this result. Propinquity undoubtedly affects the likelihood that a pair will come into contact at all, and it is usually correlated with the similarity of their backgrounds and values. There is also some evidence indicating that part of the contribution of proximity is to reduce the costs (effort and expense) required to interact when separated by considerable distance.

Recent research has shown that similarity of attitudes and values is promotive of friendships. (Other evidence, to be reviewed later in this book, shows the reverse effect, friendship being conducive to increased similarity ) The evidence suggests that (expressing agreement with another person's opinions or supporting his values often constitutes a reward for him,) but value support may also reduce the costs he incurs in the relationship by reducing his concern for expressing unacceptable opinions ) From the strong tendency for expressions of liking to be reciprocated, we might infer that being regarded positively by another person also has reward value for many individuals, and again, this can be interpreted in terms of the principle of value support the positive regard serves to confirm or validate an individual's positive feelings about himself.

Although some pair relationships seem to be based upon similarity of attitudes and background and presumably involve an exchange of value support, others constitute symbiotic relationships in which the rewards one person provides the other are quite different from those provided in the reverse direction This kind of relationship requires that the two individuals differ in certain respects (e g in their respective predominant needs and abilities) and in ways that are complementary, each being able at low cost to provide the special kind of product valued by the other )

Several lines of evidence indicate that persons are most comfortable (incur least cost) when associating with persons from their own social class and status levels However, there also appear to be instances in which rewards are higher if one associates with persons of higher status A number of explanations suggest themselves, but these have not yet been systematically investigated as to their validity or generality.

# 4.

# *Interference and Facilitation in Interaction*

In Chapter 3 we discussed the exogenous factors that determine the potential rewards and costs of members of a dyadic relationship    These exogenous factors may be construed as setting the boundary conditions, the outside limits, within which at any given moment other processes that are internal or endogenous to the relationship may operate to affect further the rewards and costs of the members    We contend in the present chapter that the maximum rewards and minimum costs that are potentially available under given boundary conditions are achieved only when certain endogenous factors are optimal    These endogenous factors, when they are less than optimal, attenuate the most favorable reward-cost possibilities    They are thought to arise mainly from particular combinations of sets, or response sequences, adopted by the members of the dyad

A person often cannot do two things at the same time and do them efficiently and well    This is the phenomenon referred to as *response interference,* by which is meant that the performance of one response (or even the existence of a tendency to make that response) may be incompatible with the performance of another)    Response interference is important in the analysis of dyadic interaction because for each individual the behaviors of the other constitute powerful instigations to responses. These may be incompatible with other responses which, by virtue of other instigations (events in the social or physical environment or internal events such as need or drive stimuli), the individual

51

happens to be performing at that moment  Any two behavioral sets
(or pairs of items) from the repertoires of A and B may be described
in terms of their incompatibility. Set $a_1$ in A's repertoire is said to be
*incompatible* with set $b_1$ in B's to the degree that when the two sets
are simultaneously enacted $a_1$ instigates some response tendencies (or
set) in B that interfere with his making the responses in $b_1$, and, vice
versa, $b_1$ instigates some response tendencies (or set) in A that interfere with his performance of $a_1$

Interference will frequently operate symmetrically in an interaction.
if what A is doing interferes with B's activities, B will also often interfere with A's activities  If interference effects are symmetrical in this
way, they would be expected to produce a correspondence between
A's and B's outcomes over the various cells in the matrix, that is, a correlation tends to exist between the paired entries in each of the several
cells in which such symmetry of interference occurs  It should be
mentioned, though, that interference need not be symmetrical  In
numerous situations such effects are asymmetrical, for example, when
one participant to an interaction teases or criticizes the other or exhibits annoying mannerisms, such as scratching, belching, or snoring
—in fact (when any behavior is performed which interferes without
being interfered with )

Before continuing with a discussion of the various effects of interference on the outcomes to the participants in an interaction, it should
be emphasized (if it is not too obvious) that *facilitative* effects also
occur in interaction  The husband's greeting is completed by the wife's
countering in an appropriate way, hence the reward value to the husband of this bit of interaction is maximal only if the wife's response is
satisfactory  The reader is asked to remember that these positive enhancing processes of the pairing of optimal responses are necessary if
rewards are to be maximized  The concentration in the present chapter on the effects of interference is based not on any conviction that
facilitative effects are unimportant but rather on an impression that the
effects of interference are more complex, hence require more careful
analysis

## 4.1  EFFECTS OF RESPONSE INTERFERENCE

In specifying more exactly what we mean by interference we should
first state that interference may exist at the level of the production of
the behavior associated with a given set and also at the level of the
consumption or appreciation of the behavior.  On the production side,
interference will be directly related to cost and will secondarily affect

the quality or reward-value of the produced behavior. On the appreciation side, interference may affect both the perceiving or apprehending
of the reward-value of behavior as well as the consummatory experience itself.

Return to the dyadic situation in which person A is producing set
$a_1$ from his repertoire while person B is enacting set $b_1$ from his. We
will analyze the relationship from the point of view of A's production
of behavior that is potentially rewarding to B with the understanding
that the process would ordinarily be bilateral and that any conclusions
about A's rewards for B would also apply to B's rewards for A.

### 4.1.1 COST TO A

The cost to A of set $a_1$ will be greater than minimum to the degree
that there is interference from set $b_1$, that is, to the degree that set $b_1$
is incompatible with set $a_1$. The reader will recall that by *minimum
cost* we mean the minimum cost as defined by the optimal conditions
discussed in Chapter 3. To paraphrase slightly, we are simply assert-
ing that inhibiting or incompatible response tendencies accompanying
the production of behavior increase the optimal cost of the behavior,
whether in the form of annoyance, embarrassment, anxiety, or the increased effort required to make the appropriate responses.

The main evidence on this point comes from industrial research on
the costs of noise and other distractions. Chapanis, Garner, and
Morgan (1949), in summarizing the work of Stevens and others, remark that: ". . . subjects require more energy to perform the same
kind of work in a noisy environment than in a quiet one. A number of
studies have shown quite consistently that the basal metabolism of
subjects working in a noisy environment is higher than those working
in a quiet one," and ". . . this seems to indicate that subjects in a noisy
environment . . . require more energy to do the same amount of
work" [p. 417]. The danger of accepting evidence of this sort is that
we have no assurance that interpersonal interferences will act in the
same way as interference from impersonal "noise."

Evidence on the effects of another person's activities, such as laugh-
ing, mumbling, humming, and walking around, is provided by Cason
(1938). His subjects were given tasks of reading, paired-associate
learning, addition, and arithmetic-problem solving. As contrasted to
a quiet period, introduction of the above forms of distraction caused
the subjects to exert greater effort (in spite of which they showed
lower efficiency). On the basis of this and other similar evidence, we
are strongly inclined to believe that interpersonal interference will
raise costs.

One superficially discrepant finding is reported by Bradney (1957) in her study of salesclerks in a large department store. Bradney's analysis suggests that three sets of external factors control the sales-clerk's activities  (1) the spatial layout of her department, which provides physical barriers and prescribed pathways, (2) the sales procedure which requires her to learn the location of the various goods, how to prepare the sales slip, etc , and (3) the demands made on her by other members of her work group   Each of these factors determines a type of interruption and interference.  In sections with counters there is

. . hindrance in the form of blockades unavoidably made by other members of the department when they open a drawer in a narrow gang-way or stand talking on the only opening leading to the other side of the department [p 180]
There is so much to learn and know about where things are situated in both the department and the store as a whole, so much to know about the sales procedure, etc., that working side by side as the assistants do, it is inevitable that they refer to each other from time to time about these matters, often interrupting a sale in doing so [p 181]
The buyer may at any time ask to see an assistant or get her to do a special job, and the underbuyer   .  frequently has to interrupt an assist-ant to tell her, for example, that a special order has arrived and may be dispatched or to ask her how a particular "line" is selling [p. 181].
It is at this point, then, when an interruption comes from another mem-ber of the staff to hinder a sale or waste valuable selling time that one would expect to find friction in the department   .  But what *do* we find?  We find a "joking relationship" [p 182]

Bradney's interpretation of this effect may be paraphrased in this way  the more or less irreducible interference that occurs among these people who are constrained to work together gives rise to high costs which threaten to break out into open conflict   The "joking relation-ship" develops as a social institution which protects the group members from the disastrous effects of such irreducible interferences.

The determinants of the amount of cost increase under conditions of set incompatibility are suggested by theoretical analyses of conflict. No doubt the reader will have noted a similarity between the present discussion of response interference and the usual treatment of con-flict   We suggest that the excessive costs induced by interference are proportional to the amount of conflict produced by the situation   The tendency to avoid high costs, postulated here, is then another way of describing what might be called a "conflict-avoidance" drive.

Following Brown and Farber (1951) and Berlyne (1957), we take the amount of conflict to be an increasing function of four variables  (1) the number of competing responses, (2) their degree of incompatibility) or interference, (3) their (absolute strengths) or intensities, and (4) the degree to which their strengths approach equality) From these considerations, it follows that A's costs when performing set $a_1$ are not likely to rise much if the incompatible response tendencies comprising the set instigated by B's activities are relatively weak The husband's costs of watching an exciting boxing match on TV will be little affected if the wife only barely arouses in him an impulse to engage in whist On the other hand, conflict will be maximal when both the original responses and the newly induced incompatible ones are very strong Costs become high when both the boxing match and whist succeed simultaneously in instigating their "appropriate" sets

Assuming the existence of a basic tendency to avoid high cost, we would expect A to take all available measures to avoid the arousal of incompatible sets. Stated more conventionally, A will avoid conflict-arousal Assisting A in his reluctance to pay the increased costs of conflict is the fact that concentrated and intense enactment of the behaviors in a given set may prevent his receiving instigations from the other person's behavior A wife thoroughly engrossed in a novel may not notice her husband's attempts at seductive flattery (Of course, she thereby loses whatever she might have gained from this bit of interaction ) Individuals can learn means of avoiding conflict and have numerous opportunities to do so. These include giving close attention to relevant stimuli and selectively excluding the irrelevant The cues which tend to keep one in a single set may be multiplied and other cues avoided, either by (surrounding oneself with appropriate behavioral "props") or by (moving into an environment in which all cues act uniformly to support a single behavioral sequence.)

In brief, because of cost considerations, individuals try to do "one thing at a time," and, to this end, they try to control their environments and perceptual responses so as to eliminate instigations to mutually interfering activities However, there are limits to the effectiveness of these perceptual-selection and cue-control measures The external cues presented to a person are in large part determined by other persons and the physical world Moreover, some of the most powerful instigations to sets, in the form of need or drive stimuli, are internal to the individual and largely beyond his control

Interference is, of course, a problem for both members of any dyad If it exists for A, it will often exist at the same time for B, and the two are likely to share (though not necessarily to verbalize) a concern about avoiding the high costs incurred. Later in this chapter we consider what the two might do jointly in the interests of reducing interference.

### 4.1 2   REWARD PRODUCED BY A

Rewards may be considered from two points of view: first, in terms of the quality of the product created by A and, second, in terms of B's appreciation of the product created by A.

The reward value of set $a_1$ will be less than maximum to the degree that there is interference from set $b_1$ in the production of it. This statement is a prediction that the (interferences (e g, disturbances or distractions) will lower the quality of performance of the set) As we shall see later, this prediction will have to be severely qualified

First let us look at some empirical evidence. There are clear indications that worry and anxiety are disruptive of many behavior sequences Experimental subjects who are threatened with failure or danger find that their preoccupation with the possible consequences interferes with their concentration on the task at hand (Lazarus, Deese, and Osler, 1952). On some tasks there is an increase in speed but also an increase in the number of errors  This would account for the finding that industrial accident rates are disproportionately high when workers are worried or apprehensive (Hersey, 1955)   Intermittent loud noise is reported to have similar effects on work in standard performance tests the rate of productivity is increased but the percentage of accuracy decreases (Smith, 1951).

Perhaps the most relevant data are those on the effects of *social facilitation,* in which the performance of subjects working alone is compared with that of subjects working before a passive audience or with other persons at the same task  In regarding these findings as relevant to our present concern, we assume that in working alone the subject is focused more or less exclusively on the task at hand (i e., he is rather fully aroused in set $a_1$), whereas with social participation the subject is not only focused on the task itself but also on the various social tasks of competing with, defending against, affiliating with, and otherwise generally coping with the social stimulus (i.e., the other person's activities arouse some *social* responses which may be assumed to interfere in some degree with task set $a_1$)

A summary (Kelley and Thibaut, 1954) of a number of such "social facilitation" studies reveals that working in a social context, as compared with working alone, has the following main effects.

(a) Greater quantity of work where physical output is involved, suggesting increased motivation to perform the task

(b) Lesser quantity or quality of work where intellectual processes or concentration are involved, suggesting that social stimuli are able to compete successfully with the task stimuli

(c) Inhibitions of responses and qualitative changes in the work, which suggest that the person somehow "takes account" of the others as he goes about his work, e g , he has fewer idiosyncratic thoughts, exercises moderation in judgment, and gives more "popular" or common associations

(*d*) Greater variations through time in his output, indicating the presence of periodic distractions and/or the effects of working under greater tension [p 750].

Evidently there is at least partial confirmation of our assertions that interfering social responses are elicited and that these operate to reduce the quality of the performance The main difficulty is with the first finding summarized that quantity of physical output is often increased. Ordinarily, such quantitative increases would be expected to increase the reward-value of the performance, assuming quality of work to remain constant Our difficulty partly resolves itself into one of specifying more clearly the criterion of reward-value and how A's performance mediates this criterion

Let us return to some theoretical considerations. When the performance of a given set is interfered with by the partial or complete arousal of another, incompatible set, the result is conflict manifested in tension, strain, and discomfort. The amount of conflict is a function of the degree of incompatibility of the two sets and of their intensities (which depend upon the strength of instigations to the sets)

Further, we have stated that increasing conflict leads to increasing costs, and, through a cost-minimization assumption, conflict will be avoided or reduced when possible Conflict thus acts very much like a need or drive state· it tends to reduce itself. We have said that need or drive states are a source of instigations to a set The question arises Into what set do the instigations from conflict-drive feed? The answer must be Into whichever is momentarily prepotent, that is, whichever momentarily has greater intensity. But the additional instigations from conflict-drive will increase the intensity of the prepotent set, and thus we would expect that in proportion to the amount of conflict the responses of the prepotent set will be discharged with greater intensity than if no conflict had existed In other words, there will be an increased amplitude in the responses accompanying the reduction of conflict

We are now in a better position to evaluate the effects of incompatible sets on the reward-value produced by A Any of the usual costly forms of conflict (anxiety, frustration, stress, fear, or intense self-consciousness) will generate high drive and lead A to produce behaviors of heightened intensity Whether this will result in increased or decreased reward to B (or to A himself for that matter) is mooted by a further consideration. Smock (1956) summarizes a series of studies by Spence and his colleagues with this comment.

> A number of recent investigations concerned with the functional relationship between anxiety level and performance in a variety of learning tasks    . indicate that anxious Ss tend to perform at a lower level than non-anxious Ss on tasks that elicit multiple competing response tendencies (i e , complex tasks) [p 192]

Stated somewhat more generally, any increase in drive will improve the performance of activities that are simple, easy, or well integrated (overlearned) but will lead to deteriorated performance of activities that are complex, difficult, or in general not well learned. This would seem to imply that for any given type of activity, such as speaking French, the greater A's skill, that is, the lower his costs of production, the more likely it is that an increase in drive (through conflict or any other source) will lead to improved performance, the less the skill the more likely that drive increases will impair his performance

Thus it may be predicted that if the task is sufficiently simple and the appropriate behavior sufficiently automatic an increase in drive will lead to greater performance   The problem is to assess how pervasive this phenomenon is   In a summary of a large number of studies of the effects of stress and conflict on performance, Lazarus, Deese, and Osler (1952) conclude that· "   . it does seem likely that some individuals will show a facilitation of performance under such conditions, but it also seems probable that these individuals will be in the minority in any randomly chosen sample of people" [p 306]   If this is a fair assessment of the evidence, we may conclude that the presence of incompatible sets or conflict will usually tend to lead to a deterioration in performance and, therefore, to lower rewards.

### 4.1.3   APPRECIATION BY B

On the appreciation side, in general, the reward-value to person B of A's enactment of $a_1$ will be less than maximum to the degree that B does not make the appropriate attentive, interpretive, or consummatory responses   B's failure to make such responses is attributed to interference from the simultaneous arousal of response tendencies incompatible with them   The costs of making whatever appreciative responses he does make are likely also to be higher as a consequence of the interference.

Research evidence on interference with appreciative responses comes from several quarters   Music has been found to reduce reading efficiency (Henderson, Crews, and Barlow, 1945, Fenduck, 1937)   The individual typically encounters difficulty in attending to two dif-

ferent streams of input to the same sensory modality   For example,
in one experiment (Cameron and Magaret, 1949) subjects were given
sentences to complete orally and at the same time listened to a re-
corded story   Fewer items of the story were recalled under these
conditions than when listening only to the story.   The learning of
nonsense syllables has also been shown to be more rapid when the
person is strictly alone than when closely observed by the experimenter
(Pessin, 1933).   Investigations of this sort suggest that the attentive
and possibly the interpretive behavior necessary to appreciate the
performances of others is likely to be disrupted by cues arousing
irrelevant sets

It is not clear whether on the appreciation side conflict-drive may
also operate to increase set intensities and, thereby, increase the intensity of the pleasures experienced   In principle, there is no reason to
doubt that conflict should have motivational properties in consummatory behavior if it is accepted as having these effects in other (instrumental) types of behavior   Animal studies (e g , Siegel and Brantley,
1951) do show increases in food and water intake immediately after
"teasing" faradic stimulation   However, these studies do not necessarily involve the simultaneous arousal of interfering sets

It is obvious, perhaps, that the behaviors of other persons sometimes enhance one's enjoyment of other events.   For example, more
people laugh aloud at jokes heard over the radio when there are
others listening in the same room   Similarly, most people feel radio
humor to be improved if they can hear the laughter of a studio audience (Cantril and Allport, 1935)   The importance of the appropriate
setting and preliminaries for the enjoyment of sexual relations has
been emphasized by marriage counselors and investigators of marital
difficulties (Dickinson and Beam, 1931)   These examples illustrate an
important fact which the present emphasis on interference might lead
one to overlook. on numerous occasions the behavior of another person serves to facilitate the full assumption of a set   In the absence of
this or other instigations the set is likely to be enacted in a rather
slack way and its reward-values to be less than maximal

To summarize our discussion of incompatible sets, we have suggested that they will increase the actor's costs and will usually impair
both the quality of his performance and the other person's appreciation of the performance, thus reducing the reward-value of the product   In those instances in which a possibility exists that the actor's
performance and the other's appreciation are improved by interfering
sets it seems necessary that the task be simple and the behavior highly
automatic.

### 4 2  MEANS OF AVOIDING INTERFERENCE IN INTERACTION

If a dyadic relationship is to form and survive, it must provide minimally satisfactory reward-cost outcomes to its members   The preceding discussion suggests that the likelihood of the formation and survival of a relationship is, in part, contingent on the success of social interaction in providing for the participants combinations of sets that are compatible   A relationship might be expected to develop most cohesion and morale when the two individuals discover and employ some means of moving from one pair of compatible sets to another

The question arises   How can compatible sets be attained in a relationship?   Very generally, we can say that the presence of compatible sets in the relationship will depend on either of two processes Sets incompatible with all or most other sets must be eliminated from the interaction  or pairs of sets must be synchronized so that incompatible sets will not be simultaneously aroused   In relationships that can be severely restricted as to the domain of relevant activity all incompatible sets might be eventually eliminated from the repertoire of interaction   However, in most relationships it would seem that a combination of mechanisms, including the elimination of some sets and the synchronizing of most sets, would be used to reduce response interference

#### 4.2 1  SYNCHRONIZING SETS

Let us deal first with the ways in which synchronization of pairs of sets can take place   There seem to be two closely related types of factors that support synchronizing   The first of these has to do with the availability of synchronizing cues in the environment.   More specifically  good synchronization would be expected to be found when the reciprocal sets are aroused by cues that occur at the same time, for example, when the social behavior associated with eating is aroused by the dinner bell   A variant of this would be observed when the cue is provided by one member of the pair and the other member is in the versatile set of adjusting to the cue, for example, in identification behavior (the doting mother) or when there are expectations of future rewards (the employment interview)

A further word is necessary to indicate the limits of probable success of this mechanism for synchronizing sets   It appears that we must distinguish between sets the instigations to which are beyond the control of the member (e g , instigations from urgent and recurrent need states) versus those over which the member exercises a measure of control (e g, instigations arranged for oneself by providing external cues, such as an appropriate work place, tools, clocks, and materials). (On the latter mechanism of self-control, see Skinner, 1953 ) Needless to say, synchronization will be more difficult to arrange when the sets of both members are governed only by strong need states, since the needs themselves are unlikely to be synchronized But in the absence of such coercive needs, and by virtue of exercising control over instigation, moment-to-moment compatibility can often be achieved, that is, in many instances incompatibility can be converted at the next moment into compatibility Thus, if one fails to instigate the other member to the appropriate set, one can adapt by providing self-instigations to the appropriate set.

A second way of achieving synchronization is provided by the rules for behavior specified in social roles. (We deal specifically and in some detail with roles and norms in Chapter 8. We introduce *role* here as it is defined by everyday usage ) A main contribution of role to the achievement of set-compatibility is that roles frequently suggest (when they do not clearly specify) a synchronized order of interaction ) We refer to the whole range of role attributes having to do with rights, privileges, responsibilities, precedence, seniority, and so forth In the later chapter on roles and norms we define role in terms of norms and suggest that the activation of any given role often implies the coactivation of a role compatible with it (often referred to as a reciprocal role ). When this occurs, the cues that activate a given role in A also serve to activate a reciprocal role in B or the role behavior of A serves to activate reciprocal role behavior in B. Thus, because of the high serial dependence of items of behavior specified by a role, synchronization cues are necessary only to activate the roles and are not necessary on a moment-to-moment basis. This mode of synchronization probably occurs very widely and may be illustrated by such diverse situations as are observed in the interaction among factory workers on a production line and in that between doctor and patient

Before leaving this discussion of social role, we should mention a further function which roles contribute in maintaining the reward positions of the members We have noted that roles facilitate synchronization, but, should synchronization fail, there is another way in which roles can operate to avoid severe loss of rewards This is the opportunity afforded by many roles for much rehearsal, hence for adequate overlearning of the behaviors specified by them By virtue of this routinization of behavior, role behaviors should be less susceptible to interference, hence if any conflict-drive should arise from incompatible sets it might be expected to result in facilitated rather than deteriorated performance of the behavior Some theory such as this appears to underlie the intensive practice and drill which soldiers, firemen, and policemen undergo in preparation for meeting emergency situations

### 4.2 2 ELIMINATING SETS

We have said that one way to reduce the costly and reward-impairing effects of incompatible sets is by synchronization. Another more direct way is to eliminate such sets from the relationship If it is true that a relationship does not survive if it provides chronically unfavorable reward-cost positions to its members, it is also true that there is a tendency for sets to be eliminated from a relationship when they persistently impair the members' reward-cost positions. Hence incompatible sets would tend to be eliminated from the flow of interaction, except when in spite of interference effects the incompatible sets yield reward-cost positions above the members' comparison levels for alternative relationships

In suggesting that incompatible sets have low likelihood of survival in a relationship, we are not proposing either a model of random trial-and-error behavior or one of an hedonic calculation of rewards and costs with its purposive and rationalistic overtones What we have in mind is a model of "natural selection" of low-cost, high-reward sets rather than one of deliberate optimization through planful decisions at every moment We do not deny that major decisions projecting optimizing strategies do occur, but they do so only at certain critical junctures in the lives of the members when major alternatives with long-term (contractual, irrevocable) consequences are clearly perceived. But routine day-to-day interaction consists more of coping with the immediate situation and accomplishing intermediate instrumental goals We view this process as one in which pairs of sets and synchronizing conventions that are found to have satisfactory reward-cost consequences are retained (have high survival value) in the relationship, whereas those that prove to be unsatisfactory are eliminated from the relationship. Thus these endogenous processes may lead to a progressive restriction in the domain of paired sets operative in the relationship and to more or less ritualized modes of activating these sets

Furthermore, (role-prescribed) combinations of sets that are highly adaptive resultants of this endogenous process tend to be taught to the young of the next generation, thus providing exogenous means of eliminating incompatible sets even before they occur

— Although the above process would lead to a stabilization and rigidification of the content and style of the relationship, we can safely assume that any such stabilities will be intermittently upset or disrupted by exogenous influences (e.g., changes in other relationships, acquisition of new tastes or needs) as well as by unanticipated events in the interaction itself. Such shiftings and disruptions may be expected to provide for variety and innovation.

## SUMMARY

In dyadic interaction the behavior of each person may instigate responses in the other, and these instigated responses may be incompatible with other (ongoing) responses. When, for either member, tendencies to perform such incompatible behaviors exist, response interference will occur. If the behavior of each member interferes with that of the other, response interference is said to be symmetrical and will produce a correspondence between the outcomes of the two members over the cells in the matrix.

Although the present analysis emphasizes the effects of interference, interaction may also result in facilitation, for example when a member's rewards are maximal only if the other member performs in an appropriate way.

In interaction response interference may have effects both on the production of behavior and on the appreciation of behavior. With regard to the former, interference may be expected to increase the costs of performing the behavior and, usually, to decrease the reward-value of the behavior. On the appreciation side, interference may usually be expected to decrease the reward-value of the behavior.

Altogether, then, interference often increases costs and reduces rewards to the interacting members. Therefore, if a dyadic relationship is to form and survive, some means must be found to avoid excessive interferences. Two such means appear to be available.

(1) Behaviors may be synchronized so that only compatible responses are simultaneously performed. Such synchronization may be produced by cues that simultaneously arouse reciprocal or compatible behavior or by the existence of normative prescriptions which co-activate reciprocal role behavior.

(2) Persistently interfering behaviors may be eliminated from the relationship.

# 5.

## *Forming the Relationship*

It is obvious that it is impossible for the dyadic relationship even to begin to form unless some contact is made between the prospective members. The discussion in Chapter 3 of propinquity and least effort attempts to establish the basis for this minimum condition. Naturally, this does not mean that minimizing the cost of communication between the members totally governs the likelihood that a dyad will be formed. If rewards are sufficiently high in relation to total costs, then dyads may form at a distance, for example, by written communication or by traveling great distances to meet intermittently.

Once contact has been made, the fate of the relationship—its likelihood of formation and survival—depends on the level of outcomes the two persons experience. We have asserted that individuals will remain in a relationship only as long as the outcomes it yields are superior to those obtainable in their respective best alternative relationships. Put more simply, we assume that each person enters and remains in the best of the relationships available to him. Documentation for this basic point is provided in a study of the International Typographical Union by Lipset, Trow, and Coleman (1956). The authors first present evidence that for Roman Catholic printers the main alternatives to associating with other printers are in other lower status manual trades, whereas for Jewish printers a large number of alternatives are available in higher status, middle-class groups: the business and professional community. Considering only those persons for whom associations with high-status individuals are rewarding, we would expect them to establish relationships with the highest status persons available to them. The evidence bears out this expectation. Among those one might expect to be most oriented toward high status (those of native origin, good education, and middle-class background), the Roman Catholic printers associate more with other printers than do Jewish printers. This difference does not appear among printers with attributes suggestive of little orientation toward high status. In our terms, because of the alternative relationships available to them, the $CL_{alt}$ of (certain of the) Jewish printers is too high to permit them to form extensive associations within the printing trade, whereas the $CL_{alt}$ of Roman Catholic printers is low enough for them to accommodate such relationships.

In the formative stage, as later, the fate of the relationship presumably depends upon the outcomes experienced by the prospective members as they interact, and the experienced outcomes in turn depend on the matrix of possible outcomes (such as represented in Table 2-1). If, in fact, the objective matrix provides for each of the prospective members possibilities of outcomes that are superior to those obtainable in their best alternative relationships, then formation of the dyad will be determined by how well the objective possibilities are represented in the early phases of interaction. This early interaction may be viewed as a process of exploring the matrix, of learning its values, by (1) *experiencing samples of the outcomes* in various parts of the matrix as a basis for making inferences about its present adequacy and (2) *forecasting trends* in the outcomes and, in particular, evaluating their stability. This process of exploration is not, of course, unique to the early stages of the relationship. However, with repetition and routinization as the interaction proceeds, the necessity for continued sampling and forecasting declines sharply.

In a preview of this process it may be said that the first contact of two persons provides each of them with a sample of the outcomes in the matrix. This initial contact is often a chance encounter, a side effect of individual pursuits; hence it is not a rationally planned affair designed to maximize the sampled outcomes of the two persons. Instead, it is as though the samples of outcomes experienced initially were presented to the two participants as an implicit test of the survival-value of the tentative contact. If the first samples of outcomes are definitely below $CL_{alt}$ for one or both members, then the relationship will die aborning: no reinforcement will be given to the behavior of approaching one another again, for the initial outcomes do not successfully compete with alternative adaptations.

On the other hand, if the initial sample is definitely above $CL_{alt}$ for both participants, there will be motivation for repeated approaches. Especially as dependence on the relationship begins to develop, it becomes increasingly important to take account of the future course of the relationship—of its stability and irreversibility. Alternatively, if the initial sample of outcomes is only marginally acceptable, that is, hovering ambiguously in the neighborhood of $CL_{alt}$, the likelihood of repeated interaction will depend on a confidence that the present outcomes are transitional to an improved state of affairs.

## 5.1  AMBIVALENCE IN COURTSHIP

To enter a new relationship is also to abandon an old adaptation—an earlier relationship or a state of independence  Some degree of conflict may be inevitable between putting on the new and putting off the old.  Waller and Hill (1951) describe in detail a pervasive ambivalence that they feel dominates courting behavior  As each partner begins to experience his growing dependence on the other, as his outcomes begin to derive exclusively from the other, he begins also to experience acutely the threat to his independence  Not yet ready to give up independence for the incompletely sampled advantages of dependence, each partner attempts to deny or disguise or at least delay the steady increase in dependence before it overwhelms him  Thus each partner is careful to keep his indebtedness covert, to express his appreciations only in stereotyped language (the "line")  In this manner each one gradually becomes dependent on the relationship without knowing how the other one really feels about it  This state of *pluralistic ignorance* leads to intermittent crises, or "lovers' quarrels," in the course of which each partner, by means of temporary withdrawal or separation, tests the other's dependence on the relationship  If adequate demonstrations of affection are provoked, the dyad is strengthened.

As the conflict between the new dependence and the old adaptation builds up and becomes unbearable there are explosive developments which often surprise the participants themselves  These explosions occur either in the direction of "falling in love" or a disruptive "falling out"  In either case the final temper of the relationship is far more extreme than if no conflict had existed.

Although this conflict may be ever present in any relationship, it is particularly high during the formative stages because (uncertainty of the consequences of the relationship is then maximal)  If one looks for the sources of this uncertainty, it will be seen that they are twofold:

(1) Uncertainty whether outcomes in the prospective relationship are significantly superior to those in the best available alternatives, including the state of free, unaffiliated independence

(2) Uncertainty about the stability of the outcomes in the future

A further word about the second source of uncertainty is in order. Stability is a particularly acute problem in instances in which the eventual relationship may become highly irreversible or *nonvoluntary*. This occurs when entering a given relationship has the effect of making less available certain of the better alternatives, and it becomes more costly to leave the present one (e.g., the social and economic costs incurred in dissolving a marriage) or to enter alternative ones (in "going steady" or engagement relationships the persons who were once alternatives tend to become unavailable through withdrawal to *their* alternative relationships). The consequences of being in a nonvoluntary relationship are detailed in Chapter 10, but they include most prominently the possibility of being forced to endure low outcomes. (This situation is most threatening when an individual believes it to be one-sided, he being highly dependent upon a relationship that can be arbitrarily disrupted by the other person.) Such arbitrary disruptions are frequent, and the attendant pain is commonly known. Waller and Hill (1951) quote one young lady as having said to her lover: "If you ever let me down, I'll kill you. Oh why did I ever allow myself to love anyone so much?" [p. 232]. "Letting down" the other person is an apt characterization of what are often the effects of disruption, as viewed theoretically. Through unavailability of alternative relationships, the person "let down" may be forced to take a sharp drop in outcomes. This is especially difficult for him to accept if he has become adapted to the previous high level so that the new outcomes are far below his CL.

To summarize: the formation of a dyad will be most likely if good outcomes promise to be irreversible. Motivation to form a relationship perceived to be highly reversible will depend on the prospective member's having at least partial control over revocation.

These two sources of uncertainty are reduced by the processes of *exploring* the objective matrix of outcomes, noted earlier. The more unbiased the initial sample of outcomes appears to be, the greater the reduction in the prospective member's uncertainty whether the present relationship offers outcomes superior to those in the available alternatives. And the firmer the basis on which trends in the matrix are forecasted, the more the uncertainty from the second source is reduced.

Let us now turn to a consideration of some of the broad factors that affect the process by which prospective relationships are explored and discuss the process first from the point of view of the *production of behavior* (the "stimulus side") and then from that of the *perception of behavior* (the "response side"). Admittedly this division between production and perception does violence to the two-way flow of inter-action, but it seems justifiable for the purpose of analysis and the organization of topics.

## 5.2 PRODUCTION OF BEHAVIOR

What factors in the formation stages of a relationship affect the behaviors each person selects from his repertoire to contribute to the interaction?

The acts presented will certainly depend upon the task each person is engaged in at the time (e g, shopping or traveling) and the social setting of the encounter (e g, cocktail party or sporting event) For reasons external to the relationship, they may be thrown together as co-workers or as competitors Indeed, the different possibilities such as these are too numerous to mention. Let us instead consider some conditions more especially pertinent to the early stages of interaction.

### 5 2 1 STRANGENESS

Apart from other factors, such as the possibility of innate fears and aversions (Hebb and Thompson, 1954), strangeness between the part-ners of a prospective relationship increases uncertainty of both types and therefore at least delays formation of the relationship. It is a common observation that first meetings are often characterized by formality and constraint This everyday observation is supported by systematic investigations, for relationships between children and strange adults (Wiche, 1935, Jersild, 1954) as well as within groups of adolescent and young-adult strangers (French, 1944) Even when only temporary laboratory groups were involved, Nash and Wolfe (1957) found a decrease in inventiveness suggestive of constrained behavior immediately after a subject was moved from a familiar group into a new one

It may be readily seen that such inhibited and stereotyped behavior leads both to a reduction of sample size and to a biasing of the sample of outcomes ) (The seriousness of this biasing depends much on the degree to which the prospective relationship is ceremonial rather than spontaneous. Large cultural differences would exist here.) Since, under such circumstances, little information about the stranger's repertoire of behaviors is transmitted, the process of dyadic formation must await other developments

The same biasing effects might be expected to appear even more strongly when strangeness is compounded by adding ethnic or religious differences to the interaction. This supposition is borne out by a number of studies of interviewing in which interviewer and respondent differ in ethnic or religious membership. Hyman (1954) reports a study done in Memphis in 1942 by the National Opinion Research Center with a sample of 1000 Negroes. By random methods, half of the sample was assigned to Negro interviewers, the other half to white interviewers. The survey focused mainly on opinions and attitudes about the war but also contained questions of a factual nature. The analysis of the answers revealed that when interviewed by Negro interviewers Negro respondents were freer in expressing resentment about discrimination in employment and unions, beliefs about the good intentions or possible victory of Germany and Japan, and sympathy for the CIO. It appears that when giving their opinions to white interviewers Negroes were more inhibited about expressing their resentment, disloyalty, or radicalism. The tendency to give answers that might be more acceptable to the white interviewers extended even to responses to the factual questions on auto ownership and reading of Negro newspapers.

Similar results were obtained in a study by Robinson and Rohde (1946). Questions like "Do you think the Jews have too much power?" were put to four equivalent samples of respondents. Interviewers assigned to the first sample were "Jewish appearing" and used Jewish names to introduce themselves, those assigned to the second sample were "Jewish appearing" but mentioned no name in the introduction, those assigned to the third sample were "non-Jewish appearing" and mentioned no name, those assigned to the fourth sample were "non-Jewish appearing" and used non-Jewish names to introduce themselves. Frequencies of anti-Semitic responses to the questions varied with the characteristics of the interviewer, the lowest incidence of such responses occurred when the interviewer both "looked Jewish" and used a Jewish name.

Hence we see in these observations a tendency for strangeness, whether merely as nonacquaintance or as a disparity in group membership, to lead to a distortion of behavior, hence to biased samples of initial outcomes. This distortion is not always, however, in the direction of constricted, less frank responses. Simmel (1953), Maccoby and Maccoby (1954), and others have observed that interaction with a stranger is sometimes more open and objective than with an acquaintance, as in the easy conversations between strangers on a train or the extremely frank revelations often made to door-to-door interviewers. Observations such as these refer to situations in which the out-group characteristics of the stranger give him an air of objectivity or perspective so that one anticipates no evaluation or censure from

him  In addition, these observations seem to refer exclusively to the
stranger *passant*, with whom there is no future and whose total impact
on one's life is in this brief encounter  Because the relationship with
the stranger *passant* is inevitably brief, ambivalences between a developing dependency on him and a nostalgia for a fading autonomy
cannot occur, except perhaps in fantasy  Hence for this fleeting relationship the usual constraints are unlikely

The importance of concern about dependency in early stages of
relationships is well documented by Polansky and Kounin (1956) in
their investigations of clients' reactions to the first interview with a
counselor or psychotherapist  In a field study in which clients were
interviewed immediately after their first contact it was found that
their willingness to maintain the relationship with the counselor depended not only upon the progress made and the likeableness of the
counselor but also upon how much the client felt at ease and free to
reveal himself during the interview  These last factors were found
to be positively related to the client's felt power in the relationship
In a subsequent experimental study (Kounin  Polansky, Biddle, Coburn, and Fenn, 1956), the power of the counselor was varied  in the
*nonpower* condition he was nothing more than a counselor, in the
*power* condition the subjects acting as clients were potentially dependent upon him for such things as grades, job assignments, and letters
of recommendation  The results confirmed those of the field study.
Subjects felt more at ease with the nonpowerful person and more willing to reveal bad things about themselves  The suggestion is strong.
then, that the amount of constraint a person exhibits in an initial contact with a stranger depends upon the extent to which the person
may be dependent upon the stranger in future situations.

However, for interaction with the stranger who is a member of the
"field of eligibles," uncertainty about the future course of the interaction must be high. Will it provide adequate outcomes?  Will it be
possible to work out satisfactory synchronization and trading arrangements, and so forth?  In view of these uncertainties, it is expected that
participants will limit their "investments" in the relationship by restricting themselves to low-cost behaviors  In this lies the functional value
of politeness and other stereotyped forms of interaction in the early
stages of the relationship.

### 5.2.2  ACCESSIBILITY AND CULTURAL NORMS

Insofar as relationships in a society are given a built-in reversibility,
for example, in the frequent disruption of relationships occasioned by
high social mobility, social techniques may develop to protect mem-

bers from the damages caused by uncertainty of the stability of relationships. Since politeness may serve as low-cost protection against premature commitment to an intimate relationship, so ready-made and stereotyped social gambits for initial conversation may assist the person to manage relationships that are especially subject to revocation. Consistent with this is Lewin's (1948a) analysis of differences in social accessibility between Americans and Germans, if we assume the latter to be less socially mobile. Lewin remarks on the readiness and seeming effortlessness with which Americans strike up conversations with strangers (a phenomenon rare in Germany) and accumulate friends. "Compared with Germans, Americans seem to make quicker progress towards friendly relations in the beginning, and with many more persons. Yet this development often stops at a certain point; and the quickly acquired friends will, after years of relatively close relations, say good-by as easily as after a few weeks of acquaintance" [p. 20].

One obvious feature of initial conversations constructed of culturally provided stereotypes is that they convey very little information about the rewards and costs ultimately attainable in the relationship. Stereotyped topics and phrases will, of course, result in high interindividual uniformity of the initial sample of outcomes, and therefore little is transmitted about the outcomes unique to the given relationship. British observers have commented on the anonymity of the B.B.C. accent, and Cantril and Allport (1935) have noted the difficulty with which judgments are made about radio announcers, presumably because of their special training and practice in standardized speaking. Merton's (1940) description of the *depersonalization* of the bureaucrat is in the same vein.

> Another feature of the bureaucratic structure, the stress on depersonalization of relationships, also plays its part in the bureaucrat's trained incapacity. The personality pattern of the bureaucrat is nucleated about this norm of impersonality. Both this and the categorizing tendency, which develops from the dominant role of general, abstract rules, tend to produce conflict in the bureaucrat's contacts with the public or clientele. Since functionaries minimize personal relations and resort to categorization, the peculiarities of individual cases are often ignored. But the client who, quite understandably, is convinced of the "special features" of *his* own problem often objects to such categorical treatment. Stereotyped behavior is not adapted to the exigencies of individual problems [pp. 565–566].

Of course, there will be individual differences within cultures in interpersonal openness or expressiveness. Estes (1937) reports "openness" of a stimulus person to be an important determinant of the accuracy with which he can be judged.

To conclude this brief discussion, easy peripheral accessibility, though it conveys little information, appears to have functional utility. Potentially unstable relationships may be entered with relative impunity, and at the same time, for relationships promising stability, the transition to more adequate sampling of outcomes can be accomplished at low cost.

### 5 2 3    AUTISTIC HOSTILITY

Any failure to communicate adequately and fully in the initial phases of a relationship will affect the representativeness of the outcomes sampled    One process suggested as affecting the openness of interpersonal communication is proposed in the autistic hostility hypothesis of Newcomb (1947)    This hypothesis asserts that an initial state of hostility protects itself from change by reducing the communication of information capable of changing it    Hostility is maintained, then, by the mechanism of reduced and constrained communication    A study by Thibaut and Coules (1952) shows that the initially hostile subject is relatively less communicative to a standard stimulus person and relatively more self-disparaging than the initially friendly person. Insofar as the hostile person is not uniformly and permanently hostile, his communicative behavior leads to a biasing of the sample of outcomes attainable through interaction with him as well as a reduction in sample size )    A relationship with a momentarily hostile person may thus be rejected prematurely

### 5.2.4    AUTISTIC FRIENDLINESS

The initial sample of outcomes may also be biased by what may be called "autistic friendliness"    For example, predispositions to friendliness may be induced by a technique like Back's (1951) in which the experimenter privately informs each of two subjects that (on the basis of some previously administered psychological tests) each will very probably like the other    Contrasted with a less enthusiastic introduction, this preparation leads to a more active production of behavior (longer time spent together) and the selection of better items from their joint repertoires (greater care in the interaction), thus generating a large sample of superior outcomes to each other    It may be surmised that these outcome samples are biased in that they very likely underrepresent the unfavorable outcomes in the objective matrix and overrepresent the favorable ones.    However, the consequences are likely to be rather different from those following the opposite kind of biasing, as from autistic hostility    When the preponderance of initial outcomes is unfavorable, there is no evidence to the participants that favorable outcomes even exist or are possible in the relationship. Unfavorable outcomes, on the other hand, are always possible and probably always appear in the matrix as resultants of unmotivated performance or response interference. So a favorable initial sample in a sense provides more information about the matrix.

Furthermore, once participant A initiates a behavior contributing a very favorable outcome to B, the probability is high that B will counter with a similarly favorable outcome to A. The prognosis then is good that a relationship will form or at least that approaches will be repeated.

Consideration of the interdependence of events such as those just noted has led a number of social psychologists, most notably Homans (1950) and Newcomb (1953), to formulate theories interrelating communication and attitudes. To oversimplify somewhat, we may paraphrase two of their propositions as follows: as the attitudes of persons A and B toward one another become more favorable, communication between A and B becomes more frequent; and, conversely, as the rate of communication between A and B increases, attitudes toward one another become more favorable.

## 5.3 THE PERCEPTION OF BEHAVIOR

We have surveyed some of the broad factors that affect the likelihood of dyad formation through their influence on the behaviors produced in the relationship. We now turn to look at the formative phases of a relationship from the point of view of the recipient toward whom the behaviors are directed. What factors affect his appraisal of the other's behaviors and the forecasts he can make of future outcomes in the relationship?

### 5.3.1 SPECIFIC CUES

The first obvious answer to this question is that various specific cues are presented during early interactions from which the observer may make inferences about the other person's ability to perform adequately and with versatility. [For example, one could cite Thornton's (1944) research on the effects of wearing glasses and smiling as these cues affect judgments of intellectual ability, friendliness, etc.]

It is impossible to consider or even to list all of the cues that might be relevant to the relationship, but it *is* possible and probably more profitable to present some generalizations about the availability of cues during early interactions and their use in the perceptual process.

## 5.3.2 AVAILABILITY OF CUES

The factors noted in the discussion of behavior production have a direct bearing on this question because the cues available as a basis for evaluation and inference are in part determined by the specific behaviors emitted in the interaction. At the outset, superficial cues of an "external" sort (appearance, etc ) are readily available and (very nearly, at least) in their total supply  Then, depending upon the action of those factors indicated earlier as affecting the production of behavior (strangeness, accessibility), more behavioral cues become available  This change makes it increasingly possible for persons to make their extrapolations and forecasts from observed instances of behavior rather than from external appearances

As the interaction develops, there is also more information available to each individual about the *context* of the other one's actions  There is considerable evidence that in judging emotion the more information the observer has about the situation in which the emotion is being expressed the more accurate and reliable the judgments. (For a summary of these studies, see Bruner and Tagiuri, 1954 )  Thus, given knowledge of the stimulating conditions, the common confusion between such emotions as love versus mirth and happiness is likely to be eliminated  These data suggest that the accuracy of judging the effects upon another of one's own behavior is likely to increase as interaction continues

With increasing numbers of cues available, one might expect people to become more differentiated in their judgments of each other  This is consistent with the observed decreases, from early to later judgments, in the correlations between different dimensions used in evaluating one's associates  For example, Lippitt (1951) cites data showing a drop over time in the correlation between judgments of most productive associate and most desirable leisure-time companion.

The cues from certain kinds of behaviors may not become available, however, if there exist cultural norms against their enactment  For example, Lippitt, Polansky, and Rosen (1952) present a comparison of two boys' camps in terms of the basis for making judgments of fighting ability.  In one camp where a good deal of fighting took place judgments were based on performance  In the other camp where there was little fighting these judgments were based on external cues of physical size.

Even at the beginning of interaction, systematic individual differences appear in preferences for "external" cues (by high authoritarians) as opposed to preference for "internal" cues (of ability, competence, etc., by low authoritarians) in making inferences about another person's power (E. E. Jones, 1954, and Thibaut and Riecken, 1955a). For as yet unanalyzed reasons women seem to be more willing than men to make inferences from superficial cues (Sarbin, 1954).

### 5.3.3 THE PRIMACY EFFECT

Much of the preceding discussion implies that inferences about other persons will become better (e.g., more accurate and more differentiated) as the interactions proceed. On the other hand, there is some evidence that early information about a person provides a core of meaning to which later information is more or less assimilated. We may speculate that the mechanisms underlying this *primacy effect* are similar to those governing the perceptual processes in general. If this is so, it is possible to interpret the disproportionate weight given to early information as a special case of the general principle that perceptual processes operate to minimize the costs of information intake (Attneave, 1954). As soon as the perceiver has received sufficient information to permit him to locate the stimulus person in a category or compact set of categories, the task of categorizing appears to terminate and, as far as possible, further information is used only for redundant elaboration.

Asch (1946) has studied the effects of variations in the order of presenting a list of adjectives attributed to a person on the different impressions that subjects form of him. The disproportionately great effect of adjectives occurring early in the list is unmistakable. (The relevance of this method to our present topic rests on the assumption that the intake of actual information about a person is similar to the intake of a list of adjectives said to characterize him.)

Luchins (1957) provides a demonstration of a very striking primacy effect by varying the order with which two verbal descriptions of a person are presented to subjects. Each description is a single paragraph, one showing the stimulus person as extroverted, the other showing him as introverted. Whichever was presented first quite overwhelmingly dominated the impression formed of the person. Luchins also found that he could dissipate this primacy effect by initially warning the subjects that premature impressions might be contradicted by later evidence and asking them to suspend judgment until all the evidence was in.

### 5.3.4 ORGANIZATION OF PERCEPTION

The primacy effect is a special case of the general rule that some items of information are given more weight in judging a person than others. The core around which one's view of another person is organized need not be the earliest information received (Some information has a powerful organizing effect whenever it is received  In other words, some pieces of information are used to make inferences about a broad variety of behaviors or outcomes, as if they constituted a larger sample of the possibilities than other items )

Asch (1946) and Kelley (1950) have demonstrated that the adjective "warm" (or "cold") when offered as a personality description has very strong effects on the impression formed of the person, regardless of serial position in the list of adjectives ( Such adjectives apparently have *central* organizing characteristics to which other information is assimilated, )whereas concepts like "polite" or "blunt" exert little such effect  Haire and Grunes (1950), by employing a research procedure similar to Asch's, show the consequences of presenting observers with incongruous, mutually unassimilable elements of information about a stimulus person  Their results confirm the general point that many observers tend fairly strongly to establish an organized, internally consistent view of other persons  Gollin (1958) finds that the introduction of organizing concepts to account for incongruity of an observed person's behavior increases markedly with age, few ten-year olds but about two thirds of the sixteen-year olds doing so.

The adequacy of these simplified, organized views can be evaluated only in terms of how much people actually *are* organized and consistent. This, of course, has an important bearing upon whether judgments made on the assumptions of organization and consistency are verified by further interaction with the person evaluated.

The tendency for one's general attitude toward a person to influence more specific evaluations of him has been called the "halo" effect  As this has been a persistent problem in the use of ratings for practical purposes, such as selecting among job applicants, investigations have been conducted to determine how to minimize the effect  These studies, in general, showed that halo is maximal when difficult or abstract judgments are required or when the judgments have moral implications

More recent investigations of the halo phenomena have stemmed largely from the theoretical work of Heider (1946, 1958)  Heider's general theory is that observers tend to maintain similar attitudes toward a person and toward things he is seen to cause, possess, or like (his actions, friends, or possessions)  Horowitz, Lyons, and Perlmutter (1951) report a study exploring this thesis of a tendency toward "balance"  Friendship patterns in a group of twenty persons were estimated by sociometric methods  Then, after a (systematically observed) discussion by the group, the investigators presented to the group three of the assertions actually made during the discussion, each with the name of its originator. Questionnaire responses showed that there is a close relationship between the degree to which a member likes the originator of an assertion and the member's tendency to agree with the assertion. Further, a member perceives liked members as agreeing with his evaluation of the assertion and disliked members as disagreeing. A number of studies show that liked persons are perceived to hold views similar to one's own. For example, Davitz (1955) found that children perceive their best friends to be more similar to themselves (in attitudes toward camp activities) than they actually are.

A related line of investigation inquires into the ways available to persons for the resolution of unbalanced states, for example, when a liked person expresses a bad attitude or a disliked person performs a good act. Osgood and Tannenbaum (1955) show that changes occur in one's evaluation of the actor, the action, or both. They also present a theory for predicting how the adjustment or resolution will take place. An additional possibility is that the actor's responsibility for causing the action may be denied, as in Zillig's (1928) classic demonstration that a mistake made by a popular child is attributed by the classmates to an unpopular one. Harvey, Kelley, and Shapiro (1957) present evidence for the denial of causal responsibility when a friend makes negative evaluations of oneself.

### 5.3.5 STATES OF THE OBSERVER

A great deal of research has been done on the question of what personal characteristics produce accurate judgments of emotions, personality, and future behavior. Much of the evidence is either self-evident or contradictory. For the present purposes it is more important to know whether systematic biases in evaluation may exist in early phases of interaction. An early investigation of this question was conducted by H. A. Murray (1933). He found that fear induced in adolescent girls (by playing a frightening game) led them to attribute more maliciousness to strange men pictured in photographs. Experimentally induced hostility has also been shown to affect evaluations of people, increasing the number of unfavorable qualities attributed to them (Miller and Bugelski, 1948, Jones and deCharms, 1957). These phenomena are, of course, related to the autistic hostility effects. An initial state of mild hostility may be preserved by discontinuance of interaction, but it may also be furthered by attribution of undesirable qualities to the other person.

## SUMMARY

Whether a dyadic relationship is formed depends upon the outcomes experienced in the early stages of interaction. This preliminary interaction is viewed as a process of exploring the matrix of possible outcomes by (1) experiencing samples of the outcomes in various parts of the matrix as a basis for making inferences about its present adequacy and (2) forecasting trends in the outcomes. This process of exploring the matrix is analyzed first from the point of view of the *production* of behavior and then from that of the *perception* of behavior

The representativeness of behavior produced in early stages of the interaction is affected by a variety of factors. Strangeness in a social interaction, whether it derives from mere nonacquaintance with the other person or from his belonging to a different ethnic or religious group, usually produces formality and constraint, thus biasing the sampled outcomes. Easy peripheral accessibility in the early stages of a relationship provides little information about the quality of potential outcomes. However, such accessibility permits persons to enter tentatively (without becoming dependent upon) relationships that are potentially unstable, while at the same time furnishing low-cost transition to improved sampling of outcomes in relationships promising stability. Autistic hostility refers to the tendency of an initially hostile person to maintain his hostility by reducing his communication with the person toward whom he is hostile. This biasing of the sample of outcomes potentially attainable in interaction with him may lead to the premature rejection of a relationship with a momentarily hostile person. "Autistic friendliness" also leads to a biasing of the sample of outcomes experienced and heightens the occurrence of superior outcomes. (The effects, however, are to facilitate the formation of the relationship by motivating the prospective partner to reciprocate by returning superior outcomes)

On the side of the perception of behavior several factors are considered as they affect the appraisals made by the person toward whom the behavior is directed in the early stages of the relationship. Specific cues seem to be too numerous to be profitably analyzed. In general, though, as interaction proceeds, a greater diversity in types of cues becomes available, with behavioral cues supplementing the more external cues (physical appearance, etc.) that dominate first impressions. The primacy effect is discussed to illustrate the superior weight given to first impressions. The analysis is then extended to include other contributions to the organization of perception The chapter concludes with a brief discussion of some of the ways in which states of the observer (e g., fear) may affect his attribution of qualities to another person.

# 6.

# *Evaluation of the Dyad*

The outcomes a person receives in the course of interaction have a certain absolute significance to him If they are offered to him, he will always prefer outcomes better than those he has, no matter how favorable the level of outcomes he has reached, for if they are offered they are instigated, and if they are better it is true by definition that he will prefer them Further, he will attempt to repeat the activities he finds to yield good outcomes, and he will try to avoid activities that produce unsatisfactory ones) However, a good deal of what social psychology knows about how people evaluate themselves and their circumstances indicates that these evaluations also involve a good deal of *relativity of judgment* Much of the work on the level of aspiration (e g, Lewin, et al, 1944), reference group effects (Merton, 1957), and status behavior (Hollingshead, 1949) suggests that the person typically evaluates his circumstances in relation to those he believes other people achieve or in relation to those he has experienced in the past) He strives especially hard to reach certain levels, (e g, those attained by his siblings), and he is particularly unhappy if he falls below a certain minimum (perhaps the standard of living he had achieved several years ago)

To take account of these phenomena, we introduced in Chapter 2 the notion of *comparison level* (CL) as a standard or reference point against which, in some sense, the relationship of the moment is evaluated There we distinguish two special instances of CL that seem necessary for the analysis of interpersonal relations The first, referred to merely as CL, provides a standard against which an evaluation is made of how satisfactory or unsatisfactory the relationship is) The second, referred to as CL$_{alt}$ provides a standard in terms of which

80

decisions about remaining in or leaving the relationship are made.) In Chapter 7 we consider $CL_{alt}$ in connection with the discussion of power and dependency. The present chapter focuses upon the CL, its relation to satisfaction and attraction, and its determinants. The distinction between these two types of standards has not been made in the literature on attraction, power, and the like, and there is often some unclarity about the kind of reference point dealt with. Those (studies which are concerned largely with subjective states reflecting satisfaction, personal morale, etc., are considered here) Those that delve into dependency and the exercise of power come in for discussion in relation to $CL_{alt}$.

The reader will also note the bearing of the present discussion upon Chapter 10's analysis of nonvoluntary relationships. There we consider the case in which, for various reasons, the person's existing outcomes are considerably below his CL. This has a number of consequences the interpretation of which relies upon the present general analysis of CL.

## 6.1 THE COMPARISON LEVEL

In defining the CL the (primary intention is to locate a psychologically meaningful mid-point for the scale of outcomes—a neutral point on a scale of satisfaction-dissatisfaction.) If the outcomes in a given relationship surpass the CL, that relationship is regarded as a satisfactory one. And, to the degree the outcomes are supra-CL, the person may be said to be attracted to the relationship. If the outcomes endured are infra-CL, the person is dissatisfied and unhappy with the relationship. If possible he would leave the group, so we may say his attraction to the group is negative. Locating the CL, then, enables us to analyze the subjective consequences of membership in a dyad. Although we can expect feeling tone to deteriorate as the person receives increasingly poor outcomes, the CL indicates a point (or at least a region) on the outcome continuum where the mood changes from positive to negative and where the orientation changes from *toward* the dyad to *away from* it.

How, then, should the CL be defined if it is to be a neutral point in this sense? We have chosen to (define the CL as being some modal or average value of all the outcomes known to the person (by virtue of personal or vicarious experience), (each outcome weighted by its salience) (or the degree to which it is instigated for the person at the moment).) A person's CL depends not only upon outcomes he has experienced or seen others experiencing but also upon which of these are actively stimulating to him—are obtruded on him, are vivid and perhaps implicitly rehearsed as he makes an evaluation of his circumstances  This salience depends in part upon momentary cues which serve as reminders of certain relationships and alternatives  To the degree this is true, (CL is subject to situation-to-situation and moment-to-moment variations ) Perhaps more important, because of their relative stability, are the outcomes the salience of which is independent of the immediate situation—outcomes for which the person provides dependable self-instigations or, so to speak, self-reminders

In Section 6 2 of this chapter we examine some of the evidence pertaining to the effect upon CL of experienced outcomes.  On the assumption that instigations are supra-threshold for all experienced outcomes, we would expect to find a direct association between the quality of the known outcomes and the location of the CL, the latter being reflected in feelings of satisfaction with presently attained outcomes   In a subsequent section we consider those outcomes which are likely to be salient, both in specific circumstances and generally. Because there are important and pervasive individual differences in this regard, we then consider the personality predispositions that may be interpreted as affecting the particular set of experienced outcomes the person tends to maintain generally at a high level of salience.

For readers of Helson (1948), we might say that the CL represents the adaptation level to the instigated outcomes   This adaptation level is affected mainly by direct or indirect information available to the person about the goodness of outcomes in other relationships, but it is also conditioned partly by outcomes in the present relationship   Finally, there are what Helson calls "residual" considerations, idiosyncratic factors such as, in our case, individual differences in the weights assigned to the reward- versus cost-components particularly for favorable unattained outcomes—individual differences, that is, in "optimism" versus "pessimism."

## 6 2  EXPERIENCED OUTCOMES

If all of the outcomes a person has experienced or knows about are salient, then the CL reflects the quality of these outcomes   A person who has experienced superior outcomes, for example, in alternative relationships, will have a higher CL and, therefore, will be less satisfied with the level in the present relationship than will another person who has known only the mediocrity of the present situation

This interpretation may be made of discrepancies between parents and children in evaluating the standard of living in the home    Koos (1946) provides observations of families with foreign-born parents and low-income families in which the children have opportunities outside the home to learn to expect a higher material standard of living. This leads the children to be dissatisfied with the level of living attained in the parental home

Data from the studies of the American soldier (Stouffer, et al, 1949) may also be interpreted in these terms.. For example, as compared with the less well educated soldiers, better educated ones were less satisfied with their status and opportunities for promotion    The authors interpret this greater dissatisfaction with the same circumstances in terms of the higher aspirations that the more educated men bring to the army    As compared to the outcomes they had enjoyed or anticipated enjoying as civilians, considering their relatively superior social and economic backgrounds, the better educated found their army status to be quite poor

The results from level-of-aspiration studies are also relevant to this point    The level of aspiration consists of a person's statement about his expected level of performance on some task, for example, the number of arithmetic problems he will solve, the number of hits he will make on a target.    Because the person's rewards (from recognition or experience of achievement) are presumably closely related to his performance level, the (aspiration level is essentially an indication of the outcomes the person expects from interaction with the task)    Because of this close relation with the CL, the evidence on determinants of aspiration levels probably reveals much about the factors underlying CL

Two main results issue from the most pertinent of such studies (Chapman and Volkman, 1939, Festinger, 1942)

(1) Subjects tend to expect to do about as well as others similar to themselves, better than people they consider generally inferior to themselves, and poorer than people they consider generally superior to themselves

(2) The effects of information about the performance of others is reduced by having direct experience with the task itself    If a person has enough experience with the task, information about how others perform on it will have relatively little effect on his future level of aspiration.    Thus both one's personal experience and knowledge about others' experience play a role in these levels, but personal experience seems to be given priority.

6 3  SALIENT OUTCOMES

We suggested earlier that (not all of the outcomes experienced are likely to be equally salient, hence not all equally weighty, in the determination of CL.) Certain outcomes will be highly salient because of the particular circumstances in which the person is asked to make an evaluation of his situation    Others are likely to be salient under almost all circumstances because of some special significance they have to the individual

Consider first the specific instigations and reminders which, by their immediate or recent presence, heighten the salience of some outcomes Perhaps the best evidence on the effects of such instigations comes from studies in which people from similar backgrounds and presently receiving objectively similar outcomes are asked under different circumstances to evaluate their outcomes   For example, if a person is asked to say how well off he is considering the plight of the displaced peoples of Europe, he is almost certain to give a different response (a more "satisfied" one) than if the question suggests a more opulent set of outcomes for the comparison   Many such variations in "frame of reference" produced by different question wordings indicate fluctuations in CL as a function of the particular outcomes, persons, or relationships the question brings to mind   For example, Hyman (1942) found that an individual's judgment of his status changes as the reference group provided in the instructions was varied

Variations in the other persons who are in one's immediate vicinity may have similar effects    For example, Stouffer and his associates (1949) found several instances in which outcomes were evaluated in a manner inconsistent with their objective quality   These findings are interpreted in terms of the effects of other persons near at hand. Among the many similar comparisons that appear in the data, let us take Negro troops stationed in northern versus southern installations and noncombat troops in the United States versus those in rear-areas overseas.  In these cases a relatively high degree of satisfaction was found under what were objectively poorer conditions   Noncombat troops overseas showed higher satisfaction with army life than did noncombat troops in the United States, presumably because the salient alternatives for the overseas troops were the rigors and hardships of the combat soldier, whereas the troops at home compared their plight with that of a prosperous civilian population   Similarly for Negro soldiers

Relative to most Negro civilians whom he saw in Southern towns, the Negro soldier had a position of comparative wealth and dignity   His income was high, at least by general Southern standards Moreover, in spite of the Army carryover of many civilian practices of segregation, the Negro soldier received treatment more nearly on an equality with the white soldier than the treatment of the Negro civilian in the South as compared with the white civilian. Officially, the Army policies always insisted upon equality of treatment of the races, even when this meant separate treatment, and throughout the war repeated though often unsuccessful efforts were made by the War Department to translate these policies into practice and to enforce them even against the private wishes of some white commanding officers

Consider, on the other hand, the Northern Negro stationed in the North The differential in income and status between soldier and civilian was not the same as that in the South The industrial earning power of one's Northern Negro civilian acquaintances was at an all-time high, very often far exceeding that of the Negro soldier Moreover, the contrast between the racial practices of the Army and the racial practices of Northern civilian society was, frequently, the reverse of the contrast in the South Although the Northern Negro was accustomed to countless irritations and instances of discrimination in Northern civilian life, he was not confronted to the same extent with official policies of racial segregation as existed in the Army [pp 563–564]

## 6 3.1 SALIENCE AND CONTROL

Consider next the question of which outcomes are likely to be salient whether or not there exist momentary instigations to them An hypothesis proposed here is that the generally and persistently salient outcomes are those perceived by the individual as instances of variations in rewards and costs for which he himself is primarily responsible —variations over which he has some degree of control. The following considerations are offered in support of this hypothesis.

As a person's outcomes fluctuate with changes in interaction and in his memberships, he adjusts his behavior in an effort to maintain better outcomes and avoid poorer ones Of the total variability in his outcomes, only part is responsive to such attempts, namely, the portion that is in some manner under his control The remaining variability is introduced by the exercise of external control over him by other persons or agencies. (See Chapter 7 on *fate control* ) As his behavior has no effect on these variations, the adaptive solution would seem to involve a recognition of external control and an acceptance of its indocility to his efforts

We might imagine that it would be highly adaptive if the human organism, in the course of his evolution, had developed the capacity to respond with acceptance toward such arbitrary incursions into his life, being gratified by some events and hurt by others, but responding always in a consummatory rather than an instrumental way This mode of responding has the adaptation value of avoiding costly attempts to adjust or rectify unalterable outcomes.  On the other hand, it is highly useful for the organism to be able to give full attention to variations in outcomes that lie within his own range of control  A high sensitivity to such variations has the value of enabling him to attain more nearly the level of outcomes that is maximal in view of his ability to control his environment

Our hypothesis suggests this to be true that the person is indeed especially sensitive to variations subject to his own control and relatively insensitive to variations caused by others over and beyond his control.) The outcomes under his control will tend to be highly salient under most circumstances; those under the control of others are salient only if they are currently being experienced or if obtrusive cues are present in the immediate situation  It is, then, the former variations that will predominate in determining the CL)  The level forming the transition from satisfaction to dissatisfaction depends, according to this view, primarily upon the rewards and costs seen as instances of variations in outcomes for which one is himself responsible.  By virtue of the tendency for selective salience or instigation of the different classes of outcomes, the CL depends in part upon the person's conception of his own power, his ability to cope with the contingent demands of others, and the realms over which he believes his own causal efficacy extends )  The CL thus begins to approximate the modal value of the range of outcomes over which the person believes his control prevails. ( It is largely an indication of what the individual feels he "deserves") and only in small part an indication of what he expects or anticipates on the basis of all the outcomes he has experienced  The reason is, to repeat, that the outcomes are weighted (instigated) according to perceived responsibility for them.

What implications does this line of reasoning have for the kinds of outcomes that would be likely to be especially salient, hence heavily weighted in the CL?)  To begin with, outcomes the person receives by virtue of temporary ascribed status will have less effect on CL than those received by virtue of achieved status.  (See Linton, 1945 for the distinction between "achieved" and "ascribed" status )  When the individual is indulged with magnificent rewards by a generous fate, his CL will be relatively little affected, or, when he is deprived of favorable outcomes by the action of external control, his CL will be relatively little affected  Of course, with repeated experiences of either sort, the instigations to them become so strong that CL ultimately will move in the direction of the good or bad fate.  All we suggest is that in the short run these experiences change the person's outcomes without greatly affecting his CL. Consequently, with entrance into a high or a low ascribed status, there is initially a period of great satisfaction or dissatisfaction as the CL lags behind the experienced outcomes As the CL finally catches up with the repeatedly experienced outcomes, the situation becomes more neutral in feeling tone. (See Chapter 10 for a more extensive discussion of this process.)

Outcomes the person has commonly experienced are also more likely to be perceived as within the realm of self-determination than those he has rarely experienced or only heard about. The latter would include most of the extremely high and extremely low outcomes, especially the high ones, which are outside or close to the limits of the individual's personal experience These ordinarily appear to be outcomes a person would not attain (or be forced to endure) without the intervention of either a kind or cruel fate. Thus extreme outcomes, particularly the high ones (for anyone can assure himself of low outcomes) and those the individual person has never personally experienced, are not likely to be viewed as outcomes he reaches by employment of his own control Subjectively these are the outcomes that have a low probability of attainment It is on these grounds that we believe that outcomes of low perceived likelihood of attainment carry little weight in the determination of the CL Outcomes of high probability of attainment, on the other hand, are perceived to be part of the range covered by one's control and are ordinarily heavily weighted in determining the location of CL.

If there exists a high subjective probability of attaining a very favorable outcome, the CL should rise. Failure to achieve such an outcome should then place the person below CL By contrast, had the person's subjective probability of success been lower, his CL would not have risen, and failure to attain the outcome would be less likely to place him below CL Spector (1956) has stated a variant of this hypothesis as follows:

> On *failing to achieve* an attractive goal, an individual's morale will be higher if *the probability of achieving that goal had been perceived to be low than if it had been perceived to be high* [p 52, author's italics]

In an experiment designed to test this hypothesis and a set of closely related ones Spector varied the perceived probability of being promoted up a hierarchy of simulated military rank His results confirmed the hypothesis stated above among the subjects who were not promoted, those who had perceived the probability of their being promoted as high were more dissatisfied than those less sanguine about their chances

An earlier report of the same relationship between expectation and morale comes from field research. In their study of the American soldier in World War II, Stouffer, et al. (1949), found a higher degree of satisfaction with the promotion system among enlisted men in the Military Police, in which promotions were relatively infrequent, than among Air Corps enlisted men in which the rate of promotion was quite high. In line with the hypothesis stated above, the airman's discontent may come from the dashing of too high hopes.

Our analysis of the relation between control and CL further suggests that (another person's outcomes will have an effect upon CL to the degree that the other's realm of power is seen to coincide with one's own). This is akin to Festinger's (1954) hypothesis that a person will tend to compare himself with others whose ability or competence is very similar to his own. Because similarity in ability is likely to induce a perception of similar power vis-à-vis the fates, we might expect the circumstances of persons similar in ability to the individual to contribute heavily to his CL. This would also be true of persons who occupy a social position similar to that of the individual, since similar social positions usually carry roughly equivalent power implications. Consistent with these expectations are Hyman's (1942) findings that friends and work associates are used more often in evaluating one's status than is the total society or the population at large.

The findings of Stern and Keller (1953) contain the further suggestion that there are (societal differences in the range of persons with whose outcomes an individual compares his own). In a study conducted in France a count was made of the social groups spontaneously mentioned in interviews regarding living conditions and aspirations. Most frequently mentioned were social class and family, followed by references to occupational groups, age groups, and friends or colleagues. The authors suggest the generalization that, "In a society where there is little social mobility, one's horizon of possibility is relatively limited, thus confining comparison between oneself and others to members of one's family, occupation, and social circle. In a society of greater social mobility, the self-other comparison is allowed freer range and takes in more groups, as well as groups outside of one's membership or 'in-group' environment" [p 216]. We would interpret this to mean that in a society in which the typical individual's realm of control over his outcomes is rather extensive there is considerable breadth to the class of persons whose outcomes contribute to his CL.

The effect of another person's outcomes will depend, of course, upon what (causal interpretation) is placed upon their occurrence. For example, a man who wins the Irish sweepstakes and thereby comes into

a laige sum of money would by our reasoning, have little effect upon
his brother's CL. However, if the man acquires wealth by virtue of
his own skill and effoits, his brother is likely to think of these rewards
when evaluating his own outcomes

## 6.4 Individual Differences and the Comparison Level

Consider two quite extreme cases lying on a continuum of power or
control. at one end is located a person having much power and at the
other a person having very little  We can say that the person having
much power is able dependably to insure himself of a wide range of
outcomes, from very unfavorable ones (anyone can get these in abun-
dance) to very favorable ones  The person having little power is able
dependably to insure himself of a much more modest range of outcomes, from very unfavorable ones to mediocre ones.

If we assume that the person holding high power has a veridical perception of it, he will appear confident and sure of himself and will experience a high subjective piobability of attaining favorable outcomes.
Fuitheimore, he may be expected to respond diffeiently to the reward
and the cost components of very superioi outcomes which he above
his present level of attainment  For he will have learned that thinking
about and anticipating better outcomes creates only temporary tension
which, by virtue of the effectiveness of his ensuing instiumental activities, is usually followed by actually attaining them  From the point of
view of thorough mobilization of action, it is even advantageous for
him to emphasize the positive aspects of new ventures and de-emphasize the negative ones.  Thus, for a person with such high competence and confidence, (instigations to behavior may be expected to
come primaiily fiom the reward components of superior outcomes.
Instigations from the cost components should be very slight)  This
means that the reward components of such outcomes will carry relatively heavy weights, and the cost components relatively light ones, in
determining this person's CL  The CL, then, is likely to be high.

For the person holding very little power, the prediction is quite diffeient (Instigations to his behavior will very likely deiive mainly fiom
the cost components of supeiioi outcomes and only neghgibly fiom
the reward components)  Hence the cost components of such outcomes
will be heavily weighted, and the reward components only lightly
weighted, in locating this person's CL  The CL is likely to be low.

As intimated above, these two diffeient oiientations toward rewards
and costs may be quite adaptive, each in its own way.  The ieward
orientation of the powerful person motivates him to approach all of the

favorable outcomes lying within the range of his power   The cost orientation of the powerless person helps him to avoid instigations to outcomes that he cannot dependably attain

Although the preceding argument has been developed in terms of the person's actual power and his veridical perception of it, the perception will not always coincide with the fact   It is well known that there are ideological contributions to the developing percept of one's own power relative to that of external sources.   Thus the person's beliefs about this may depend upon how his parents indoctrinate him with respect to his responsibility for his own fate or upon the particular ideology about the individual's causal potency that pervades his culture (Kardiner, 1945)   These factors may create notions about one's power that are quite discrepant with the facts   In this event the present theory is to be applied in terms of the perceived rather than the actual power   We merely note here that overestimations of one's power may often be corrected in the long run. the CL will be excessively high in the light of attained outcomes, with frustration chronic until the perception becomes more veridical   Underestimations of power may go uncorrected, however   The person will maintain modest levels of aspiration and comfortably surpass them without being presented with any impressive clues as to his unrealized potential

### 6.4.1   IDEALIZATION

Suppose that each of these persons experiences a very satisfactory relationship, say in marriage   The powerful person, we may assume, will assign much of the causality for the success of his marriage (and the consequent favorable outcomes) to his own high range of control   By our hypothesis that one's own perceived realm of control contributes heavily to the determination of CL, this person's CL should be high from the outset of the relationship.

The powerless person will be more likely to assign causality for *his* happy marriage to external agencies, such as fate, good luck, unprovoked good will, and enigmatic forces.   His CL will be expected to rise very gradually as instigations from favorable outcomes in the marriage take effect

Now suppose that each of the marriages is revoked, say by the death of the spouse   The powerful person (instigated primarily by the reward components of the now unattainable outcomes) will be expected to recall the marriage in an (idealized way) (overemphasizing the rewards, underemphasizing the costs)   Consequently his CL should rise even higher than its level during marriage

The (powerless person, instigated primarily by costs,) is more likely to recall the marriage in a "debunking" way, (overestimating its costs, depreciating its rewards) (although social constraints would usually limit the public expression of outright disparagement of the late spouse). His CL should fall.

Is there any evidence for such effects on the CL from past events? We may first note that there is considerable evidence for the existence of a phenomenon that looks very much like *idealization*) Consider a study based on interviews with widows. Dickinson and Beam (1931) report that to the widow the earlier marriage experiences now appear "sexually golden." "Sex life with the husband was interesting and desirable" [p 276]. She remembers intercourse to have been very frequent and highly satisfactory—considerably more so than reported by women presently living with their husbands. "The dead sexual life takes on the value of all dead things, creates its own ideal and feeds the living desire" [p 274] Thus the widow may be " sexually avid but unwilling to marry any man who compares unfavorably with the idealization of the husband's memory . . ." [p. 270].

This apotheosis of the past has received literary documentation, notably in Daphne Du Maurier's character "Rebecca," the first wife, whose reputation for perfection continued to grow long after she had been succeeded by a wife of merely remarkable talents Following the motif of this novel, Gouldner (1954, pp 79–83) has characterized as the "Rebecca Myth" this source of employee resistance to new industrial managers  Gouldner describes a situation in one of the plants of a large industrial corporation in which the old manager "Doug" had been succeeded by a new manager "Peele." "Doug" was remembered as a model manager  he set a comparison level that "Peele" had difficulty meeting  "Almost to a man, workers in the plant were in the spell of a backward-looking reverie  They overflowed with stories which highlighted the differences between the two managers, the leniency of Doug and the strictness of Peele" [p 80].

An English study (Scott, et al , 1956) on the social consequences of transferring steelworkers from two obsolete plants to one large new plant revealed the (same effect of idealization on the comparison level ) Of the two managers of the older plants, one became manager of the new plant and the other was given a less important post outside the new plant hierarchy  The men whose old manager had been removed—". occasionally referred to the new  . manager in a disparaging way, more often, indeed much more often, they spoke of their past manager . . . very favourably" [p 235]  Summing up their observations, the authors conclude. "It is not unreasonable to assume that a tendency to idealize the virtues of a past plant manager and to

magnify the failings of the present one was in operation here,   .  "
[p 235]

The comparison level may be elevated as much by idealizations of the future as of the past   It is generally thought that persons facing marriage tend to develop fantastic expectations of how their partner will behave in marriage and of the satisfactions to be achieved there One of the main objections made by marriage counselors to premarital autoeroticism is that it is likely to involve fantasies of beautiful and talented partners whom an actual husband or wife will be unable to replace (Dickinson and Beam, 1931)   Stories are also told of soldiers who, having been isolated from real women and limited to fantasy association with pin-up girls of movie magazines and fiction, find the women they return to rather disappointing

Regarding this phenomenon, as it occurs with young people with limited social contacts, Sullivan (1953) has the following comment.

> Some of these isolated early adolescents suffer a particular handicap from this reverie substitution for the interpersonal experience, in that they develop quite strongly personified imaginary companions, and the singularly personal source of the idealized characteristics may be a severe barrier later on to finding anybody who strikes them as really suitable for durable interpersonal relations [p 277]

A quite different type of research, which may not at first sight seem particularly relevant, is reported by Pepitone (1950).   Adolescent boys appeared before an experimentally controlled board of adults who were to decide whether the subject-applicant would receive a prize (a ticket to an important college basketball game)   Subjects who were highly motivated to win a prize, as contrasted with those not so highly motivated, showed marked "facilitative" distortions in their judgments of the adult board members   For example, in the first part of the experiment, highly motivated subjects judged the board member who played a friendly role toward the subject as having a disproportionate amount of power over the prize-awarding decision   And in the second part highly motivated subjects judged the board member who held the greatest power (i e., the "head" member) as being more friendly toward themselves than did the less highly motivated subjects.   This facilitative distortion resembles idealization in that the persons who most want the prize are optimistically judging the situation to be favorable to their attaining it   We would expect this to characterize the powerful person described earlier, who indirectly reveals his confidence by overestimating the power of the board member who is friendly to his interests or, alternatively, by emphasizing the friendliness of the most powerful board member   But what of low-power persons?   Why are there not some pessimistic individuals who magnify the amount of unsympathetic external control present in the prize-attainment situation?

Both kinds of persons *do* appear in an experiment by Klein (1954), thereby calling into question the generality of Pepitone's findings. Klein administered the Stroop test (which measures the degree to which performance on a sorting task is impaired by interference from irrelevant information) to a large group of male college students On the basis of these test scores, he then selected two extreme groups of subjects, one of which showed maximum and the other minimum impairment of performance, that is, a high-interference and a low-interference group On the basis of more or less good evidence, the first group could be characterized as "compulsive" and "constricted," the second group as "outgoing," "confident," "exploratory" Just prior to the experiment itself, half of the subjects in each group were made thirsty by experimental means and the thirst of the other half was fully satiated In the experiment the subjects made size estimations of pictures of objects, some of which were thirst-relevant (e g , an ice-cream soda) Klein's results show that his low-interference subjects (exploratory) yield data that roughly parallel the Pepitone findings with increasing need (thirst), there was an increasing tendency to overestimate the size of need-relevant objects. However, his high-interference (constricted) subjects showed the opposite relationship as need increased, the size of need-relevant objects was increasingly *underestimated*

To speculate further, the overestimations characteristic of Klein's low-interference subjects and the underestimations of his high-interference subjects are suggestive of recent interpretations of differences between those who score high and those who score low on the McClelland-type measure of need-achievement For example, Atkinson (1953) summarizes experimental results by describing high need-achievement in terms of a confident orientation which " is essentially positive motivation to experience feelings of accomplishment and success . " and low need-achievement as an avoidant orientation which implies " relatively greater anxiety about failure" [p 389]. If this interpretation is correct,* Atkinson's research on the relationship

---

* We hesitate to take any definite stand on the disagreement between interpretations like those of Atkinson and those of Alper (1948, 1952, 1957) Alper provides experimental and clinical evidence for the thesis that high need-achievement represents fear of failure and low need-achievement represents self-confidence, thus reversing the polarity that Atkinson describes The issue awaits further research and standardization of measurement. Here we are interested only in raising the question as to the relationship, whatever its direction, between achievement motivation and a dimension the extremes of which may be labeled "hope for success" and "fear of failure."

between achievement motivation and recall of tasks may reveal further facets of our powerful-confident and powerless-constricted types   One way of summarizing part of Atkinson's findings and interpretations is to say that when the achievement motive is aroused (by presenting tasks in a formal, serious way as having important consequences for the subjects' college careers) those subjects whose achievement motivation is high tend subsequently to recall a relatively high proportion of their failures, whereas subjects with low achievement motivation tend to recall relatively more of their successes   These findings are quite consistent with our view that the confident, powerful person can afford to entertain instigations from unattained outcomes (important but incompleted tasks), whereas the less powerful person learns to avoid such instigations and quickly puts such experiences out of mind. The latter might not have undertaken such tasks in the first place had not the experimental situation required it.

It is probable that the complexity of the Klein and Atkinson results, as contrasted with those of many of their predecessors, can be attributed at least in part to their recruiting procedures, as Atkinson [pp 388–389] himself remarks.  The subjects in many of the earlier studies, which relied heavily on volunteer recruits, would be expected to include large numbers of confident, outgoing persons who were unafraid of failure, whereas Klein and Atkinson both used preselection procedures that insured not a random or representative sample but at least one which contained the pertinent extremes

An experiment reported by Horwitz (1958) provides a fitting capstone to this discussion because it deals simultaneously with a number of the variables considered separately in the studies just summarized. In this experiment all subjects performed a series of tasks on which success would presumably be highly rewarding to everyone.   Each subject's goal was to learn how to do the tasks so that he could improve his performance on a later retest   Each subject was permitted to complete correctly half the tasks and the other half was not completed at all   This score of 50 per cent was interpreted to some subjects as indicating almost certain *success* on the retest and to others, almost certain *failure*. Persons in the success condition would be expected, then, to be little concerned about their wrong answers (the incompleted tasks), but in the failure condition these same items should be the occasion for considerable concern   However, a fair number of subjects in the success condition were found to express considerable concern over their wrong answers and a sizable number in the failure condition, to express little concern.  These subjects, whom Horwitz describes as having nonveridical attitudes toward their success or failure, might be viewed as being pessimistic about success, even though it is promised them, or, when failure is in the offing, as devaluating the loss sustained in doing poorly. Thus they resemble the personalities we have described as powerless and lacking in self-confidence. The remaining subjects, exhibiting "veridical" attitudes, might be considered as powerful, outgoing persons.

The resemblance is further manifested when "veridical" and "nonveridical" subjects are compared on their responses to a TAT picture. veridical subjects tend to give active themes (e g , working on a problem) and nonveridical subjects, passive themes (e g , worrying, daydreaming, activity unrelated to an achievement task). On the assumption that all subjects are originally instigated to do well in the experiment, Horwitz interprets the nonveridical subjects as inhibiting tendencies to engage in goal-striving behavior. When failing, they are said to block off attempts to improve and to inhibit awareness that they care about doing well. When successful, they feel "in luck" and are afraid that their own activities might destroy their lucky streak. It must be obvious to the reader that this pattern corresponds closely to our description of the person who perceives his own power to be inadequate relative to that of external agents.

Finally, Horwitz reports that the nonveridical subjects performed more poorly on the retest, and, in line with Atkinson's findings, their recall of the tasks consisted of a larger proportion of successes than did that of the veridical subjects.

The evidence cited in the disparate array of studies mentioned above leads us to reaffirm our view of the way in which individual differences affect CL. There will be wide individual differences in personal attributes at one extreme, *positive motivation to experience success or* the confidence and outgoingness, and, at the other, *constriction* and a *fear of failure*. The positive attributes might be expected to dispose the person to emphasize (to weight heavily) the rewards and/or to de-emphasize the costs that were associated with a past activity or that will be associated with a future one. This is idealization. Similarly, we would expect the person at the other end of the continuum (constricted, fearing failure) to de-emphasize (to weight lightly) the rewards and/or emphasize the costs of future or past situations. From such individuals we would expect pessimism about the future and "debunking" of the past.

## 6.5 Generality of Comparison Level

We may propound the general hypothesis that the more satisfactory any given relationship has been found to be, the higher will be the comparison level for evaluating any new relationship.

Let us begin by considering the (quite opposite claim that a kind of substitution tendency exists such that if the person achieves very satisfactory states in one relationship then he will be more willing to settle for somewhat less satisfactory states in others) Conversely, then, those who achieve quite unsatisfactory outcomes in one relationship might be expected to demand compensatory advantages in others    The only relevant evidence comes from studies of level of aspiration    Although these studies provide a very imperfect test of the hypothesis, they are germane insofar as the goal setting is affected by motivations to improve one's outcomes.    Consistent with the substitution hypothesis are the scattered findings that at least some of the individuals who repeatedly perform badly on tasks tend to set high goals for themselves, as high as those set by more successful individuals.    In general, the habitually unsuccessful people show great interindividual variability in their goal-setting behavior (Lewin, et al , 1944, pp 343–344)

However, aside from this special effect of very little success, the original hypothesis appears to be somewhat better supported than the substitution one  highly successful persons tend to set higher goals than moderately successful persons

Another kind of evidence can be approached through Benoit-Smullyan's (1944) status equilibration hypothesis, which is stated as follows.

> As a result of status conversion processes which are normally at work in every society, there exists a real tendency for the different types of status to reach a common level, i e., for a man's position in the economic hierarchy to match his position in the political hierarchy and for the latter to accord with his position in the hierarchy of prestige, etc [p  160].

Benoit-Smullyan's hypothesis is slightly different from ours, since it emphasizes the tendency to equalize positions on different status dimensions within a given society or organization rather than a tendency to demand equally good outcomes, whatever their type or dimension, from different social organizations or relationships.

In a study designed to test this hypothesis Fenchel, Monderer, and Hartley (1951) asked subjects (sophomore men) to rate their present and desired standing in each of five specific groups. a school group, social club, friends, family, and the college student body  If we assume that the rating of present standing reflects the satisfactoriness of the reward-cost position the person is attaining in a given group, we would expect the statuses desired in the different groups to converge upon a common level    This follows from our (hypothesis that the satisfaction a person achieves in each relationship will tend to set the standard (comparison level) of what he expects and wants in other relationships. Although the results are beset with methodological problems which can only partly be met within the limits of the data in hand, they are consistent with such a convergence effect. The data were analyzed by determining the discrepancy between desired and present standing and comparing this for groups in which present standing is *low* versus those in which it is *high*. This discrepancy score was found to be greater for those of low, as compared with high, present standing—a finding taken to indicate that although present standings vary over most of the scale the ratings of desired standings tend to be relatively concentrated at the upper end of the scale. If this effect is a real one, it appears to operate in the upward direction, that is, convergence toward the more satisfactory outcomes. This may be true of desired statuses but not true of realistically expected statuses.

The phenomenon we are pointing to here is a special case of the tendency for aspiration levels in different situations to be interdependent. How well a person does on one task affects not only his aspirations for further performances on it but also, to some degree, his aspirations with regard to other tasks, the degree of transfer effect depending upon the amount of similarity between the tasks (Lewin, et al., 1944, pp. 339, 343–344).

The general conception a person has about how well he can perform on tasks in general, which has been referred to in the literature as his "ego-level," is probably related to his general feelings of self-esteem. Our present suggestion is that a similar ego-level exists with regard to individual attainment in social relationships. As a result of many experiences in many relationships, the person develops a general and relatively constant expectation of the satisfaction he can achieve in association with others—a generalized conception of his worth in interpersonal relationships.

## SUMMARY

Although a person is always assumed to prefer better outcomes to poorer ones, certain levels of outcome are of special significance in his evaluation of a relationship. This chapter defines and discusses the comparison level (CL) which constitutes a kind of zero or neutral point on the outcome scale. To the degree the outcomes an individual obtains in a given relationship surpass the CL, to that degree he is attracted to and satisfied with the relationship. To the degree obtained outcomes fall short of the CL, he is dissatisfied with the relationship.

The comparison level depends in general upon the outcomes which are salient (actively stimulating or vividly recalled) at any given time. If we assume that all the (recently experienced outcomes are salient,) then the better they have been, the higher the CL and the less the satisfaction with any given level   Thus (CL tends to move to the level of outcomes currently being attained)  In other words, the person adapts to the presently experienced levels  after a shift upward to a new level, the once longed for outcomes gradually lose their attractiveness, after a downward shift to a new lower level, the disappointment gradually wears off and the once dreaded outcomes become accepted

The foregoing generalizations do not always hold, however, because of the fact that not all the outcomes a person has recently experienced or learned about are equally salient   With variations in the particular instigations or reminders that are present (e g., the particular persons brought to mind for comparison), there appear to be corresponding fluctuations in CL.

It is also proposed that salience of outcomes depends upon the person's conceptions of his power or control over his own fate   This is based on the assumption that it is highly adaptive for a person, on the one hand, to pay attention to and remember outcomes for which he has had major causal responsibility and, on the other hand, simply to accept and forget outcomes determined by external forces   A number of consequences follow from this proposition   For example, with an improved level of outcomes, the person's CL will rise more if he believes them to represent products of his own causal potency than if he views them as resulting from (arbitrary actions of the external world.) It is speculated that the latter category usually includes both infrequently received and extreme outcomes and those of low probability of attainment   This analysis is consistent with evidence that dissatisfaction with failing to attain a desired state is less if there was little optimism about attaining it in the first place

There are, of course, individual differences in optimism and confidence about attaining good outcomes   These are viewed as tending to reflect the power the individual perceives himself to have and, in some degree, his actual effectiveness vis-à-vis his environment   It is also suggested that these individual differences are reflected in the manner in which the person permits himself to think about good, but presently unattainable, states   Arguing again from an adaptation and learning viewpoint, we may hypothesize that more powerful and confident persons will tend to emphasize the reward aspects of such states and de-emphasize the cost components   Conversely, less powerful and confident persons will emphasize costs and play down the rewards   A number of lines of evidence reveal the former tendency—to *idealize* unattainable states    Furthermore, recent work on personality variables points to an individual difference dimension at one extreme of which are found persons exhibiting an idealization tendency and at the other, persons who show the opposite, "debunking" tendency    It is to be expected that CL will tend to be higher for the first kind of person than for the second, with a consequent difference, on the average, in their evaluations of the relationships and situations they experience

The question is raised as to whether an individual's CL is general over different relationships (with attained levels in one relationship affecting the CL operative in evaluating others) or specific to different types of relationships    Some indirect evidence suggests that there is at least some generality, a given CL representing the outcomes expected in a broad variety of relationships.

# 7.

# *Power and Dependence*

If two persons interact, the pattern of outcomes given in their interaction matrix indicates that each person has the possibility of affecting the other's reward-cost positions and, thereby, of influencing or controlling him. In other words, the matrix reveals that each person has certain possibilities for exercising power over the other, assuming that they do, in fact, interact. (Whether they do depends upon how the outcomes in the matrix compare with those existing in the available alternative relationships.) Unless each person receives outcomes better than those specified by his $CL_{alt}$, we assume that interaction will not occur. (Therefore, when the outcomes in the matrix are scaled with the $CL_{alt}$ as a zero point, the matrix values indicate each person's possible dependence upon the relationship, and the pattern of values indicates, as we shall see, the possibilities for influence within the relationship.)

(The objective conditions that are the basis for the $CL_{alt}$ lie in the outcomes that the person can achieve in his best available alternative to the present relationship.) This best alternative will be the most favorable of any of the alternatives to the present relationship, including the state of being alone. If the $CL_{alt}$ represents the average outcome of the best alternative, then it should represent approximately the least that the person will "settle for" in the present relationship. If the outcomes in the present relationship fall so that they approximate more and more closely the $CL_{alt}$, the person will find it increasingly difficult to maintain his decision to stay in the present relationship: he will begin to be tempted to disrupt it. At this point, the person's dependence upon the dyad will be very small indeed, if not nonexistent. If he does leave the relationship and enters his best alternative relationship, his $CL_{alt}$ is dropped to the next best alternative.) Thus the average level of outcomes cannot fall below $CL_{alt}$, except perhaps briefly, during the period of shifting from one relationship to another. As his outcomes in a relationship rise, his dependence on that relationship also rises.) However, as we have stated in Chapters 2 and 6, his average level may lie either above or below CL, and not until his outcomes have surpassed his CL will he be *positively attracted* to the dyad. (CL, then, is crucial in his attraction to the dyad, but $CL_{alt}$ is crucial in determining his dependency upon or, conversely, his power within it.)

In this chapter we analyze the kinds of power one member of a dyad may have over the other and consider the ways in which power can be used to produce changes in the other's behavior and attitudes. Then we describe various strategies for increasing or maintaining one's power. Throughout this discussion, the predictions and generalizations presented depend upon what the two members perceive and believe to be the facts about their interdependency.) For example, person A's promise of reward to B will be effective in changing B's behavior only if he perceives that A can truly deliver the promised outcomes. To simplify the presentation in the discussion of types of power, its consequences, power strategies, etc., we assume that both members of the dyad have accurate understandings of the facts represented in their matrix. Then, in a final section on perception of power and dependence we consider the principles and factors governing the formation of perceptions and beliefs about these aspects of the relationship.

## 7.1 Types of Power

We will first define power in an approximate way and then try to specify it more exactly. Generally, we can say that the power of A over B increases with A's ability to (affect the quality of outcomes attained by B.) From this it follows that our treatment of power is at once somewhat broader and somewhat narrower than that of many other writers on this topic. It is narrower in that, by relating A's power to his effects on B's outcomes, we do not deal with a certain class of means by which A can alter B's behavior. In the present treatment we ignore such sources of the control of B's behavior that are not contained in variations in B's outcomes (Chapter 2). Specifically, we will not treat A's ability to control B's behavior by controlling the direct instigations to B's "innate" responses. This means that we will exclude from the discussion such events as A's ability to cause a startle response in B or to cause any such reflexive responses.

Our treatment is also somewhat broader than some others in that by relating A's power to effects on B's outcomes we focus not only on A's ability to control B's behavior but also to control his fate. We now turn to these two types of power: fate control and behavior control.

### 7.1.1 FATE CONTROL

If, by varying his behavior, A can affect B's outcomes *regardless of what B does*, A has *fate control* over B. Consider the matrix in Table 7-1 in which only B's outcomes are represented. (This may be considered as a portion of the total matrix existing for A and B, and the outcomes are scaled in terms of reward-cost units above B's $CL_{alt}$.) By changing his behavior from $a_1$ to $a_2$, A can increase B's outcomes from 1 to 4. He can also, of course, later reduce B's outcomes from 4 to 1, and in neither case can B do anything about it.

The larger the range of outcome values through which A can move

TABLE 7-1

ILLUSTRATION OF A'S FATE CONTROL OVER B

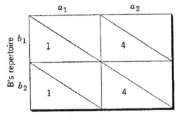

A's repertoire

B, the greater his fate control over B. The lower end of this range is zero, since one possible behavior for A is that of "leaving the relationship." On the assumption that B's $CL_{alt}$ is a fairly realistic representation of outcomes he can receive in his best alternative relationship (and we deal later with the factors that produce nonveridical perceptions of such outcomes), A's leaving will drop B's outcomes to the level of his $CL_{alt}$, which is given a value of zero in the matrix. In assessing the upper reaches of this range, it seems reasonable to use a modal value, for example, the average outcome value attained by B. Thus a possible index of A's general fate control over B might be the distance from B's $CL_{alt}$ to the average reward-cost position he achieves in the relationship. The reader will note that this index is similar, though not identical, to that proposed earlier for B's attraction to the dyad. The difference is simply that B's attraction to the dyad is estimated by comparing his average outcomes with his CL, whereas his dependence on the dyad—hence A's fate control over him—is estimated by comparing his average outcomes with his $CL_{At}$. Since outcomes from the best alternative relationship are included among those that determine the CL, the CL and $CL_{alt}$ will tend to be positively correlated. The language of conceptions of power like those of Ross (1921) and of Waller and Hill (1951) seems to indicate that these writers believe dependence and attraction to be closely associated.* To the degree that they *are* correlated, formulations of power (like those of Festinger, Schachter, and Back, 1950, pp. 164 ff) which are based on attraction to the relationship will yield results similar to ours.

TABLE 7-2

ILLUSTRATION OF A'S BEHAVIOR CONTROL OVER B

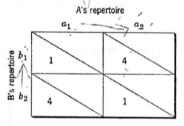

### 7.1.2 BEHAVIOR CONTROL

A second kind of power is called *behavior control*. If, by varying his behavior, A can make it desirable for B to vary his behavior too, then A has behavior control over B. (We use "control" here in the sense of ability to affect the likelihood of occurrence of one or more behaviors.) Consider the matrix in Table 7-2 in which, again, only B's outcomes are shown. By changing his behavior from $a_1$ to $a_2$, A can motivate B to make a corresponding change in his behavior from $b_2$ to $b_1$.

The amount of this behavior control will depend upon the values to B of the various outcomes. A's behavior control is greater the more B stands to gain by adjusting his behavior in accord with A's behavioral choices. This form of power is manifested in the matrix as a set of values that show what is, in the statistical sense, an interaction effect. That is to say, B's outcomes vary not as a function either of A's be-

---

* E. A. Ross states the "Law of Personal Exploitation" as follows: "In any sentimental relation the one who cares less can exploit the one who cares more" [p. 136]. Waller and Hill propound the "Principle of Least Interest": "That person is able to dictate the conditions of association whose interest in the continuation of the affair is least" [p. 191].

havioral choices (fate control) or of his own but as a function of the
interaction between them (This provides another way of distinguishing behavior control from fate control on the basis of their determinants ) A's fate control rests on his ability to supply high rewards to B
at low cost to himself  A's behavior control rests on this same ability
*plus* an interaction effect contributed by interferences or facilitations
which (as described in Chapter 4) reduce or enhance B's outcomes in
certain cells of the matrix

This interaction effect suggests the possibility of adapting a measure
of statistical interaction from the analysis of variance in order to provide an index of behavior control   A similar index (suggested to us
by Richard Savage) comes from game theory  assuming that B can
select only one item from his repertoire, how valuable is it to him to
know before making his choice what behavior A is going to perform

It may be noted in passing that A's behavior control over B requires
B to discriminate A's behavior choices and to make appropriate choices
himself.  If B is unable to do either of these (i e , if the problem is too
difficult for him for either reason), then the situation resembles that of
fate control insofar as there are fluctuations in B's outcomes which he
is unable to control or counteract.

### 7.1.3 CONVERSION OF FATE CONTROL
####      TO BEHAVIOR CONTROL

Fate control can be used to control behavior.  Refer again to Table
7-1.  Person A can make it desirable for B to perform set $b_1$ rather
than $b_2$ by always performing $a_2$ when B does $b_1$ and $a_1$ when B does
$b_2$   In other words, A must see to it that only two of the four combinations in Table 7-1 occur.  $a_2b_1$ and $a_1b_2$.  To do this, A must obtain
information about B's behavioral choices and follow a certain rule in
matching his own choices to B's.  After the rule has been applied several times or otherwise conveyed to B, he will find that he can affect
his outcomes by behaving one way rather than another.  Hence A's
fate control, under which B could not affect his own outcomes, becomes "converted" to control B's behavior.

To change the situation from one in which B will prefer doing $b_1$
to one in which he will prefer $b_2$, (A must change the rule he is following in matching his behavior to B's)  This suggests one characteristic
of converted fate control which should be noted and emphasized
There are always several matching rules that A can apply (in Table
7-1 there are two)  Which of these he chooses to apply may be more
or less arbitrary  Thus it is probably clear to B that A may change
rules at any time, in which case there is the possibility that A will

misapply the rule by inadequate monitoring or careless choice of behavior. In brief, the converted fate control situation is not always a completely comfortable and predictable one from B's point of view. Rather, it may involve considerable uncertainty and conflict.

To have the desired effect on B in any given instance, A must determine B's behavior and modify his own behavior accordingly. (Whether or not active *monitoring* is required of A depends upon whether he places emphasis upon an *augmentation* of outcomes for compliance or a *reduction* for noncompliance.) (See McGregor, 1948, for a discussion of these two modes of influence.) This distinction is not adequately illustrated in a 2 x 2 matrix, but the notion is a simple one. In the course of the interaction A may promise to augment B's outcomes if B performs the indicated behavior or he may threaten to reduce them if B fails to perform as requested (and, of course, A may do both). If B is controlled solely by augmentation (say he is offered rewards for compliance), he will monitor himself. The situation then becomes very similar to straight behavior control; in both situations B applies a matching rule to himself, that is, he monitors both A's behaviors and his own. The difference is that in converted fate control with augmentation for compliance B will present evidence of his compliance to A to validate his claim for the "reward." In contrast, when reduction (decreased rewards or increased costs) is threatened for noncompliance, A must keep B's compliance under surveillance.

If A is intent on controlling B's behavior, he may find it efficient to insure that B learn the appropriate matching rule by explicitly communicating the rule to B. However, it is possible for fate control to be converted implicitly, that is, without A's explicitly instructing B in the rule. This is done by repeatedly applying the matching rule until B learns that he can affect his own outcomes by behaving one way rather than another.

Implicit conversion of fate control can be illustrated by Table 7–3, which depicts a situation in which each member of a dyad exercises fate control over the other. Whenever A performs $a_1$, he rewards B, and, whenever he performs $a_2$, he punishes (i.e., adds high costs to) B, regardless of B's behavior. B's behaviors have the same effects on A. Whenever B performs $b_1$, he rewards A, and, whenever he performs $b_2$, he punishes A, regardless of A's behavior. In a situation of this sort, through conversion of fate control, the interaction can eventually stabilize in the mutually satisfactory cell ($a_1b_1$), and this can be achieved implicitly, without any discussion or explicit communication. Consider the two cells in the matrix, $a_1b_2$ and $a_2b_1$, in the first of which A is punished and B is rewarded and in the second of which A is rewarded and B is punished. In $a_1b_2$, since A is punished, he will cease performing $a_1$, and, since B is rewarded, he will continue to perform $b_2$. This shifts the joint behavior to the $a_2b_2$ cell in which both are punished. Similarly for the cell $a_2b_1$. Since A is rewarded, he will continue to perform $a_2$, and, since B is punished, he will cease performing $b_1$. The joint behavior again shifts to the $a_2b_2$ cell. But, since both A and B are punished in $a_2b_2$, both should cease *that* behavior, and the joint behavior should shift to $a_1b_1$. In this cell both are rewarded, hence stability should be achieved.

Sidowski, Wyckoff, and Tabory (1956) have performed an experiment which may possibly be interpreted as the implicit conversion of mutual fate control. In each experimental session each member of a

TABLE 7–3

AN ILLUSTRATION OF MUTUAL FATE CONTROL WHICH GIVES RISE TO
IMPLICIT CONVERSION

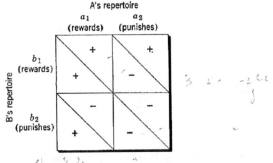

pair of subjects was placed in a cubicle isolated from the other. Each member was in fact unaware of the existence of the other. In each cubicle the subject was provided with two push buttons, one of which delivered a score and the other an electric shock to the other subject. A subject was told only that he could push the buttons in any way he chose and that he should try to make as many points as possible. For half of the dyads, the shock was strong, for the other half it was weak. The main results of the experiment were that under the strong-shock conditions members of dyads learned to give one another predominantly more scores than shocks, whereas in the weak-shock condition no evidence of learning occurred. Although data on sequential patterns are not presented in this experiment, the results are consistent with expectations based on our analysis of the implicit conversion of fate control.

### 7.1.4  USABLE POWER AND PATTERNS OF INTERDEPENDENCE

As we have seen in analyzing the implicit conversion of fate control, a person will not use his power to affect the fate or behavior of another person without regard to the effects of this use upon his own outcomes. Consider Table 7–4. Here A has the same degree of fate control over B as that shown in Table 7–1. However, from the pattern of A's outcomes in Table 7–4, it is quite apparent that he will be reluctant to use this control because to do so would require his affecting his own outcomes in a major way.

Individual A may also be deterred from using his power by the fact that B possesses counterpower over him. Table 7–5 shows two instances in which A has fate control over B and C, respectively. B has an equal amount of fate control over A, so, if, for example, A uses his power to reduce B's outcomes, B can counter by reducing A's outcomes

TABLE 7–4

A AFFECTS HIMSELF IF HE EXERCISES HIS FATE CONTROL OVER B

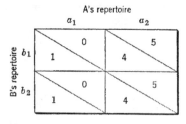

to the same degree. Person C, on the other hand, has behavior control over A. This does not give C any guaranty that he can reduce A's outcomes, but it does give C the opportunity to keep his own outcomes high by providing incentives to A to continue enacting $a_2$. The case in which each person possesses behavior control over the other is illustrated in Table 7–6.

These examples indicate the desirability of considering each person's *usable* power, by which is meant (following Webster's definition of "usable") the power that it is convenient and practicable for him to use. (Power is not usable to the degree that its use penalizes the possessor, either directly or because of counterpower held by the other person.) (The latter might be covered by the notion of *relative power*, that is, A's power over B in relation to B's power over him.)

The two matrices in Table 7–6 raise another problem, that of the pattern of interdependency between A and B. In both matrices they have the same degree of behavior control over each other, but in the first their outcomes are positively correlated and in the second, negatively. The first situation might be generated by a cooperative arrangement of member goals (see Deutsch, 1949a, on promotive interdependence), by identification processes which lead one or both members to obtain satisfactions by delivering rewards to the other, or, as shown in the next chapter, by the development of norms. The second situation more closely resembles a competitive relationship, as each person attains maximum rewards at the expense of the other's attainment of relatively poor outcomes (Deutsch's contrient interdependence). These different patterns of interdependence have sharply different consequences for the relationship. In the first, in which qualities of outcome are positively related, there exists a clear

TABLE 7-5

B and C Have Power Counter to A's Fate Control over Them

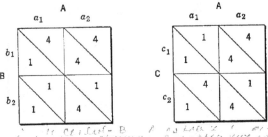

basis for working together and the only problem is that of synchronizing the shifts from $a_2b_1$ to $a_1b_2$. The second case, in which outcomes are negatively related, creates the possibility of highly unstable interaction. As soon as A does $a_2$, B does $b_1$, which motivates A to shift to $a_1$. This, in turn, motivates B to shift to $b_2$, thus shifting A to $a_2$, which starts the cycle all over again. As we explain later, an interaction of this sort is likely to be quite unsatisfactory for both persons. To avoid difficulties, A and B must work out some agreement for trading or exchanging good outcomes.

In general, the pattern of values in the matrix, considering the outcomes of both A and B, determines the degree to which each person's potential control over the other is usable and also affects the modes of interaction and kinds of agreements the two persons must work out in order to maximize their outcomes.

### 7.1.5 EXPERTNESS

One person can improve the outcomes of another in one or both of two ways: by providing him with rewards or by reducing his costs. A special case of the ability to cut another person's costs is exemplified by the "expert," an individual who has special knowledge he can impart to others which enables them to perform rewarding activities with less effort, less anxiety, or in less time—in general, at lower cost. Through the possession of such knowledge, the expert has power over his clients, for by giving or withholding information he can improve or worsen their outcomes.

However, this particular source of power has some peculiar drawbacks. If the receiver of expert advice thereby becomes enabled to provide himself with such information on later occasions, the expert's power is lost. It is as if he had a cost-cutting tool which he gives the

TABLE 7-6

DIFFERENT PATTERNS OF INTERDEPENDENCY

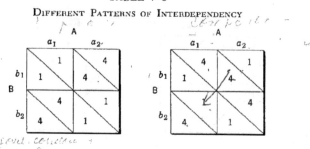

other person. Only if he retains ownership of the tool and can withdraw it at any time does he continue to derive power from it. Further, it appears from a study by Wilensky (1956, pp. 304–305) on the staff expert in labor unions that the replaceability of the expert's skill is an important factor in determining the amount of influence he will have on decision making in the union. His power is increased to the degree that his skill and experience are not replaceable. In other words, the more special the expert's skill and the poorer the client's alternatives (i.e., the lower his $CL_{alt}$), the greater the staff expert's power. Similarly, the expert retains his power only so long as he is able to keep the client from permanently acquiring expertise. This is possible under a variety of conditions, for example, when the expert has a set of general principles from which he derives his specific recommendations   These principles are never revealed and are too subtle for a client to infer from the specific suggestions he receives

Expertness raises another question of interest   Under what conditions is the advice of an expert followed?   When does a client assume that his costs will be cut by following the expert's recommendation? The general answer seems to be that compliance with the suggestions of this expert or other similar ones has in the past resulted in the achievement of desirable reward-cost positions   An experiment by Mausner (1954) shows that subjects' judgments were influenced more in a perceptual task by a partner who had been previously successful on a similar task than by one who had been unsuccessful.

## 7.2   Changes in Values and Attitudes

From the preceding discussion, it is clear that the power to affect another person's reward-cost positions often enables the possessor to influence that person's behavior or to affect his outcomes. Power also forms the basis for the production, either deliberately or unintentionally, of changes in values and attitudes.   Since a person's outcomes listed in the matrix depend in part upon his values and attitudes, fate and behavior control afford opportunities for these outcomes to be modified   The change mechanisms described are drawn largely from elementary considerations of learning   The first two involve mainly associative processes, the last mainly motivational processes

### 7 2 1   CHANGES IN THE REWARD-COST VALUES TO B OF A'S BEHAVIOR

The principle may be stated briefly   A's behavior, which is initially neutral, may acquire reward value by association with B's receiving rewards from A   Refer again to Table 7–1 in which A has fate control over B   B does not need to discriminate between his own response alternatives, $b_1$ and $b_2$, but only between the response alternatives of A, $a_1$ and $a_2$   The principle states that those discriminable aspects of A's behavior, $a_2$, associated with the production of rewards to B, will acquire reward value for B   Thus the mother's smile, the mother's act of walking toward the infant, any discriminable attributes of the mother's behavior as she feeds the infant, may take on reward value to the infant   These secondary aspects of feeding then acquire the reward properties that were originally restricted to the intake of food itself   In this manner (and as a result perhaps of other factors) the infant develops favorable feelings toward the mother and many of her behaviors.

By the same process, changes can be produced in the effects of A's behaviors on B's acts. Initially neutral aspects of A's behavior can acquire the ability to elicit anxiety or other inhibitory responses if they occur in association with other behaviors that elicit these reactions from the outset

### 7.2.2   CHANGES IN THE REWARD-COST VALUES TO B OF HIS OWN BEHAVIOR

The principle of association also explains how certain of B's own behaviors, instrumental to receiving rewards from A or occurring simultaneously with the receipt of rewards from A, may come to have reward value similar to that produced by A (This requires that A reward B in a selective and consistent manner) Thus, in Table 7-1, $b_1$ could come to have considerable reward value for B if A consistently requires $b_1$ as a condition for his performance of $a_2$   In this case B must learn to discriminate his own responses, $b_1$ and $b_2$, and the discriminable characteristics will take on reward value by association with the reward produced by A   The relevant responses of B that acquire reward value would include his verbal and other expressive behavior, and so B may gradually find it rewarding to express opinions and attitudes that have in the past been associated with receiving rewards from A.  As the reward-value of these expressed attitudes becomes relatively autonomous, B will find it increasingly comfortable and comforting to state these attitudes in settings other than those from which they arose

B's behaviors may also acquire excessive cost values through association   For example, a response that is consistently punished by A will be increasingly inhibited   After negative emotional conditioning of this sort, the response will be accompanied by considerable tension and discomfort

### 7.2.3   CONFLICT AVOIDANCE

The concept of conflict has already been introduced in Chapter 4. The same meaning of conflict is intended in the present discussion, although its application is changed   Earlier we were concerned with some of the reward-cost effects of response interference that may exist when a member is instigated to two incompatible sets at the same time. The conflicted member was involved in little or no decision making· rather the two sets (or at least one of them) were obtruded on him   The general form of the present interest, in the consequences of conflict for attitude change, can be exemplified by turning again to Table 7-1. Suppose A is in set $a_2$ and B must decide whether to enter into the activities associated with set $b_1$ or those associated with set $b_2$. Both alternatives entail B's moving to a position four reward-cost units above his $CI_{alt}$, hence are indistinguishable to him in their overall favorableness. Assuming the alternative activities to be incompatible, this choice is expected to arouse conflict in B. The conflict might be either an approach-approach type (in which only rewards and no costs are involved) or a double approach-avoidance type (in which each alternative involves both rewards and costs). In any case, conflict is assumed to result in excessive costs—costs over and above those associated with the separate alternatives.

Let us suppose the conflict is the double approach-avoidance type and try to make the example more concrete: A, the father, offers two alternatives to his son, B. In the first alternative, $b_1$, B will receive a two-year-old palomino pony if he agrees to substitute for the hired hand during his two-week vacation, and in the second, $b_2$, B will receive a small, fast, but aging mare if he agrees to work one week of the hired hand's vacation. These two alternatives are by our initial assumption equally attractive to B; hence we expect considerable conflict.

We may suppose that as B thinks about the alternatives he will begin to lean slightly toward one of them, say the palomino and much work. Once this trend has begun, he will attempt to reduce the high cost of conflict by further separating the merits of the two alternatives. This may conceivably take the form of his beginning to value the palomino more, or the mare less, than he did at the outset or of reducing his appraisal of the disvalue (cost) of the hired hand's work. Each time B makes a response in favor of the first alternative (whether this response is an implicit private event or a verbal comment) the conflict will be somewhat reduced. By virtue of this reduction of conflict (cost), the favoring response (e.g., "I think the palomino would be much better because it will last me longer") will be reinforced, hence will have a heightened probability of occurring subsequently. When, by this kind of process, the two alternatives become discriminably different to him in their over-all favorableness, he will make the decision.

To the extent that the conflict still exists at the point of decision, conflict drive (as defined in Chapter 4) will provide greater vigor or amplitude to the activities corresponding to the chosen alternative, that is, greater vigor than if no conflict had existed. (There is a problem in determining just how much of the apparent effect of conflict drive is attributable directly to drive and how much to drive-reinforced habit

strength or, for that matter, to habits strongly conditioned to past conflicts of a similar sort, but we will not try to solve this problem here.)

### 7.2.4  DISSONANCE REDUCTION

Besides heightened vigor of activity, there is another possible consequence of unresolved conflict at the point of decision. This is a residual state of tension which Festinger (1957) calls *dissonance*. All
of the items of information that favor the chosen alternative are consonant, and all of the items of information that favor the unchosen
alternative are dissonant with the choice behavior. In the example
just described, the boy's judgment that the palomino is preferable to
the mare is consonant with his decision, whereas his judgment that the
mare is still a pretty good horse and that additional farm work is not
so good is dissonant with his decision. The greater the information
favoring the unchosen alternative, the greater the post-decision dissonance. Festinger analyzes several ways by which the individual
may attempt to reduce dissonance, and later we will be discussing some
of them, but we are concerned here with the effects of dissonance on
the alteration of values and attitudes. Brehm (1956) reports an experiment which bears on this point. Subjects rated each of eight
articles (e.g., an electric sandwich grill, an automatic toaster, or a book
of art reproductions), made a choice between two of them, and rated
each article again. The results bore out the prediction that subjects
would attempt to reduce the dissonance created by choosing between
alternatives by making the chosen alternative more desirable (rating
it higher the second time) and the unchosen alternative less desirable.
The results also showed that dissonance and consequent attempts to
reduce it would be greater the more nearly the two alternatives approached equal desirability.

Thus we conclude that both conflict between alternatives and the
unresolved residual effects of conflicts that produce dissonance will
produce changes in the degree to which objects of choice are valued.
As conflicts are engendered in interaction by the exercise of power,
these mechanisms provide possible means whereby attitudes and
values undergo modification.

## 7.3  SOME CONSEQUENCES OF POWER

### 7.3.1  CONSEQUENCES FOR THE DYAD

What are the effects on the dyadic relationship if the two persons
are highly dependent upon each other (hence have high power over
each other) rather than only slightly interdependent?

A traditional way of beginning this discussion is to relate the "cohesiveness" of a group (including the dyad) to the *internal power* of the group and then to predict various outcomes, such as conformity behavior, from internal power (Festinger, Schachter, and Back, 1950) Cohesiveness has been defined as an increasing function of the attractiveness of the group to its members, that is, cohesiveness will be greater to the degree that rewards are experienced in belonging to the group. These rewards have sometimes been classified by their sources: attractiveness of the (members) to one another, attractiveness of the (goals achieved by belonging to the group, and attractiveness resulting from positive evaluations of the group by relevant nonmembers (prestige)). Back (1951) has performed an experiment in which dyads were arranged to have high or low cohesiveness, some dyads deriving their (high or low) cohesiveness from one of these three sources of attractiveness, some from another of the sources Observing the verbal interaction of the members in attempting to resolve their differences (about the best way to write a story), Back found that his highly cohesive dyads, regardless of the source of dyadic attractiveness, showed a greater change toward agreement than did the less cohesive dyads Perhaps a more striking finding was that the members of highly cohesive dyads also showed a greater overt resistance to one another's suggestions than did members of less cohesive dyads.

Let us look at these results from our point of view. (In our terms, a highly cohesive dyad is one in which each member can move the other through a relatively great number of reward-cost units above $CL_{alt}$, each can (potentially affect the outcomes of the other to a relatively large degree over and above the alternative possibilities expressed in the $CL_{alt}$) Thus each one has high power over the other and their power is equal (This is an "ideal-type" description and of course, the power would usually be somewhat greater either for A or for B; but this makes no difference to our argument) Another way of describing this power equality (or near equality) is to say that although both A and B can affect the other's outcomes both can also counter this effect Thus, from one point of view, each *does* have power, but each also has counterpower, or each member's ability to make demands is matched by the other's ability to resist those demands.

In high cohesiveness both the ability to make demands and the ability to resist them are greater than in low cohesiveness Therefore, a potentiality for conflict exists in high cohesiveness (We will see in a moment, though, that over the long term highly cohesive groups tend to develop a high correspondence of outcomes, hence reducing the likelihood of severe conflict) This theoretical expectation is borne out by Back's finding that his highly cohesive dyads showed not only more strenuous influence attempts but also greater overt resistance to influence than did his less cohesive dyads.

Theoretically, this capacity of highly cohesive dyads to counterpose resistance could lead the members to a mutually unsatisfactory standoff, but it is reasonable to suppose that with a relatively great (and costly) potential for conflict highly cohesive groups will quickly find a working procedure that permits conflict avoidance. This *modus operandi* may take any of several forms, not mutually exclusive.

(1) In any actual dyad the power of the members will hardly ever be exactly equal, and so the procedure for reducing conflict finally adopted may be to permit the prepotent member to be more influential. This is in accordance with Back's finding that in highly cohesive dyads one member was much influenced, the other little, whereas in less cohesive dyads the influence was low to intermediate and relatively equal for the two members.

(2) The cohesive group may rather quickly determine a "zone of conformity" (Bovard and Guetzkow, 1950, Bovard, 1951) which defines the range of issues about which conformity is important and expected, whereas for all other issues no conformity is required. Bovard's data show this differentiation.

Back's finding that greater agreement is reached in highly cohesive groups than in those of low cohesiveness is consistent with the results from several other investigations (e.g., Festinger, Schachter and Back, 1950). In general, the greater the power the members have over one another, the greater the trend toward similarity of values and attitudes. Thus ability to reward each other seems to create further ability to do so. One might say that interdependence begets further interdependence. How this comes about is already implied in our description of attitude change processes: A will reward B in order to get B to produce behavior that he, A, finds rewarding. By so doing, A creates conditions under which, through association learning, B is likely to learn to like this behavior himself. The greater A's ability to reward B, the more this learning will occur. This process tends to produce a correspondence among their outcomes which, as noted earlier, produces a highly satisfactory and stable relationship in which the pair need influence each other only about *when* to do various things and not about *what* to do.

Closely related to the above is the fact that certain value changes insure that each person will produce behaviors desired by the other without the need to maintain surveillance. For example, in Table

7–1, by proper use of his fate control, A can get B to produce $b_1$ when A wants him to. But the overt compliance we observe on B's part does not necessarily imply covert acceptance ("internalization") Only if B spontaneously emits $b_1$ in the absence of the influencing agent A have we evidence that $b_1$ has acquired special reward value for B   A can deliberately or accidentally create conditions in which this value will be acquired and thereby heighten the likelihood of B's performance of $b_1$ whether or not A monitors his actions.

The association mechanism also extends the range of activities which each member can use to provide rewards to the other   As A's words of reassurance or praise, words that initially have no special value to B, come to have reward value, A can substitute them for other, perhaps more costly means of reward provision and control   Of course, through generalization from other relationships, such words are likely to have reward value at the outset of the relationship (Verplanck, 1955).

### 7.3.2 CONSEQUENCES FOR THE INDIVIDUAL

In the preceding section we considered the consequences of the members of a dyad being highly interdependent (with high power over each other) rather than only slightly so   Now we turn to the consequences to the individual of having much versus little power in the relationship. Is high power desirable, and, if so, what difference does it make?

Common sense indicates that power is useful to enable its holder to gain more favorable reward-cost positions. If one postulates the existence of a need for power or dominance, then this would be true by definition  the possession and exercise of power would be rewarding in itself   There may well be such a need or drive, but we shall attempt to account for the advantages of power in terms of the assumptions implicit in our theory. In the long run any such advantages may be expected to lead, by association, to the acquisition of a "need for power," but first it is necessary to establish that such advantages exist.

At first glance it may seem that our theory is contrary to common sense on this point   For example, in Table 7–7 A is shown to have greater fate control than B   But in the course of their interaction it appears that B may achieve higher reward-cost positions on the average than A   This, of course, is true only in relation to each member's $CL_{alt}$   If A has a higher $CL_{alt}$, even though he can exceed it by only two outcome units, his absolute quality of outcomes may be considerably superior to B's   The opposite may also be true  the less powerful member of the relationship may achieve higher absolute outcomes (which probably also means having higher status).   The point to be emphasized here is that there is no *necessary* relation between a person's power and his absolute level of outcomes.

Our theory does suggest, though, that the person with high power will be able to enjoy more frequently the best reward-cost positions available to him in the matrix. Having more to offer (or to threaten to withdraw), he is better able to induce the low-power person to perform such behaviors as he, the high-power person, desires rather than vice versa.

The high-power person also gains considerably from his ability to set the pace and "call the changes" in the interaction. This is often spoken of as the advantage a high-power person has from being able

TABLE 7–7

A Has Greater Fate Control over B than B Has over A

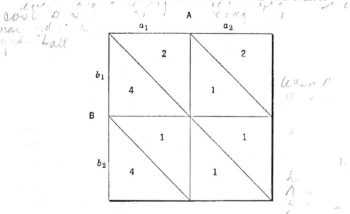

to predict with great certainty the behavior of his vis-à-vis. Our interpretation of this is as follows: Power, either in the form of behavior control or converted fate control, enables the holder to motivate the other person to change behaviors whenever the holder desires it or changes his own behavior. Thus, in Table 7–2, assume that all of A's entries have the same value so that he has considerable behavior control over B but B has no counter power. Given this state of affairs, when A shifts behaviors, B will tend to shift also in an attempt to attain high rewards. But when B shifts, A may or may not shift. He can afford to continue his activity to completion, disregarding B's shifts. B will tend to interrupt his behavior sequences in order to synchronize with A, but A will not do so. Now, assume that during the course of behavior sequences costs are usually incurred early and rewards received late   This is simply a statement that instrumental activities tend to precede consummatory ones.   If this assumption is correct, a person who interrupts his sequences will tend to incur most of the costs but not receive all of the rewards potentially available)  On the other hand, the (high-power) person who can (disregard the other's untimely changes and carry his sequences through to completion will enjoy his potential reward-cost positions to the fullest.)

It might also be assumed that interrupted, incomplete behavior sequences tend to persist (the Zeigarnik effect) and produce interfering cues and responses that raise the costs of subsequent behaviors   This would raise even further the costs of the person who has to interrupt himself at inappropriate times in order to adapt to the other person's changes

(There is also probably some reward from the symbolic value of being able to initiate interaction.)  At least in Western culture, the prerogatives of command plus the enhanced self-esteem go to him who sets the task for others.   Whyte (1949) shows how the counterman in a restaurant strives to avoid taking orders from waitresses.   For example, the counterman will make up a batch of drinks at one time presumably to avoid being asked to make up a single drink each time a waitress brings him an order   It is not at all unusual for personages of high power and social status to find means of avoiding the behavior control of others   For example, the high-level executive has one or more secretaries who interrupt and control other persons' intrusions upon him and arrange a schedule of appointments so that his day can proceed according to the pace and in the manner he prefers.

One of the common disadvantages of low power is that the person finds it desirable to exercise great care in his interactions with those upon whom he is dependent   Hurwitz, Zander, and Hymovitch (1953) observed a tendency for persons of low "status" (where this also meant being low in power) to be "ego-defensive" in their interactions, participating rather infrequently in a discussion in which high-power persons were present and addressing their remarks mainly to the high-power persons when they did participate  (This is interpreted as reflecting uneasiness in relations with persons of higher power.)  In an experiment designed to study this particular effect Cohen (1958) found that persons whose upward mobility was controlled by others tended to communicate with these others in a manner apparently calculated to create a favorable impression.   The general point to be drawn from these studies is that for the low-power person the careful monitoring of his own behavior necessary to avoid offending or annoying more powerful persons probably adds considerably to the costs he incurs during interaction with them.

One further advantage of high power may be briefly noted. By virtue of his ability to deliver large rewards, the values and attitude changes occurring through interaction are more likely to converge upon the high-power person. (See earlier discussion of changes in values and attitudes.) This fact would be of no great importance were it not for the fact that both persons also belong to other dyads and groups and each of these tends to have certain value norms unique to itself. This condition of holding membership in multiple groups, typical of complex, modern societies, poses for the individual the problem of self-consistency. It is uncomfortable and costly to have competing loyalties and conflicting standards to live with. Although most persons undoubtedly have considerable capacity to compartmentalize their values and respond in a highly outer-directed way to each set of social pressures immediately present, it is much better for the psychic economy if a coherent set of standards can be followed consistently.

Important for the present context is that it is more feasible for a person of generally high power to maintain consistent values and attitudes than one of low power. This is a consequence of the greater influence of the former upon the values that the pair come to share. Thus the powerful person is better able to keep the values with which he enters the relationship, these being values consistent with the standards that exist in his other relationships.

### 7.3.3 THE OVERUSE OF POWER

The use of power can be self-defeating. For example, if A uses his behavior control too much, he can so reduce B's attainment of good reward-positions that he will lose his control over B. If B is interrupted so often by A's exercise of control that he incurs only the costs of his sequences and not the rewards, B will lose interest in synchronizing his behavior with A's.

Overuse of power may take another form. If a powerful person, A, too often keeps B at a low level in order to achieve outcomes he desires for himself, B's dependence on the group declines, and, accordingly, A's fate control drops. In general, power can be maintained at its maximum only if it is used considerately and sparingly.

### 7.4 POWER STRATEGIES

Let us consider some possible strategies for increasing power in a dyad. This will serve to highlight again the factors which, according to the present theory, determine this power. The general purpose of these strategies is, of course, to increase the range of outcomes through which one person, A, can move the other, B, and to decrease the range through which B can move A   This miscellaneous set of strategies and stratagems includes ploys and gambits and other gamesmanlike items as well as sounder and more durable behaviors.  Some of these may be quite deliberate devices for gaining an advantage, whereas with others power may be strictly an unanticipated consequence.  We do not pretend to exhaustiveness

(1) Developing better alternatives for A. Person A's object here is to raise his $CL_{alt}$ far enough so that B's performance keeps him just barely above it   Stephen Potter has examples of this technique in *One-upmanship* (1951).  The following is typical

> Basic Club Play as we teach it is the Two-Club approach.  In other words it is essential to belong to two clubs if you belong to one club  It doesn't matter if your second club is a 5/-a year sub affair in Greek Street, the double membership enables you, when at your main or proper club, to speak often in terms of regretful discrimination about the advantages of your Other One [p  141]

(2) Reducing B's alternatives:  By doing this, A prevents B from using the above tactic on A himself

(3) Improving A's ability to deliver rewards to B. This may involve acquiring new tools or instruments, or it may entail only the development of such relatively low-cost products as flattery.  In fact, ingratiating overtures, friendliness, and even friendship itself may be used as a power strategy   To the degree that A can motivate B to like him, B's outcomes approach correspondence with A's  B is pleased at A's happiness and is saddened by A's grief   Hence this strategy is different from most others  it is based on making B's power less usable rather than on increasing A's power or reducing B's   This type of strategy may conceivably be at work in sociometric findings such as those reported by Hurwitz et al (1953), in their study of friendship relations within a group of mental-hygiene specialists   Although there are serious methodological problems in this study, it is possible to interpret their finding that low-prestige persons express a disproportionate amount of liking for high-prestige persons as a device for immobilizing the power of the latter   Blau's (1954) study of officials in a government agency is perhaps more pertinent.  He found that the least competent officials had more extensive informal relations in the agency than did the more competent ones   This might be viewed as an attempt by persons with low ability-based power to compensate

for this lack by developing some friendship-based control Fiedler (1958, p 44) suggests the possibility that the high-power person, the leader, is sensitive to the potentialities of friendship as a power strategy and that the social distance often maintained by leaders (and in particular by leaders of effective groups) is partly motivated by this perceived threat.

Closely related to ingratiation is the strategy of gaining support through entering a coalition This requires that A locate a person with high power whose outcomes are in close correspondence with his own, so that A can depend on his using his power *in* A's interests and not *against* them.

(4) Reducing B's skills This is easier but dangerous if overplayed. It requires interfering with, distracting, disturbing, stealing useful instruments from, and otherwise sabotaging B while he is performing It may also be possible to limit his opportunities to acquire new skills or instruments.

(5) Building up the value of A's product. This may consist of "propaganda" about A's products or may involve careful creation of the proper conditions for maximal appreciation of his rewards. In courtship this is termed "setting the stage," whereas in advertising it is called "creating a need"

A related strategy is that of forcing A's product upon B if, for example, he is trying to avoid being placed in a weak power position This is also illustrated by Potter in *The theory and practice of gamesmanship* (1948)

> The rarer form ('counter-drink Play') is for use *only in the following situation*, where, however, it is a gambit of the first value
> Take a young opponent (optimum age twenty-two) He must be pleasant, shy and genuinely sporting (The Fischer Test will tell you whether his apparent character is real or assumed—see 'Nice Chapmanship,' p 29 ) Then (1) Place him by the bar and stand him a drink. (2) When he suggests 'The other half,' refuse in some such words as these, which should be preceded by a genuinely kindly laugh 'Another one? No thanks, old laddie No, I certainly won't let you buy me one No— I don't want it ' Then (3) a minute or two later, when his attention is distracted, buy him, and yourself, the second drink. The boy will feel bound to accept it, yet this enforced acceptance should cause him some confusion, and a growing thought, if the gambit has been properly managed and the after-play judicious, that he has been fractionally put in his place and decimally treated as if he was a juvenile, and more than partially forced into the position of being the object of generosity [pp 52–53]

(6) Devaluating B's product This is, of course, related closely to (5), and both are well illustrated by the comments of Waller and Hill

(1951) on the "covert consumption" of rewards during dating behind the screen of standardized repartee known as the "line."

> The "line" has a further function of covering up a real emotional involvement by exaggeration. Both sexes use the "line," although conventionally the man takes the initiative. The use of such conventionalized and highly exaggerated forms of speech has something to do with "pluralistic ignorance," the ignorance of each concerning the real attitudes of the other, which is an important factor in such relations.
> In this early period there takes place an important conflict. Beneath the superficial exchange of pleasantries, beneath the soft words and euphemisms of the "line," there is a resounding clash of one human will upon another. Each is determined not to be caught by the sugared words of the other. Each wishes if he can, to dominate the fantasy of the other. Each one strives to break down the previous patterns of experience of the other and to set him to dreaming. Each one tends to become involved through his own ego drives, through his conditioned reflexes, through his sexual impulses, through his sense of moral obligation, and at the same time each one wishes to entangle the other before being caught himself [pp. 184–185].

The devaluation of B's products need not be merely a superficial "ploy" in which A attempts to convince B that he is providing A with things of little value while all the time A continues covertly to enjoy them. The power advantage which is gained by repudiating worldly rewards has been noted often enough in religious literature.

(7) Lengthening A's time perspective. If A can defer his attainment of favorable outcomes to the relatively distant future, then he can afford to give up present pleasures, even to the point of dropping below $CL_{alt}$ for awhile. This is effectively the same as lowering A's $CL_{alt}$, devaluating (or covertly consuming) B's rewards, or reducing his skill. In every case A's dependence on him is lowered. Person A must, of course, hide from B the fact that he is taking positions below $CL_{alt}$, or B's power over A will be, at least temporarily, increased.

## 7.5  PERCEPTION OF POWER AND DEPENDENCE

Many of the statements in the foregoing sections involve assumptions about the perception of power. For example, the effectiveness of a promise or threat based upon fate control depends upon whether the recipient perceives the influence agent to have the necessary control. Similarly, for behavior control to operate, the person whose behavior is being controlled must be aware of the possibility that his reward-cost positions can be improved by proper synchronization of his behavior with the other's. The power strategies just considered can often be effectuated merely by manipulating the other person's perception without any change in the objective conditions of inter-dependency. Rather little empirical evidence exists on the topic of perception of power; hence this discussion must rely largely on speculation.

The present theory suggests that the basic data from which impressions of power are formed consist of variations in one person's behavior and emotional states that coincide with or follow upon variations in the other's behavioral choices. When A exercises fate control over B, variations in A's actions affect B's outcomes; hence the degree of power should be reflected in B's expressive behavior (signs of glee, anger, dismay, pleasure, etc.). On the other hand, when A's behavior control is exercised (and this would include that derived from conversion of fate control), the amount of control at A's disposal should be reflected in the latency or motility of changes in B's behavior, given a change in A's. Both kinds of cues are, of course, available to the influencer and the recipient, so there is some reason to expect their perceptions of the influencer's power to be in agreement.

There is a considerable literature in social psychology on judgments of expressive behavior. Apparently, there is some standardization, within broad cultural limits, in the modes of expressing emotional states and considerable agreement among observers in their judgments of different expressions (Bruner and Tagiuri, 1954). In the experimental work on this topic it has been difficult to obtain records of natural expressive behavior and to be certain of the underlying state; but we can at least assert that persons agree pretty well in their judgments of different emotions portrayed by actors and are able to guess the state the actor was trying to express.

When a person has high power, his various outcomes are relatively homogeneous. He is subject neither to much external behavior control nor to large swings in his expressive behavior. Therefore, such a person is likely to appear to others as "inscrutable." The converse seems also tenable: an inscrutable person, one who shows little variation in mood or enigmatical changes in behavior, will be viewed as powerful. Much expressive behavior, on the other hand, is said to be a "sign of weakness."

Heider (1944) and Michotte (1954) have given an intensive analysis of the perception of phenomenal causality. From this analysis it is possible to distinguish between perceptions in which the locus of causality of a social effect is "internal" to a given person and perceptions in which it is "external" to a given person, that is, between perceptions of *spontaneous* and *coerced* changes in behavior. Thibaut and Riecken (1955b) have performed an experiment which shows that person A perceives causality for compliant behavior as external to a less powerful person B and as internal to a more powerful B. (As a result of these differing perceptions of causality, A's liking and acceptance of the more powerful B, who complies with his request, increases significantly more than his liking and acceptance of the less powerful B who also complies.) Whether the converse is true—that a person perceived as changing his behavior because of external pressure is seen to have lower power than one perceived as making the same change in response to internal forces—has not been investigated. Our theory suggests that it would be.

## SUMMARY

An individual's power over another (derives from the latter's being dependent upon him.) Person A has power over B to the extent that (by varying his behavior he can affect the quality of B's outcomes.) Two basic kinds of power, fate control and behavior control, can be differentiated on the basis of whether or not B can, without exercising counterpower, attenuate the variations in his outcomes caused by A.

When A has fate control over B, he can affect B's outcomes regardless of what B does. The (general amount of fate control) A has over B in their relationship depends upon the average level of outcomes B attains there in relation to the level he might attain in the best alternative situation available to him—the level designated as $CL_{alt}$.

When A has behavior control, it is possible for B to (reduce the variations in his outcomes by adjusting his behavior to that of A.) Thus, when A varies his behavior, the effect is to make it desirable for B to change his accordingly. It is also possible for A to employ his fate control as a means of controlling B's behavior; this requires him to keep track of B's behavior and make appropriate modifications in his own.

In any dyad both members are dependent upon the relationship to some degree, so we speak of their being interdependent. This means that each one has some power over the other which places limits on the extent to which each may with impunity exercise his power over his colleague. The pattern of interdependency which characterizes a relationship also affects the kinds of process agreements the pair must achieve if their relationship is to be maximally satisfactory.

Person A's ability to affect B's outcomes makes it possible for him, deliberately or unintentionally, to create conditions in which his own or B's behavior changes in its reward or cost value to B. Changes of this sort are thought to occur through modifications in the temporal and causal associations between behaviors and outcomes and through arranging situations in which behavior is instrumental to reducing conflict and dissonance

The ability to affect one another's outcomes thus provides a basis for producing mutual changes in values and attitudes This is of great importance in dyads where the interdependence is quite high as values converge through mutual influence, the relationship tends to become more satisfactory because of reduction in interpersonal conflicts and related costly activities.

From the point of view of the individual member of a dyad, the possession of superior power has a number of possible advantages It tends to relieve him of the necessity of paying close attention to his partner's actions and of being careful in his own actions His power also makes it possible for him to determine the course and pace of the interaction and to insist upon receiving the better of the outcomes potentially available to him in the relationship However, with continued use, power tends to be *used up* in the sense that its possessor loses his ability to make further demands or to induce further behavior changes in his colleague

The analysis of power presented in this chapter suggests a number of *power strategies*—ways of maintaining or improving one's power over another person and of reducing his counterpower In part, these strategies depend upon an understanding of the cues which people employ in making judgments of power Basically, the perception that a person has great power stems from evidence that he undergoes little variation in outcomes as a consequence of the actions of others and that his behaviors are largely internally rather than externally caused.

# 8.

# *Norms and Roles*

.

The concept of *norm* has been central in social psychology, serving as a rallying point for both psychological and sociological approaches to the study of group phenomena In spite of this (or perhaps because of it), there has been a great deal of confusion and ambiguity in the use of the concept, as has been ably documented by Rommetveit (1954) Whereas a detailed discussion of these difficulties and their roots would be out of place here, one point must be made in this connection Norms can be described from several different points of view For example, they may be described in terms of the social processes or mechanisms they involve (pressures, sanctions, felt obligations), they may be described in terms of their immediate effects (behavioral uniformity, shared frames of reference), or they may be described in terms of their more distal consequences or *functions* (provision of support for opinions, facilitation of group achievement) Unless these different modes of description are carefully distinguished, misunderstandings may develop, some persons may define a norm in terms of *what* it does (either immediately or in the long run) and others in terms of *how* it produces various effects

In agreement with others (e g , Homans 1950, Rommetveit 1954), we conceptualize norms from the "how" point of view, that is, in terms of the processes they involve In the present chapter we content ourselves with a brief introductory account of these processes, reserving a more detailed analysis for Chapter 13 In the remainder of the present chapter we shall consider the general, long-term functional significance of norms advancing the view that they serve as substitutes or replacements for informal influence This provides a background for treating in greater detail the properties of norms and the more

immediate effects they typically have  After a brief discussion of the
development of norms, the chapter concludes with a consideration of
the concept of role

## 8 1  CONCEPTUALIZATION OF NORMS

Consider two people in a dyadic relationship and assume that the
pattern of their outcomes is such that they cannot achieve their best
outcomes at the same time  For example, this might be a husband
and wife whose problem is that the wife likes to go dancing in the
evening and the husband prefers that they go to the movies  The
outcomes are illustrated in Table 8–1  It is apparent that trading is
necessary if both are to obtain good outcomes even occasionally

Trading can be established through exercise of the power that each

TABLE 8–1

ILLUSTRATION OF RELATIONSHIP REQUIRING TRADING

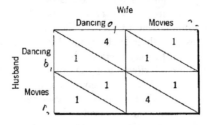

possesses, if this power is adequate  For example, the husband can
use his control over the wife's outcomes by promising to go dancing
if she will go with him to the movies. Or he can threaten to go to the
movies anyway if she fails to cooperate, in which case she will have
poor outcomes  Similar influence opportunities exist for the wife

The moment-to-moment use of personal power can be obviated if
the two can agree upon some rule for trading  For example, they
might agree that they will alternate between dancing and attending
the movies, making the shift upon some mutually acceptable signal,
for example, a word from the momentarily favored person to the effect that he or she is satiated with the present activity  Once agreement is reached on a rule of this sort, shifts are likely to proceed
smoothly and predictably and, in view of the limitations inherent to
the relationship (noncorrespondence of high outcomes), each person
is likely to feel that his own outcomes are satisfactory.

Agreements of this sort may be matters of mere convenience, repeated for their immediate value in reducing the costs involved in face-to-face influence and in smoothing out the course of the interaction  However, as Waller and Hill (1951) so aptly put it, "The *usual* quickly becomes the *right* . . " [p. 49]   The rule is likely to take on the characteristics of a moral obligation (or even to have them from the start).  This means, in brief, that conformity to agreements becomes rewarding in and of itself.

Just how this transformation occurs is a complex matter   It probably has some basis in the fact that conformity to rules and agreements has proven rewarding in past relationships) in which some external agent has delivered extrinsic rewards for conformity   For example, two brothers disagree about what to play because they prefer different games   Their mother steps in and says, "Play what Jimmy wants for awhile, and, after you've done that, give Johnny a chance," and rewards them if they follow her rule.  Agreement to rules is also reinforced by the value they have for the relationship in cutting costs and enhancing rewards   We shall elaborate this shortly

These reinforcing conditions make it likely that the two boys will learn to value "fair play "  They will *accept* the rule in the sense that their equitable turn-taking behavior will no longer occur simply as a result of their compliance to external sanctions but also because they have *internalized* the rule (Chapter 13 and Kelman, 1956)

Thus a predisposition to value and abide by a trading rule may exist at the outset of the husband and wife relationship   Norms need not be invented anew for each relationship but may often be transferred from other ones   These learning conditions also make it likely that a general value for agreements and rules of this sort will be acquired.

When an agreement about a matter such as trading exists between the members of a dyad and when it is accepted to some degree by both, we would say that a norm exists )  This would manifest itself to an outside observer in several ways

(1) There would be regularity in behavior (in our example, a routinized sequence of shifts in activities of the pair )

(2) In the event of disruption of this regularity, the "injured" person would attempt to restore it by appealing, at least initially, to the rule) and he would (exercise his personal power as an enforcer of the rule )

(3) The person disrupting the regularity would be likely to feel some obligation to adhere to the agreement and might even (exhibit some conflict or guilt about deviating from it, as if he were punishing himself for his nonconformity.)

Once a norm exists, it appears to the pair almost as if a third agent had entered the relationship, a feeling which undoubtedly is reinforced by the fact that in earlier relationships the enforcers of rules often actually were third persons (e g , the mother in the case of the two brothers ) The third agent exercises power over each member in the usual sense of making it desirable for him to act in certain ways at certain times and does so in an impartial way without regard to the special interests of either one This normative power, when the rule has been accepted or internalized, seems to be exclusively behavior control, except in the case we discuss later in which the person is unable to make the necessary discriminations or perform the specified behavior In one sense this power accrues to the norm because the two persons give up some of their individual power to it This is evidenced by their exercising personal power in the name of the norm rather than to advance their personal interests In another sense, the norm may have power over them independently of their enforcement of it: to the degree that the norm is accepted by individuals to whom it applies, conformity is more rewarding, other things being equal, than nonconformity

From the preceding discussion the reader can deduce our definition of norm A norm is a behavioral rule that is accepted, at least to some degree, by both members of the dyad (A rule which one person advances and tries to enforce but which the other person does not accept cannot be called a norm, at least in a dyad In large groups, on the other hand, acceptance by all members is not an essential part of the concept, although acceptance by a sizable number is.) Thus both members feel some obligation to adhere to it Nonadherence is met with the use of power to attempt to produce conformity, but the influence appeal is to a supra-individual value ("Do it for the group" or "Do it because it's good") rather than to personal interests ("Do it for me" or "Do it and I'll do something for you")

The reader may wish to compare the present treatment of norm with similar conceptualizations advanced by other social scientists Most similar is Homans' (1950) definition

> A norm, then, is an idea in the minds of the members of a group, an idea that can be put in the form of a statement specifying what the members or other men should do, ought to do, are expected to do, under given circumstances A statement of the kind described is a norm only if any departure of real behavior from the norm is followed by some punishment [p 123]

In the Lewinian tradition, Festinger, Schachter and Back (1950) give a definition in terms of forces " . a uniform set of directions which the group induces on the forces which act on the members of the group" [p 166]. Rommetveit (1954) distinguishes carefully between the individual acting as enforcer of a norm, on the one hand, and the individual subject to it, on the other. "A social norm is a pressure existing between a norm-sender and a norm-receiver's behaviour in a category of recurrent situations" [p 45] The last phrase excludes accidental and temporary interpersonal pressures. Pressure is said to be manifested in the norm sender's expectations that the norm receiver will behave in a specific way, or in his wish for this behavior, and in overt sanctions applied by the norm sender in response to the norm receiver's actions [pp 45 ff ]

## 8 2   Norms as Substitutes for Informal Influence

The foregoing discussion illustrates the characteristics of normative processes and also implies what we take to be the major broad functional value of norms—that they serve as substitutes for the exercise of personal influence and produce more economically and efficiently certain consequences otherwise dependent upon personal influence processes    Let us now consider this point in detail by examining the various problems created by the use of informal, interpersonal power and the ways in which norms may avoid or solve them.

In the first place norms may function to prevent or delay the development of any of the dependencies on which interpersonal power is based.    Particularly in the very early stages of the relationship, when it is not yet clear whether the relationship will be formed, norms may assist in preventing premature commitments )    As Hiller (1947) says "      norms supply a means for evading an implication of affectional relations.    This is accomplished by treating with strict politeness or rigid etiquette a person who wishes to occupy a position which is too intimate  .      Formality indicates a categorical rather than a unique personal footing, and unwanted approaches are repelled by confronting the other with decorous conduct      " [pp 105–106].

Let us go on though to consider a relationship that has formed    Assume first that A has greater power than B, at least within some limited segment of the matrix    From B's point of view a number of problems exist    If A has behavior control over him, the unbridled use of this power tends to reduce the quality of B's outcomes    This follows from the interruption effect noted in an earlier chapter    If A has fate control and converts it in order to control B's behavior, the unstandardized use of this converted control places B in an uncomfortable situation    As noted in Chapter 7, A's conversion of his fate control is more or less arbitrary, that is to say, he has several alternative ways in which he can use it  If he shifts among these in an unpredictable way, B may on any given occasion act upon the wrong assumption about what A intends and thereby suffer reduced payoffs  Even without actually making incorrect behavioral choices, B may worry about the possibility of doing so, and this tends to raise his costs for all the activities involved  The uncertainty is most extreme, of course, when A uses his fate control willy-nilly.  If A converts and uses his control in one standardized manner, B's situation becomes that of having control over his *own* outcomes.

From the point of view of A, the more powerful individual, there are also problems, but of a different sort  If he is not careful in the use of whatever behavior control he may have, it will be reduced or even lost entirely.  Because of the effects of interruptions in reducing B's outcomes, A must use his behavior control sparingly if he is to conserve it  If, on the other hand, A uses converted fate power to induce B to respond differentially, A must often monitor B's action, and such monitoring or surveillance is usually costly.

Given the above problems, both the weaker and the more powerful members of a dyad are likely to be somewhat dissatisfied with the informal exercise of personal power  However, many occasions arise in the course of their interaction in which some sort of control over behavior is necessary  Behavioral norms provide a means of meeting this dilemma  they control behavior but do not entail the difficulties created by the unrestrained use of interpersonal power.  For example, they may include a definite and unchanging statement that behavior x is expected from person B, the weaker of the two  Knowing this, B need not worry about a change in the rules, (he can always be confident about what to do in order to attain good outcomes or avoid poor ones  Furthermore, if he accepts the norm, B will perform the required behavior even in the absence of surveillance, thus (relieving A of the necessity of monitoring him )  (In larger groups wide acceptance of a norm has the further consequence that there can be sharing of the task of maintaining whatever surveillance is necessary, thereby reducing the cost to each individual )  The general point is that both weaker and stronger persons stand to gain from the introduction of mutually acceptable rules which introduce regularity and control into the relationship without recourse to the direct interpersonal application of power

Consistent with this view is evidence obtained by Wispe and Lloyd (1955) that structured normative procedures are preferred to more informal and spontaneous ones by low-power members  Forty-three life insurance agents were interviewed about their preferences for various types of interactions between agents and managers  The main result of the study was that, as compared with highly productive agents, the less productive ones preferred their interaction with managers to be structured and normative rather than informal and spontaneous.  Since the productivity of the agents fluctuated over time rather erratically, nearly all of the agents performed poorly from time to time  The authors interpret their findings to mean that those who are currently producing poorly, hence are very vulnerable, experience less anxiety about their vulnerability if there are structured procedures to protect them from managerial power.

The general contention advanced above can be argued from a slightly different point of view  Consider a dyad in which one member, A, performs a certain special behavior that is highly rewarding to B  As long as A continues to perform this sequence, there will be no problem, B will come to *expect* it in the sense of predicting that A is likely to repeat it in the future  However, if A is somewhat undependable or even merely exhibits covert tendencies not to perform his special function, B's dependency upon him is dramatized and becomes somewhat difficult to tolerate.  This might be explained by assuming the existence of a need for autonomy (Murray, 1938) that motivates people to avoid interpersonal situations in which they are dependent upon others.  Perhaps it is simpler merely to suggest that dependency upon an unreliable person is cost increasing  In interaction with such a person one often begins behavioral sequences without being able to consummate them, and one frequently does things for him without getting anything in return  On the other hand, dependency is no problem with a perfectly reliable deliverer of rewards, for example, a bountiful environment or the corner grocer with his stable prices.

So B's problem is to strengthen A's tendency to perform the desired sequence without making too apparent his dependency upon A, that is, without suffering (power loss)  This is done by an appeal to a supra-individual value connected with the welfare of some third agent, set of persons, or organization rather than with B's own welfare  Such appeals as "Do it because it's good," "People expect it of you," or "Do it for the group" are essentially power-maintenance strategies  They play down the value of the behavior to the person making the appeal or request but at the same time insure that the performance will continue  Allport (1954) summarizes an extremely cynical version of this point, advanced by Le Dantec  Moral standards such as those expressed in the Ten Commandments are described as being promulgated merely for the convenience of those who have some interest to protect, as, for example, property owners—"Thou shalt not steal"—and persons who have sexual partners—"Thou shalt not commit adultery" Thus B attempts to change the basis for A's performing the behavior from that of doing B a personal favor to that of satisfying social or moral obligations

This process of transforming the value basis for compliance is probably supported and reinforced by conflict reduction on the part of A, the performer If he has impulses not to help his partner, he has a recurring conflict between incompatible activities, those rewarding to B versus those which are not. This conflict is costly and can be reduced by mobilizing powerful instigations to only one kind of behavior These are provided by the moralistic or social value appeals used by B which give A a justification for overvaluing the desirability of the behavior Thus acceptance of supra-individual, depersonalized values as the basis for behavior has functional value both for the actor and the one dependent upon his actions

Norms have similar functional values in many dyads in which power is evenly distributed. In Chapter 7 we noted that in highly cohesive groups the great power the two members have over each other not only gives them ability to carry out strong influence measures but also to resist each other's influence, This situation potentially leads to interpersonal conflicts and unresolved "stand-offs" in which neither one is able to get the other to engage in desired activities This type of conflict can be avoided by procedural rules in which power is transferred, so to speak, from personal agents to the norms Then, when A tries to induce B to do something, B is expected to perceive the locus of causality for the influence attempt not as internal to a whimsical or self-aggrandizing A but as existing in the depersonalized norm on behalf of which A is acting We might expect that the counterpower (or resistance) that B might mobilize against A's suggestion would not exist for an impersonal set of rules Alternatively stated, in a highly cohesive dyad B's counterpower derives from his ability to affect A's fate, this source of resistance is eliminated when power is depersonalized by transfer to a set of procedures or rules (Note the implication that norms will develop more rapidly and more surely in highly cohesive groups, assuming that the majority of the members have about the same degree of dependence on the group, than in less cohesive groups ) Frank (1944) provides evidence that an appeal to an impersonal value encounters less resistance than does the direct exercise of personal power.

Even if equal power does not lead to interpersonal impasses, the interaction process is likely to be characterized by a good deal of argument and informal litigation Unless argument and uncertainty happen to be rewarding in themselves, they merely represent unnecessary costs These costs can be substantially reduced by agreements that enable the individuals to run off their most frequent interaction sequences according to automatic routines, without moment-by-moment decision making Green (1956) comments on this point, "What an utter chaos human life would be—it could not long endure—if every day we had to settle by family debate or authoritarian decision how many meals we would eat *this* day, at what hour of the day or night" [p 75] In a similar vein, MacIver and Page (1949) write of norms, "Without them the burden of decision would be intolerable and the vagaries of conduct utterly distracting" [p 207] It may also be noted that for both members of a dyad the necessity of invoking power on the one hand and the necessity of complying with it on the other tend to bring to mind and dramatize the dependence of each upon the other As we have stated above, the feeling of dependence is probably something most people would rather avoid To the extent that there is depersonalization of influence, the source of power and control being external to both individuals, the basic fact of their interdependence goes unstated and probably unnoticed

In short, we may view norms as social inventions that accomplish more effectively what otherwise would require informal social influence We do not intend to imply that norms are deliberately developed for this purpose The contention is merely that there exists a basis for unconscious collusion between weaker and stronger persons, between controllers and the controlled, between persons highly dependent upon each other—a collusion that has the effect of bringing regularity and control into the relationship without the informal exercise of personal power.

### 8 2 1  SOME IMPLICATIONS

This point of view has several important implications *First*, if the central assertion is correct, that norms are means of influence and control which minimize the problems created by informal influence, then from a close examination of informal influence and its problems we should be able to infer the general *properties of norms.* This requires little explanation beyond that contained in the preceding pages Norms are, in the first place, (*rules about behavior*) They tell each person what is expected of him in certain situations, and in so doing they indirectly indicate requests that others may not properly make of him In this way, he is protected from subjugation to another's whimsically exercised power Norms are also (*stable* so that the individual knows not only what is expected of him today but what will be expected of him tomorrow. Furthermore, norms are based upon *agreement or consensus* which reduces the necessity for thorough surveillance and, in large groups, distributes the responsibility for surveillance rather widely  The enforcement of norms often involves *appeals to impersonal values or suprapersonal agents,* which reduce the extent to which compliance is viewed as a matter of giving in to a more powerful person and thereby reduces resistance  Also these values are often *widely held* among the group members, so that once they have been associated with compliance it becomes directly rewarding and the need for exercise of external control is greatly reduced. Simmel (1902) puts the last point this way·

> In the morality of the individual, society creates for itself an organ which is not only more fundamentally operative than law and custom, but which also spares society the different sorts of costs involved in these institutions  Hence the tendency of society to satisfy its demands as cheaply as possible results in appeals to "good conscience," through which the individual pays to himself the wages for his righteousness, which otherwise would probably have to be assured to him in some way through law or custom [p 19n].

The *second* implication is this. If norms are to control or replace interpersonal influence, then they should have some relevance to the things about which this influence is exercised  What norms are about, that which is commonly called the *content of norms,* should be inferable from a consideration of the things about which group members find it necessary to influence each other  This is considered in more detail in the following section.

## 8 3  The Content of Norms

In the preceding section we have described rather extensively the general latent function of norms—that of bringing control and regularity into the interaction while minimizing the use of personal power  Norms also have more obvious and immediately apparent functions that are reflected in the *particular kinds of controls* and influences they exert upon behavior and attitudes  These are effects the production of which, in the absence of norms, would be undertaken by informal influence  Hence, by considering a specific pair of persons and determining the things about which they would find it necessary to influence each other, we can obtain clues as to the things about which norms are likely to develop  These are not the same for every dyad but depend upon the particular problems the members face as a consequence of the pattern of outcomes in their matrix of interaction possibilities (their particular patterns of interdependency). We do not pretend to exhaustiveness in our list because norms can be developed to cover any of a wide range of specific problems

If it is assumed that the two persons are motivated to maximize the reward-cost positions they attain in the relationship, several difficulties must be overcome    Perhaps the most important is the common predicament that their reward-cost positions are not positively correlated over the matrix and they are unable to attain good outcomes from the same phases of the interaction. A case in point would be the husband and wife, mentioned earlier, who have different preferences for leisure-time activities    Both can achieve their good outcomes only by alternating between two different cells in their matrix, that is, by a trading process    Norms can dictate a trading procedure that both will regard as fair and just and save them the communication and other costs that would be required to make moment-to-moment decisions about what to do next.    Indeed, the very existence of a cooperative relationship may depend upon finding a mutually acceptable mode of trading    This is illustrated experimentally by Azrin and Lindsley (1956)    They placed two children in an apparatus which delivered a single jelly bean when coordinated responses were made    Because a jelly bean could not be divided conveniently with the tools at hand, some sort of alternation was necessary if both were to be rewarded for their efforts    Eight of ten pairs immediately developed a procedure for alternation    In the other two teams one member took all of the candy at first until the other one refused to cooperate.    They then reached verbal agreement on a trading scheme and proceeded to work together for the duration of the experiment

The necessity of alternation and trading can be eliminated entirely if both parties come to value the same cooperative activities    This would be reflected in their matrix by the existence of a positive correlation between the two sets of outcomes, as shown in Table 8–2    Many norms have this consequence, which may occur in a variety of ways. For example, if the trading norm involves an appeal to fair play, and this is one of the husband's values, going dancing with his wife will be rewarding on this basis and, by the associative processes described in Chapter 7, may eventually acquire autonomous reward value    Conformity with the norm may also yield other reinforcements (e.g., conflict reduction, elimination of unpleasant "scenes," or provision of extrinsic rewards by the wife) which provide a basis for its taking on reward value

In general, norms afford a basis for changes in attitudes and values,

operating through the mechanisms described in Chapter 7  Moreover, norms act to produce homogeneity of values between the two ·
members.  One circumstance under which this is a particularly im-  ↙
portant function is when one member needs social support for some
action he has taken or some belief he holds, the correctness or validity
of which has been challenged  Seeking agreement with his position,
he will try to induce his partner to support him and may deliver
rewards for doing so  This creates conditions whereby the other comes
genuinely to accept the point of view.  Thus, by the exercise of informal influence there develops a norm (agreement about what opinion to express on a given matter) that eliminates the need for further
influence of the same kind  In this manner one's opinions can be based
on a "social reality" when support for them in "physical reality"
is lacking  (On these processes see Sherif, 1936, on norms which

TABLE 8-2

<small>ILLUSTRATION OF RELATIONSHIP CHARACTERIZED BY VALUE SIMILARITY</small>

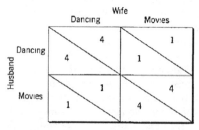

provide a structure otherwise missing from stimulus situations, Young,
1944, on social-cultural reality, and Festinger, 1950, on social reality )
    Even when two persons attain high outcomes from the same activi-
ties (as in Table 8-2) because of satiation and fatigue in each activity,
it is necessary for them to shift occasionally from one cell of the
matrix to another  If interruption and interference effects are to be
avoided, their changes in behavior must be synchronized  Special
norms develop to permit this, as discussed in Chapter 4  These norms
may consist of rules about adapting behavior to what the other person
is doing (agreements about being flexible and spontaneous) or rules
that tie behavior selections to common external cues (e g, agreements
about the time of day at which meals are served).  By these rules, the
arousal of incompatible behavioral sets is avoided, and if any communication is required between the two it consists merely of synchronizing signals, the exertion of personal pressures being largely
eliminated

Some of A's activities may be totally unsatisfactory to B. These may be items that raise his costs or that are low in reward value, either because of their intrinsic nature or because of their general incompatibility with the behavioral sets in B's repertoire For example, the husband may have the habit of responding to minor irritations with rather "strong" language, which greatly embarrasses his wife If her outcomes from the relationship are to be maximal, this behavior must be entirely eliminated from their interaction, and an agreement to rule it out may indeed develop Some activities may not, of course, be eliminated from a relationship. For example, the external demands of the local bank may make it necessary for the husband to balance the checkbook at the end of the month, even though this is rather unpleasant for his wife.

The external environment or task may require that certain behaviors be kept in the interaction and that they be performed in a given sequence (Chapter 9) Under these conditions, norms in the form of agreements about who will do what (division of labor) and when (sequence of actions) promote effective task performance The specialization made possible by division of labor may operate to reduce costs, since practice in a given activity usually tends to increase the ease with which one does it Sequence rules cut costs by reducing the amount of communication required to perform a task

Various observers (e g, Newcomb, 1950, pp 291 ff ) have noted that language consists of a special set of norms—agreements about meaning (semantics), arrangement and order (syntax), abbreviations, etc, without which communication processes would require much more time and effort For example, to understand each other with only very simple agreements, two persons might have to find and point to certain concrete objects or they might have to discuss in simpler terms the meanings of more complex words In the absence of rules about word arrangement, communication would require processes similar to reading jumbled sentences. The efficiency in abbreviations is obvious Verbal behavior serves many purposes—as a carrier of rewards in flattery or as a means of signaling in order to synchronize the interaction In all these ways it is most efficient and accurate if the speaker in his encoding and the listener in his decoding operate according to precisely the same set of rules

### 8.3.1 NORMS AND GROUP SOLIDARITY

To the extent that norms reduce interference, cut communication costs, heighten value similarity, and insure the interaction sequences necessary for task performance, norms improve the reward-cost positions attained by the members of a dyad and thus increase the cohesiveness of the dyad.

Norms may also have some less direct consequences on group cohesiveness  If the various constraints and frustrations that attend interaction are perceived to be "justifiable" in the sense that they derive from impartial and impersonal normative sources, then less aggression and hostility may be instigated than if such frustrations are perceived to originate in personal whim  (Pastore, 1952)

Norms also contribute to solidarity in another way, rendering the pattern of interaction less susceptible to disruption by external forces  This is illustrated in an experiment by Merei (1949)  Initial observations were made in a free play situation to determine which children (from four to eleven years old) exerted dominance or leadership and which were followers  Then groups comprised of three followers were formed and allowed to play together without outside interference for three to six one-hour periods.  In the course of this play together each group of three formed its own traditions or norms having to do with such things as division of toys, ceremonies about their use, kinds of games, and sequence of games.  Then one of the children previously identified as a leader was introduced into each group  In virtually all cases the group forced its traditions upon the leader and he was able to exert control and direction only by working within the framework of their norms.  Thus Merei concludes, " . . confronted by a group having its own traditions, the leader proves weak, this in spite of the fact that when confronting them singly he is stronger than any one member of the group  . " [p 26]  Although a more complex experimental design is needed to prove the point, Merei interprets his results as indicating that norms provide the necessary condition which enables these otherwise weak children to resist the demands of the more dominant one.  This seems reasonable if we recall that in carrying out norm-indicated behavior a person is not acting merely according to his own desires or to those of some other individual  Rather he is conforming to some supra-individual value, be it the shared expectation of all the others, the good of the group, or some moral value  This must provide a stronger anchorage for his behavior than he would otherwise possess and form the basis for resistance to counternorm influences.  We might also mention in this connection the considerable evidence that security in the face of external threats seems to derive from the presence of friendly powers (Aiseman, 1943, Wright, 1943)  In much the same way one can count on colleagues for support as long as one is acting according to mutually agreed-to behavioral prescriptions

### 8.3 2   THE DANGERS OF TOO MANY NORMS

We have discussed both the immediate and long-run benefits that accrue to a dyad from the development of norms  Lest this picture be painted too rosy, it must be emphasized that norms are not always a blessing to a relationship.  Difficulties are especially likely to arise when too many norms exist  Under these conditions, said to characterize bureaucracies, the rules governing behavior can be so complex that people are unable to master them fully  The result is an unwillingness to act or make behavioral decisions  The individual may also become so engrossed with the internal structure and interpretations of the norms that he loses touch with the outside world.  His behaviors become wholly governed by what is formally (i e , normatively) correct and totally unresponsive to the demands of unique situations  As norms proliferate, the individual is faced with a new kind of decision problem  which rule is applicable in this case?  At this point, norms-about-norms (or "meta-norms") may develop that specify the various domains within which the various norms are applicable.

Meta-norms have still another function.  As norms become numerous, they inevitably begin to overlap and compete, and, since they are often inconsistent, difficulties may arise in deciding which has precedence  These difficulties are reduced somewhat if meta-norms specify an hierarchical ordering to the norms, thus providing a basis for giving precedence to one or the other of the conflicting norms  Inconsistency among multiple norms is also bearable if the norms permit some latitude  Stouffer (1949) finds that the norms about appropriate performance of various roles, as perceived by the occupants of these roles, do not specify a single correct behavior but describe a range of permissible behavior.  He emphasizes the functional value of this "social slippage" in enabling persons to adapt comfortably to conflicting role requirements.

### 8.4   THE DEVELOPMENT OF NORMS

Although norms can be described in terms of their functional value to the dyad, this does not imply that the two persons deliberately develop norms with the conscious intention of achieving the benefits we have described.  Certainly some agreements are reached in this manner, for example, when a husband and wife decide that to enjoy their dinner most they will have it by candlelight every evening at seven o'clock sharp

In other cases, however, an implicit understanding is reached by a process of trial-and-error.  They have dinner when the husband comes

home and when the wife has it ready, but sooner or later they settle
down to a more or less fixed time, presumably because it is as good as
or better than other times they have tried  This process could be described in reinforcement learning terms  the pair are reinforced when
they adhere to a given rule because it cuts costs, increases dependability of rewards, or in general makes the situation more predictable and
comfortable  Thus they learn to follow it consistently

In still other instances a rule is imported into the dyad from other
relationships  For example, a married couple may adopt the dinner
time that was traditional in the home of the wife's parents. The
process here suggests "cognitive" learning  since the new situation is
seen to be similar to the old one, the behavioral rules applicable to the
old are generalized to the new.  To the extent that the problems of
coordinating and synchronizing the husband's and wife's activities are
the same from family to family, this transfer of norms from the old
to the new will be appropriate and adaptive.

The developmental processes underlying the emergence of norms
are likely to yield rules that have positive functional values for the relationship.  As norms are decided upon, imported from other relationships, and tried out, only the more useful ones are likely to be retained.
This is not to say that the norms found in any group will be the *best*
solutions to the various problems of control, coordination, and synchronization, but simply that they will generally be *adequate* solutions
leading to supra-CL positions for the members

The fact that norms are more or less stable has important implications for their developmental history  As Sherif (1936) says, "In the
initial state, norms may express the actual relationships demanded by
the situation and may serve to regulate the lives of the individual members in a group along cooperative lines with little friction  But, once
formed, they tend to persist.  Many times they outlive their usefulness"
[p 198]  This happens when changes in external conditions reduce
the functional value of the norm  For example, an agreement between
a husband and wife about the dinner hour may become completely inappropriate with the addition of a child to the family  When norms
persist under these circumstances, exhibiting "cultural lag," we may
assume that the norm still has some value to the members even though
it no longer serves its original function  For example, a secret handshake may have been important in the early days of an outlawed fra-
ternal order to permit discrimination between friends and enemies  At
a later time, when membership in the order has become a matter of
public record, the handshake may be retained for its ritualistic values
to symbolize continuity with the past and loyalty to the group  In

general, noims that were necessary for meeting the demands of a task or external environment may be preserved because of their symbolic value in maintaining group solidarity.

## 8.5  ROLES

Whereas some of the noims within a group apply to all members, others apply only to certain specific individuals or subclasses of individuals   The subclasses provide a basis for identifying different *roles* within the group   Persons are said to be in the same role if the same norms exist with respect to their behavior.   This identification of persons in the same role is facilitated by their being similar in other respects (e g , age, sex, training, and experience)

Because a large number of noims ordinarily exist in any given group, it is unlikely that exactly the same full set of norms will apply to any two individuals   Hence the criterion above must be relaxed somewhat if we are to avoid the trivial and uninteresting conclusion that every person has a unique role   The problem is illustrated for a four-person group in Table 8–3, in which an X is entered in each cell if the particular noim applies to the indicated person   As no two persons in this group are subject to the same norms, a strict application of the criterion of "same norms" would indicate that no two of them occupy the same role   However, on closer inspection of the table it can be seen that both A and B are subject to norms 2 and 3, C and D, to norms 4, 5, and 6, A and D, to norm 7, and all four, to norm 1   We might conclude, then, that there exists role I, occupied by A and B, role II, by C and D, role III, by A and D, and role IV, by all four.   This would seem particularly justified if the various norms associated with each role defined in this manner had something in common   For example, norms 2 and 3 might have to do with providing for the physical needs of persons C and D   This might be the case in which A and B are man and wife and C and D are their children   Norms 2 and 3 might be said to prescribe the role of "provider," a role occupied by both A and B   Similarly, norms 4, 5, and 6 might govern the children's efforts to meet the task demands set by their teachers, in which case these norms could be described as defining the role (within the family) of "student"   On the other hand, if 4 and 5 apply to academic behavior but 6 governs helping their mother with housework, it would be reasonable to say the children occupy two different roles

In general, we will say that two persons occupy the same role when their behavior with regard to a given problem or in relation to a given subset of group members is governed by the same norms   By a *role*, then, we mean the class of one or more norms that applies to a person's behavior with regard to some specific external problem or in relation to a special class of other persons. From this definition, it should be apparent that even in the dyad each person may be in several different roles.

This definition of role is very similar to that given by Bates (1956). After defining position as a location in a social structure associated with a set of social norms, he defines role as, "A part of a social position consisting of a more or less integrated or related sub-set of social

TABLE 8–3

MATRIX USED IN IDENTIFYING ROLES

Persons

| Norms | A | B | C | D |
|---|---|---|---|---|
| 1 | X | X | X | X |
| 2 | X | X | | |
| 3 | X | X | | |
| 4 | | | X | X |
| 5 | | | X | X |
| 6 | | | X | X |
| 7 | X | | | X |

norms which is distinguishable from other sets of norms forming the same position" [p. 314]. To illustrate this definition, Bates describes the position of a father within a family as being composed of the roles of provider, playmate, disciplinarian, spouse of mother, father of sibling, teacher, etc. A given role, such as that of disciplinarian, might also be found as part of another position within the group, that of the mother.

## 8.5.1 DIFFERENT CRITERIA FOR ROLES

Although various writers (Parsons, 1949, p. 34, Rommetveit, 1954, p. 39) define role in terms of norms or expectations about behavior, some define it in terms of actual behaviors (Davis, 1949, p 90)   This raises a rather basic question    Table 8–3 and the accompanying discussion provide a general basis for identifying roles and determining whether two persons occupy the same roles   However, the logic presented there depends in no way upon the particular criterion we gave for placing X's in Table 8–3   The question, then, is what criterion should be used?   Several possibilities come to mind

*Criterion I.*   The criterion used above   the specified norm exists in the social world surrounding the individual   This permits identification of what, following Rommetveit, should probably be called *prescribed* roles   These are the roles as they exist in the norms of the group or in the expectations of the other members, but in either case they are external to the individual to whom they apply.

*Criterion II*   The specified norm is what is perceived by the individual and is recognized as applying to his behavior   In Rommetveit's terms, this criterion would enable us to identify *subjective* roles.   With adequate communication and perception, these subjective roles would correspond closely to the prescribed ones.

*Criterion III.*   The overt behavior of the indicated individual conforms with the specified norm·  or, rather than listing norms down the side of Table 8–3, we might list specific behaviors and modes of behavior and determine which of them are exhibited by each person.   This would enable us to identify the role or roles, which might be termed *enacted* roles, actually played by each person.

*Criterion IV.*   The specified norm is one which, if the group is to deal successfully with the problems and tasks confronting it, should be applied to the indicated individual.   or, listing specific behaviors or modes of behavior in the table, we might apply the criterion that in view of the above considerations the specified behavior ought to be enacted by the indicated member   The application of either of these criteria (which, incidentally, would yield almost identical results) would entail a careful analysis of the situation, such as might be made by an industrial engineer, and subsequent judgments as to which kinds of behaviors are requisite of each member if the group is to be highly productive, well integrated, etc   This procedure would permit a delineation of what might be called *functionally requisite* roles and would provide a kind of standard against which the functional value of either the prescribed or the enacted roles might be judged

Which of these kinds of roles one should identify depends, it seems to us, upon the purposes of the role analysis   In some instances one may be concerned with prescribed roles as causal factors (independent variables) contributing to subjective and enacted roles (dependent variables) Rommetveit (1954) asserts that this is the main interest of social psychology ". human behavior as determined by patterns of normative expectation from others" [p 39] In other cases one may treat the enacted roles as independent variables and consider how they affect group achievement and morale This would be consistent with an interest in social functioning As part of a functional analysis, one might wish to consider as the independent variable the discrepancy between either the prescribed or enacted roles, on the one hand, and the functionally requisite roles on the other, relating this discrepancy to group achievement.

### 8.5.2 ROLE MODELS

Similar roles occur in quite different groups For example, the role of disciplinarian associated with the father in the family is also related to the company commander in the army or the foreman in a factory Indeed, there may be a finite list of different roles by which we could characterize most or all roles in all groups, for instance, the list of roles described by Benne and Sheats (1948).

This commonality of roles in different groups is important in facilitating the transfer of norms from one social structure to another If the roles in one group serve as models for the development of roles in another, a system of ready-made norms may be imported into the latter group The hypothesis suggests itself that the more adaptive the role models provided in former groups, the more successful will be the new groups (provided, of course, that the new situation fits the old one) The validity of this hypothesis is suggested by the consistent finding (Waller and Hill, 1951, Burgess and Wallin, 1953) that married couples are more likely to be happily married if their parents were too Each person undoubtedly carries into his marriage modes of behavior and interaction with his spouse that he has learned from his own parents. If what he borrows from these role models has enabled them to maintain a satisfactory relationship, it will ordinarily be of value to his marriage also

### 8 5 3 RELATIONS AMONG ROLES

Each member of a dyad may occupy several different roles. Thus problems concerning relations between roles exist both intrapersonally and interpersonally.

The intrapersonal problems of the relations between each person's roles have been considered largely from the point of view of consistency are the various roles a person is required to perform mutually consistent? In the case of a wife are the demands of being a "sexual partner" to the husband compatible with those of being the "housekeeper"? It is generally recognized that inconsistencies do exist and generally assumed that there is a strain toward consistency or mutual adjustment For example, Bates (1956) suggests that, in the short run, individuals may minimize the tension created by inconsistency by separating the two roles mentally (arranging that incompatible sets are not simultaneously instigated) or separating their enactment in space and time. In the long run, inconsistencies are reduced by changing roles, establishing an order of precedence, or eliminating some entirely. Bates points out that a given role is likely to be modified somewhat by varying its context For example, the father's role of "disciplinarian" may be modified to be more consistent with his role as "playmate," whereas the foreman's role of "disciplinarian" is conditioned by his other roles ("technician," "friend"). Therefore, the role of disciplinarian can include slightly different norms in the two cases

Consider now some aspects of the relations between roles held by different persons In many instances a role specifies the behavioral rules that a person should follow in interaction with others. Two roles of different people are said to be *reciprocal* if their co-enactment enables each person to attain the maximal outcomes available to him while fulfilling the obligations of his particular role This means that the behavioral sets indicated by the two roles are compatible (Chapter 4), that each is able efficiently to produce the actions required by his role, and, so far as the role permits, to enjoy fully the other's behaviors and products For example, the role of "teacher" as part of a father's position may include norms concerning when to instruct his son and what to teach him In short, the role may specify certain items in his repertoire to be performed, others to be avoided, and the proper timing and sequence of behaviors The effects of enacting this role depend upon what the son does, that is, what role he assumes If he acts according to a "learner" role, then the interaction is likely to be satisfactory both for him and his father On the other hand, if the son assumes an inappropriate role, such as that of "playmate," the outcomes may not be very good for either of them We do not intend to imply that the performance of reciprocal roles will always be positively satisfactory for both persons. The son is not likely to enjoy being the "disciplinee" when his father assumes the role of disciplinarian, but only if he assumes that role will the father be able to fulfill his role with least cost.

Many examples of reciprocal roles might be cited, for example, there are those of actor and audience and male and female sex roles. Indeed it is possible to describe much of the complex patterning in the interactions of an entire society in terms of a system of such reciprocal roles, as Hogbin (1934) has done for Polynesian society.

> . when we follow the network of services claimed and rendered within the household, within the kinship group and in the big tribal ceremonies    we shall see that it is only by mapping out a rather complicated scheme of give and take that we arrive in the long run at the picture of a well-balanced system of reciprocities . . . [pp. xxxvi–xxxvii]

## SUMMARY

A norm is defined as a behavioral rule that is accepted to some degree by both members of a dyad (or by most members, in the case of larger groups)    Both members feel some obligation to adhere to the rule, so it introduces a certain amount of regularity or predictability into their interaction    Nonadherence results in the exercise of influence in an attempt to restore conformity, and this attempt usually involves an appeal to some supra-individual value rather than to personal interests    The details of these communication and influence processes are left for Chapter 13.

The present chapter considers the general and specific functions of norms    At the most general level, norms are viewed as being functionally valuable to social relationships by reducing the necessity for the exercise of direct, informal, personal influence    Norms provide a means of controlling behavior without entailing the (costs) (uncertainties) (resistances) (conflicts,) and (power losses) involved in the (unrestrained, ad hoc use of interpersonal power    As substitutes for informal influence, norms have specific functions in providing solutions to problems about which members of a dyad otherwise find it necessary to influence each other directly    Thus norms deal with such problems as trading, synchronization, eliminating unsatisfactory behaviors, reducing differences of opinion, and communicating effectively    In all of the ways mentioned above, norms, if they are effective, can (reduce the costs of interaction) and eliminate the less rewarding activities from a relationship.)    They can act to improve the outcomes attained by the members of a dyad and to increase their interdependence.

To speak of the functional value of norms is not to say that they are deliberately developed as solutions to the kinds of problems enumerated    Instead, they are often imported from other relationships or are arrived at through a trial-and-error process. The reference to functional value is merely an assumption that, by and large, norms provide some sort of satisfactions to the members who adopt them and adhere to them. However, the kinds of satisfaction are many, and people can become attached to norms for their own sake, upholding them beyond the time and circumstances in which they retain their original value. This is one of the factors that is productive of highly complex collections of norms in most stable relationships. Such collections create new difficulties unless the various norms can be organized by the introduction of higher order norms.

To gain an understanding of the organization of the many norms that exist in most small groups, the analysis of roles is of major importance. Roles consist of clusters of norms providing for a division of labor or specialization of functions among the members of a group. A person is said to occupy a particular role when, in relation to some special social or task area, the norms applicable to his behavior are different from those applicable to his partner (or in larger groups, those applicable to at least some of his colleagues). The organization of norms into roles is to be evaluated in terms of how well the individual is able to reconcile the demands of the different roles he occupies and whether his role-specified behaviors interfere with or facilitate his partner's role performances. The further criterion of the roles that are desirable if a group is to be effective in its task environment as well as satisfying to its members is considered at some length in Chapter 15.

# 9.

# *Tasks*

It would be a mistake to suppose that a dyad is totally encapsulated in the social relationships of its two members And thus far it has, perhaps, been taken too much for granted that the members of a dyad are usually acting on their physical and social environments in various ways. There has been no explicit recognition and no analysis of the tasks with which the members of the dyad are often largely concerned. The present chapter attempts to remedy this incompleteness

We begin by discussing tasks and an individual in relation to a task he confronts We then enlarge the focus to include the dyad as a whole in relation to a joint task. The discussion is guided by the properties of the same type of simple 2 x 2 matrices or tables that have been used in earlier chapters

We recognize that a special chapter devoted to tasks is rather unusual in a book on social psychology, but we find it not only desirable but necessary to include one It is, of course, essential to consider how the external world impinges upon the social relationship and affects its structure and process The present analysis of the task sets the stage for a fuller discussion of this problem when, in Chapter 15, we consider the roles that are functionally requisite for successfully coping with the task.

The present mode of analysis also seems to bring considerable clarity to the problem of classifying tasks. We hardly need point out to most social psychologists that any reasonable system for giving meaningful descriptions to tasks is highly desirable if some order is to be brought into research performed on an ill-assorted array of more or less *ad hoc* tasks For how can results from a study with a specific task be safely generalized unless we have some means of locating that particular one within the universe of possible tasks?

A final and less obvious reason for this chapter is that by considering the parallels and, of course, the differences between a person interacting with another person and one "interacting" with a task much is learned about the person-person interaction  The understanding of the social relationship is sharpened by comparison with the individual-task relationship  We might note incidentally that this chapter, in an indirect way, begins the bridge over into groups larger than the dyad  As already implied, the starting point for this discussion is the assumption that person-task phenomena can be analyzed in the same terms as person-person interactions   To extend this argument, when the joint action of A and B upon a task is analyzed, the results are in some degree applicable to the triad in which A and B interact with a third person, C

## 9.1  TASKS

We mean by a *task* pretty much what the common-sense definition conveys  a problem, assignment, or stimulus-complex to which the individual or group responds by performing various overt or covert operations which lead to various outcomes  These outcomes may be of widely different kinds·  getting the right (or wrong) answer to an arithmetic problem, pleasing (or displeasing) the teacher, gaining a raise in pay, feeling an esthetic gratification in looking at a picture, or experiencing a reduced anxiety or moral superiority in reaching a decision about a social or political issue.  Diverse as these experiences are, qualitatively heterogeneous as they undoubtedly may be, we should like nevertheless to consider them all as eligible forms of outcome from task performance.  Note, too, that we have left room for outcomes that follow immediately from mainly *consummatory* or appreciative responses, as in viewing a picture. and those that follow *instrumental* actions on the task, as in computing sums of numbers in an arithmetic problem

With task thus broadly defined, we turn to some of its important properties

### 9 1 1  STATES OF THE TASK

Many tasks can assume different states  This means that the stimuli and situations presented to a person confronting the task vary from one time to another, either because of external factors or because of his own actions.  To give some examples, the ground thaws for the farmer planting his spring crops, the scene changes as the person contemplates a sunset, through collection and transposition of terms an algebra problem assumes a familiar form for the high school boy, and the TV set becomes irreparable by the do-it-yourself repairman, as he inadvertently crosses the wrong wires. In cases such as these it is useful to regard two states of the task as being different only if they make a difference to the person working on the task. At this point, we may take this to mean that the two different states yield different outcomes for one or more behaviors he might enact. We shall, then, define a given state of a task at any given moment in terms of its yielding a unique distribution of outcomes to a particular person over the items in his repertoire. The definition aims to emphasize those conditions of the task that fix outcomes for particular persons. A given moment of time is specified because outcomes may change with motivational shifts in the person. The definition holds only for a particular person for the obvious reason that for some tasks two persons behaving identically may receive different distributions of outcomes, although the task is objectively the same. When two persons work on a joint task, we would probably wish to distinguish as different "states" every variation of the task that affected either individual's outcomes. This is illustrated later.

Tasks may be classified according to whether their states are *steady* or *variable*. We intend by steady state only that the task has a single state. As examples, we might cite a task composed of a single arithmetic problem or one consisting of evaluating a single painting. Such a task might be represented in tabular form by a single column (the state) with as many rows as there are relevant items from the person's repertoire. If the outcomes are varied from row to row, a task in steady state would afford the person "self-control," that is, the person could vary his outcomes by changing his behavior and the task would have no countervailing power.

From our definition of *state* we would distinguish a task having variable (multiple) states by the simultaneous existence of at least two different distributions of outcomes to the person for the items in his repertoire. A very simple situation of this type would be that in which the task has two states and the person two items or response-sets in his repertoire.

Examples of tasks with such multiple states would be any in which different response-sets are required for maximum outcomes: a task in which a teacher can present either of two arithmetic problems of different types, a discrimination task requiring different responses, depending on which of two signals is given, or even a task composed of a

single complex problem involving two different operations for solution
One could exemplify a multiple-state task by taking a more micro-
scopic and analytic breakdown of a one-state task, to a certain degree
the level of analysis is arbitrary and depends on the purposes of the
investigator.

Such variable-state tasks might be represented as in Table 7-1 or
7-2, with the task and its states substituting for person A and his two
sets    (If all the outcomes across the rows were the same, the task
would have only one state, by definition.)    Granted that this representation fits,° it follows that a task can exercise fate control over the
person, as in Table 7-1, or behavior control, as in Table 7-2   To
determine the conditions under which the task exercises one or the
other of these types of power, we must look to the person's adaptability
to the series of states in which the variable-state task exists.

If, for any reasons, the person can maintain favorable outcomes by
adaptively shifting his behavior with changes in the state of the task,
then the task has behavior control over the person, as in Table 7-2.
On the other hand, if there exists for the person no possibility of so
responding to the series of states of the task, the task has fate control
over the person, as in Table 7-1   However, the objective situation
may be similar to that in Table 7-2, but the person may not be able
to change his behavior adaptively to attain systematically the most
favorable outcomes   This is equivalent to saying that the task is too
*difficult* in relation to the person's skill and may come about for either
of three general reasons.

(1) The person is unable to produce the appropriate response set
from his repertoire of sets, either because he is unable to discriminate
among them, because he lacks adequate control over their performance, or because the appropriate ones are absent from his repertoire

(2) The person is unable to discriminate between the various states
of the task, either because the cues are just not discriminably different
in relation to his skill or because of the difficulty of determining which
cues are relevant

(3) Even though the person is able to make such discriminations
and has adequate control over his behavior, he may be unable to "attain the correct concept" of the relation of his outcomes to the states
and actions considered jointly, that is, the distribution of his outcomes
over the matrix

° The numbers entered in the cells would again be scaled from a zero point at
CL₁ᵢₜ, where CL₁ᵢₜ would represent the *adaptation level* to the alternatives, in
this case the alternative tasks   In many cases the person may be operating below
CL, for example, when he is constrained to the task (Chapter 10).

### 9.1.2 POWER OVER TASKS

A person's ability to make inferences about his distribution of outcomes will be improved to the degree that he has the power to determine the states that the task will take. In their discussion of concept attainment, Bruner, Goodnow, and Austin (1956) distinguish between situations in which the individual has control over the evidence presented him and other situations in which he must try to make sense of what happens to come along. Although they present no evidence on this point, there is a strong implication that the former circumstances are more favorable to successful concept attainment.

When the task is set by another person (e g., the task is to please teacher), the principles of interpersonal power, as described in Chapter 7, would apply. And when the person determines his own task, he can also often control the number, nature, and order of the states of the task, as in the case of the painter, who can paint few or many pictures on few or many themes and in various possible sequences (Their quality, however, hence his and other people's outcomes, will depend on his skill.) But when the task itself imposes a sequential ordering on its states, in what sense would it be meaningful to speak of its being subject to the person's power, as we have defined power? It is certainly fanciful if not meaningless to speak of the task's dependence on the person for favorable reward-cost positions. One would be even more reluctant to say that the task experiences deprivation or elation with changes in the person's behavior. If, for example, the task is to start an automobile engine and in its present state the engine is "flooded," the presenting of incentives to the engine would merely illustrate the superstitions of some drivers. But the example does suggest what everyone knows that the various remedial behaviors of the driver will meet with differing probabilities of causing a change in the state of the engine. The question then arises what if, in dealing with power over an impersonal task, the cell entries in our power tables were probabilities (that a particular state will be taken when the person enacts a given behavior) rather than numbers reflecting goodness of outcome? Consider what the reward-cost numbers mean in the cells of Table 9-1. As indicators of behavior control, they refer to the motivation of person A to change sets when person B changes and for many purposes could just as well have been expressed as probabilities that the cell would be "occupied" by A. Large numbers would be associated with high probabilities and low numbers with low probabilities, enabling the investigator to make estimates of the probability that A will change or not change his set when B changes. Thus it would seem to be a reasonable extension of our representation of behavior

control to use conditional probability estimates, at least when referring
to control over impersonal tasks.

Though we can apparently speak of behavior control over impersonal
tasks, it does not seem meaningful to speak of fate control over them.
Not only is common sense outraged (as when reward-cost numbers for
task outcomes are entered in a table like 9–2), but it seems formally
impossible. If probabilities are substituted in Table 9–2 and the task
replaces person A, then the probabilities in each of the two rows, $b_1$
and $b_2$, must add to unity. (This is required by the very nature of
conditional probability statements: for any given behavior B might enact, the task must be in one or another of the designated states. If the
probabilities do not add to unity, the enumeration of the task states is

<br/>

TABLE 9–1

PERSON B HAS BEHAVIOR CONTROL OVER PERSON A

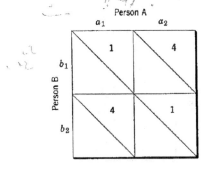

incomplete, and there must be at least one more state of the task to be
specified.) In Table 9–2, if the rows add to unity, all the cell entries
must be 0.50 because the matrix indicates that A is not influenced by
B's behavior to prefer either $a_1$ or $a_2$. If all the probabilities are 0.50,
then no fate control exists. Common sense and the formal requirement
agree.

The upshot of all this is that the person may exercise behavior control, but not fate control, over an impersonal task. This behavior control is appropriately indicated by entering in each cell of the matrix
the conditional probability that if the person enacts the specified behavior the task will assume the specified state. As we noted in Chapter
2, conditional probabilities could also be used to predict one person's
control over another's behavior, but this procedure would not permit
an analysis of fate control and all its ramifications. The reasons for

using outcomes rather than probabilities in describing interpersonal
relationships are amplified in the earlier chapter.

Table 9–3 returns to the example of the "flooded" engine to illustrate
the way in which the driver's behavior control might be represented
and the way it might relate to the task's control over him. Note that
in the example, if the engine is in a "not flooded" state, the driver can
attain his positive outcome (start the engine) by turning the key and
pressing the starter. However, if the initial state of the engine is
flooded, a certain sequence of behavior is more or less required of him:
he must first exercise his behavior control over the engine by changing
its state to not flooded by waiting for awhile; then he may turn the
key and start it. He will be able to attain his good outcome systemati-

TABLE 9–2

PERSON B HAS FATE CONTROL OVER PERSON A

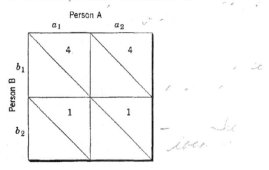

cally only if he is *well trained;* that is, if he can make the necessary
discriminations, knows the relevant cues, etc.

### 9.1.3 SOCIAL AND PHYSICAL REALITY

Festinger (1950) has proposed that *social reality* provides a way of
attaining subjective validity for one's opinions by relying on the opinions of others. He conceives of social reality as lying at one end of a
continuum at the other end of which is complete dependence on *physical reality,* that is, on the application of physical or formal (mathematical) operations to validate an hypothesis or opinion.

Although there are many factors that determine the degree to which
the person will rely on the opinions of others, instead of making direct
tests of the "correctness" or "goodness" of an opinion or hypothesis, a
major determinant is the nature of the task. Certain tasks, as in

Festinger's example of deciding on the fragility of a surface when one is equipped with a hammer, enable the person to depend upon physical tests. Others, for example, those involving moral and esthetic judgments, tend to lead the person to rely on social reality.

Consider a man wandering through a gallery of pictures. Suppose he is walking through a room of fifteenth-century Italian portraits. Some he may like somewhat better than others. But let us say that no matter how he looks at the pictures, squints, peers, glances, or studies, no matter what perceptual "operations" he performs, he likes them all about the same (and none of them very much). His outcomes for all of the pictures and for all of his sets (ways of perceiving and evaluat-

TABLE 9-3

THE DRIVER MAY EXERCISE "BEHAVIOR CONTROL" OVER THE ENGINE

|  | Task (Starting the engine) | |
|---|---|---|
|  | State 1: flooded | State 2: not flooded |
| Driver — $a_1$ waiting 5 minutes | 0.30 / 0 | 0.70 / 0 |
| $a_2$ pumping accelerator | 0.95 / 0 | 0.05 / 0 |
| $a_3$ turning key and pressing starter | 0.49 / 0 | 0.51 / 1 |

ing) are quite homogeneous. This fact will be accepted by him if the matter of judging pictures is of little importance. However, if he regards this as an important activity and believes that there is a right answer, then he will be receptive to any influence that will produce inhomogeneity in his outcomes. He will be ready, in short, to substitute social reality for physical reality.

At this point another person who might also be in the gallery can contribute to inhomogeneity in several ways. First, he may act as an expert by teaching our novice how to view and analyze paintings so that their intrinsic differences become apparent, some thereafter yielding him considerably more satisfaction than the others. If the novice heeds the expert's advice and does indeed obtain differential satisfaction from an array of paintings, he is likely to "internalize" the advice

(Chapter 13) and follow it independently of his further relations with the expert But the expert has not provided a social reality for the novice, he has merely mediated the novice's contact with the physical reality

A quite different effect would be forthcoming if the second person merely told our novice which pictures he liked and which he disliked If the second person has some sort of authority or control (by virtue of friendship, prestige, or expertness), this statement of opinion forms the basis for increasing the inhomogeneity of our novice's outcomes At first this may be only an incipient inhomogeneity in which the novice anticipates differentially good outcomes for expressing approval of some paintings and disapproval of others As these differential outcomes are actually experienced (e.g., the friend rewards his agreement and the novice finds that his new-found evaluations are shared by others), the inhomogeneity acquires a strong social basis Like all products of "identification" processes (Chapter 13), the continued existence of the inhomogeneity depends to some degree upon maintenance of the original relationships with the authority, friend, or opinion-supporters But as long as these relationships are fairly stable, the person is not likely to be very much aware of the social basis of his opinions and evaluations, and the social reality will have very much the same significance for him, the same subjective "feel" about it, as the physical reality.

In summary, then, the friend and mentor may serve in two ways to assist our novice in making discriminations leading to differential outcomes. He may function mainly to improve the novice's sensitivity and responsiveness to the pictures so that the novice begins to acquire a discriminating "taste" for pictures The novice is then able to make these gratifying discriminations independently of his mentor, whose role has been to mediate between the novice and physical reality In this extreme case a social reality has not been provided

The second way in which the friend can assist the novice is by sharing with him a social reality which is created by the novice's being rewarded for imitating the preferences of his admired friend. The discriminations leading to differential outcomes then become not so much *esthetic* as *social,* and the novice's continued ability to obtain gratifying outcomes depends on the maintenance of his relationship with his friend

Tasks which yield homogeneous outcomes may be described as highly *ambiguous* as well as *difficult.* In the foregoing example the person confronting a roomful of pictures for the first time has a difficult assignment Part of the difficulty involves the complexity of the criteria of "correctness" of his evaluations and the related problem of communicating effectively and reaching agreement about these criteria and then relative weights  Another part of the difficulty is in specifying the various response-sets in his repertoire that should be tried out on the task.  Since these ways of looking at the pictures are largely covert and implicit, they are not readily communicated.  And then another part of the difficulty is in communicating about, or having any evidence about the interpersonal comparability of, the esthetic outcomes themselves  These are likely to remain private

The operation of social reality depends upon such factors as importance of the task and the nature of the relationship with persons who provide opinion support (Schachter, 1951), but it begins with an attribute of the person-task matrix, namely, the homogeneity of outcomes. Persons who experience extreme outcomes in their interactions with tasks are undoubtedly less susceptible to social influences  For example, Kelley and Lamb (1957) found that persons having very strong taste reactions to a substance were much more resistant to social influence about it than were those having milder reactions  In fact, persons with rather strong opinions on a subject have been found to express even stronger ones when highly oriented toward being right and confronted with strong disagreement (Thibaut and Strickland, 1956).

Homogeneity of outcomes can often be traced, in turn, to ambiguity and difficulty of the task.  These attributes of problems have been shown to render the problem solver more susceptible to social influence  For example, Coffin (1941) has shown subjects to be more "suggestible" when working on tasks which, relative to their ability, were difficult and when making judgments of ambiguous attributes of stimuli  Similarly, in his study of the influence of an erroneous majority opinion on judgments of the relative lengths of lines Asch (1952) found this influence to be greatest when the objective differences between the lines afforded least objective basis for the judgments

## 9.2  DYADS AND TASKS

Thus far we have discussed the relationships between the individual person and the task without having said anything about the dyad.  In principle, what we have described for the individual holds equally well for the dyad  In Table 9-3, instead of the individual driver, we could substitute a dyad without changing the form of the diagram  In general, when this is done, two problems arise· how does the dyad decide which "response" to make to the task, and how are the outcomes divided? Again, however, these are problems that have been covered, in principle at least. Within the dyad, the problems of which member's opinion will weigh heavier in making a joint response to the task, as well as how the outcomes will be allocated between the two members, are susceptible to analysis as problems of interpersonal power (Chapter 7) or problems of normative control (Chapter 8).

A more complex analysis would deal with the task as a third party to the dyadic relationship, perhaps represented as a 2 x 2 x 2 matrix. This can be illustrated by the situation used by Daniel (1942) to investigate cooperation in rats, described in Chapter 3. It will be recalled that pairs of white rats were placed in an apparatus in which the food crock was surrounded by a grid. The electric current in the

TABLE 9–4

A SINGLE RAT IN DANIEL'S APPARATUS

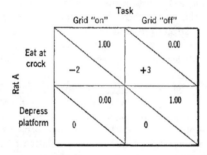

grid could be turned off only by depressing a platform located at some distance from the food crock. An analysis of this situation for a single rat placed in it alone is shown in Table 9–4. A single rat can control the states of the task but, because cells in which the probability value is 0.00 will never occur, can get outcomes of only 0 or $-2$. (The value $-2$ assumes the costs incurred from receiving the shock are greater than the rewards of feeding. The shock is assumed to interfere sufficiently with feeding so that its rewards would be much reduced.) The outcomes are potentially quite different when a second rat is placed in the apparatus. Because A's behavior also changes the state of the task for B, and vice versa, it now becomes possible for one of them (at any given moment) to achieve the $+3$ outcome. This is illustrated by a three-dimensional matrix in Table 9–5. The values in the visible cells (the "depress, depress, grid on" cell is hidden from view) represent respectively (reading from lower left to upper right) A's outcome, B's outcome, and the probability that the task will assume that particular state. Again, the circumstances described by cells with probability values of 0.00 cannot occur. From the values given, it is apparent that each animal may now achieve a +3 outcome. Both cannot, however, achieve it at the same time; hence, as we noted in our earlier discussion of this situation, some sort of alternation is necessary if both are to be successful.

This example can also be presented in the somewhat simpler way

TABLE 9-5

TWO RATS IN DANIEL'S APPARATUS

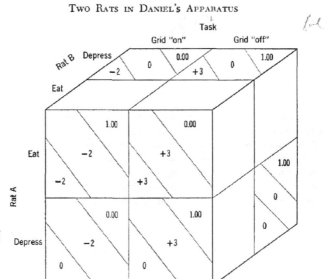

shown in Table 9-6, in which the dyad is considered as a single agent interacting with the task. The alternatives at the side of the matrix might be considered to constitute the behavioral repertoire available to the dyad.

When a dyadic task has a single steady state, it may be disregarded in the analysis. For example, in the Azrin and Lindsley (1956) experiment, mentioned in Chapter 8, only one set of task conditions exists. Each child is equipped with a stylus and is confronted with three holes arranged horizontally. Whenever the two children simultaneously place their styli in opposite holes, a reward is delivered. Let

TABLE 9-6

ALTERNATIVE MANNER OF REPRESENTING THE SITUATION IN TABLE 9–5

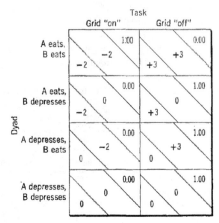

us assume (contrary to fact) that both children receive a reward on these occasions. The situation may then be represented as in Table 9–7, in which the three relevant behavior alternatives for each child are described in terms of the holes (numbered, let us say, from east to west) into which his stylus can be placed.

Now let us modify this situation. Suppose that only one pair of holes yields a reward on each trial and that this *correct* pair is chosen

TABLE 9-7

Two CHILDREN IN THE AZRIN-LINDSLEY APPARATUS

|  | Child A | | |
|---|---|---|---|
|  | Hole No. 1 | Hole No. 2 | Hole No. 3 |
| Hole No. 1 | 2 / 2 | 0 / 0 | 0 / 0 |
| Hole No. 2 | 0 / 0 | 2 / 2 | 0 / 0 |
| Hole No. 3 | 0 / 0 | 0 / 0 | 2 / 2 |

Child B

from among the three pairs of opposing holes by the experimenter.
The task would now be considered to assume three different states,
which, with the nonzero outcomes to the children, are shown in Table
9–8. From an objective viewpoint, this task has behavior control over
the children: they can, at least potentially, make adjustments in their
behaviors according to variations in the task state which will enable
them to maintain high outcomes on each trial.

They might be able, actually, to make such adjustments if some cue
were available to them as to the state of the task. This would be the
case, for example, if the states occurred in a regular sequence which
they could learn. If such cues were absent or the children were unable to "read" the cues correctly, their outcomes would fluctuate in an
irregular manner which might be interpreted by the children as the

TABLE 9–8

THE AZRIN-LINDSLEY APPARATUS CONVERTED INTO A VARIABLE-STATE TASK

fate control of the task, inasmuch as they could not dependably affect
their own outcomes.

### 9.2.1 CONJUNCTIVE VERSUS DISJUNCTIVE TASK REQUIREMENTS

As the Azrin-Lindsley apparatus is originally conceived, *both* children
have to make a certain response if they are to receive a reward. This
is a *conjunctive* task requirement. This type of requirement is manifested in the outcome matrix by the fact that rewards occur only at
intersections of certain rows and columns (Table 9–7 or 9–8).

The apparatus might have been constructed so that if *either* child
made a certain response (including the case in which both do) they
would receive the reward. This would be a *disjunctive* task requirement. The outcome matrix would be as shown in Table 9–9, which
assumes that the correct response, perhaps on a given trial, is to place
the stylus in the second hole. As can be seen, a disjunctive task re-

quirement is indicated by rewards occurring throughout a given row and the corresponding column.

Although conjunctiveness or disjunctiveness is ordinarily determined by the structure of the task, it may depend upon the subject's relation to his co-worker. For example, Lewis (1944) has shown that when a subject and another person have worked cooperatively on a task the subject tends to be as much satisfied (as indicated by the tendency to forget it) if the partner finishes the task as if he himself does. He is less satisfied when the person who completes the task is one with whom he has not been working, although this is better than leaving the task totally unfinished (Lewis and Franklin, 1944). The effect of the partner's completion seems to depend upon the nature of the task; it is more satisfying with routine tasks, such as winding thread and

TABLE 9-9

A Disjunctive Version of the Azrin-Lindsley Apparatus

copying letters, than with tasks lending themselves to individualized and varied solutions (making a clay house or drawing a map). The disjunctivity illustrated here (a person's outcomes depending on either his efforts or those of a partner) is closely related to the notions of "vicarious gratification" and, in one sense, "identification."

Whether a task involves conjunctive or disjunctive requirements has many important implications. For example, a disjunctive task permits group members to work independently without communication or coordination of their efforts. This is indicated by Deutsch (1951), who compared group discussions of human relations problems having no objectively correct solutions with those of logical puzzles for which there were unique, correct solutions. Because subjects feel they have solved the human relations problems (i.e., they feel rewarded) only when they achieve consensus, these problems may be considered as having conjunctive requirements The outcome matrix would be very much as in Table 9–7, whenever group members express the *same* solution, whatever it is, they obtain rewards On the other hand, since the answers to the puzzles are logical matters which each person can determine and check for himself, and since (at least in Deutsch's cooperatively organized groups), if any member gets the answer, they all get credit for it, the puzzle tasks can be characterized as disjunctive

Deutsch found, in line with our initial assertion, that there was more initiation of communication and more attentiveness to it in the case of the human relations ̄(conjunctive) problems than for the puzzle (disjunctive) problems. (For reasons irrelevant here, this difference was even more marked in groups in which the members were competing for scarce rewards than in those working cooperatively )

Inasmuch as group members can work independently on disjunctive tasks, when faced with a number of such tasks, they can divide them up, each member doing part of them In an earlier discussion (1954) we suggested this as one of the reasons that groups are superior to individuals on some tasks but no better on others For example, Husband (1940) compared individuals and dyads in their performance on a jigsaw puzzle and an arithmetic problem The dyads were faster on the puzzle but not so on the arithmetic problem. Our interpretation would be that the puzzle (but not the arithmetic problem) can be divided into a number of disjunctive tasks (different parts to be assembled) on which the members of the pair can work independently. This enables them to complete the task faster than an individual typically can

On the other hand, tasks which make conjunctive requirements of members' behavior may place groups at a disadvantage in comparison with individuals McCurdy and Lambert (1952) found individuals to be more successful than three-person groups on a task requiring a coordinated setting of six switches Each bit of progress on the task required changing the setting of only one switch The progress of the groups thus depended upon each member's paying rather careful attention. The investigators feel that under these task requirements the success of the group is limited to that of its least attentive member

### 9.2 2 CORRESPONDENCE VERSUS NONCORRESPONDENCE OF OUTCOMES

We have noted from time to time the importance of whether or not good outcomes are available to both A and B in the same cells of the matrix (i e, in the same positions of their interactions) This conc-

spondence versus noncorrespondence of outcomes often depends upon
the task the pair is working on. Correspondence exists when the task
requirements they must meet in order to achieve A's best outcomes are
identical with the requirements to be met for B's best outcomes. Tables 9–7 and 9–9 illustrate this for conjunctive and disjunctive requirements, respectively. Mintz (1951) used an experimental situation
which involved conjunctive requirements yielding noncorrespondence
of good outcomes. Each member of a group of subjects was given a
string leading to a cone in a large bottle, and the subjects were instructed to pull their cones out as quickly as possible. The dimensions of the cones and bottle were such that only one cone could be
drawn out at a time without the development of a "traffic jam" in the

TABLE 9–10

REPRESENTATION OF MINTZ'S "REWARD-AND-FINE" CONDITION

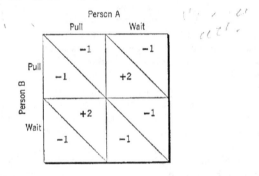

neck of the bottle. In a "reward-and-fine" condition each subject was
rewarded for removing his cone quickly and fined for removing it more
slowly. By considering only two subjects, this situation might be represented somewhat as in Table 9–10. Because there is one conjunctive
task requirement for A's best outcome and another for B's, their best
outcomes occur in different cells. Mintz found that under these conditions many traffic jams developed and a long time was usually required
before all subjects (he used fifteen to twenty-one) could remove their
cones. This was especially true when subjects were not permitted
prior discussion and were not able, therefore, to agree upon a plan of
action. The reader will note that this task requires trading or alternation to achieve good outcomes, which, as suggested in the discussion of
norms (Chapter 8), are facilitated by the existence of procedural
agreements.

In another experimental condition Mintz varied the instructions and rewards so as to create high correspondence of good outcomes. In his instructions to subjects he told them how rapidly groups at another university had removed their cones and challenged his groups to do as well. This probably created a highly cooperative motivation under which subjects derived as much (or almost as much) reward from seeing their colleagues withdraw their cones as from withdrawing their own. Thus a close correspondence resulted between their distributions of outcomes over the matrix, as shown in Table 9–11. Trading agreements, with their implications of interpersonal trust (Deutsch, 1957), are no longer necessary. The only question is who shall act first, and

TABLE 9–11

REPRESENTATION OF MINTZ'S COOPERATION CONDITION

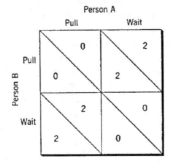

apparently this is more easily resolved than the question of who shall profit first.

The experimental results showed that under these circumstances there were no serious traffic jams, and less time was required for removal of all cones than in the reward-and-fine condition.

## SUMMARY

By using the concepts and theory developed in preceding chapters, we have analyzed the interplay of one or more individuals and a task. When individual A works on a task, the situation resembles in some respects the one in which he interacts with another person, B. One major point of similarity is that the task can assume different states, just as another person can enact different behaviors, and in both cases these can have different consequences for A  In other words, the task may have fate control over A  Another point of similarity is that A can often improve his outcomes by making appropriate adjustments to the different states of the task, just as when B has behavior control over him A can improve his outcomes by adjusting his behaviors to B's Finally, just as A may influence B's behavior by exerting behavior control over him, A may have some means of determining which state of the task confronts him at any given moment.  The analysis of person-person and person-task interactions diverges in that a person may not reasonably be considered as having fate control over a task

From this analysis of the interdependency and power relations between a person and task, it is possible to prepare a more or less comprehensive statement of what an individual must do in order to cope successfully with the task  With reference to the earlier discussion of power, these required activities are similar, on the one hand, to those involved in making adjustments to external behavior control (if the situation is largely one of adaptation to a situation over which control is minimal) or, on the other hand, to those involved in successfully exerting behavior control (if the situation is one in which control is possible).  These activities need hardly be summarized again for the reader, but perhaps their relevance for group functions and roles should be noted once more  If a given kind of task requires certain activities on the part of an individual, it requires the same activities when two or more individuals work on it.  Therefore, a listing of the required activities forms the basis for determining the functionally requisite activities which go to make up the task roles of effective small groups.

An individual's adaptation to or control of a task depends upon his experiencing different outcomes for different activities and learning to enact those which consistently yield good outcomes  However, under special circumstances, a task is *ambiguous* or *difficult* in the sense that it yields homogeneously low outcomes for the individual over the realm of behaviors which, for various reasons, he enacts toward it  These circumstances are of particular importance to social psychology because they render the person highly susceptible to social influences, as he attempts to find means of acting upon the task which yield differentially good outcomes  These social influences may take the form of expert advice and instruction to provide means of acting upon the task which the person can then independently verify as effective or satisfactory, or, the social influences may provide him with a *social reality* basis for inhomogeneous outcomes, the high outcomes deriving from his acceptance of discriminating evaluations made by highly regarded persons

When the analysis turns to several persons dealing with the same task, it is often found that the task creates internal problems for their relationship. Different patterns of interdependency are created by the properties of the task (although the task is not the only factor having this effect). Two such pattern variables were noted. The first is the variable of conjunctivity versus disjunctivity. A major consequence of a conjunctive task requirement is that coordination of the several persons' behaviors is required for them to receive good outcomes. The second variable, correspondence versus noncorrespondence of outcomes, has the effect (when noncorrespondence characterizes the situation) of necessitating an alternation in the attainment of good outcomes. These examples illustrate the general point that the interaction process necessary for several persons to establish a viable relationship may depend to a major degree upon the demands and requirements of the external situation in which they find themselves.

# 10.

# *Nonvoluntary Relationships:*
# *Frustration and Deprivation*

In this chapter we turn our attention to nonvoluntary relationships which are those in which the person is forced to stay even though he would prefer not to  In terms of our analysis, the person remains in relationships of this sort only because heavy costs are in some manner associated with being in better ones  A person would not, of course, prefer to enter the "better" ones if the heavy costs were intimately and inevitably associated with the rewards to be attained there  Our present concern is with instances in which the association is so artificial and, in some sense, arbitrary that the costs are easily dissociated from the rewards when the person thinks about or visualizes the relationships  Thus, in determining his CL, the rewards but not the costs may be salient for this person, even though when actually entering the relationships the costs inescapably have their effect  For example, the costs of leaving the present (nonvoluntary) relationship may be great (e g , if a physical barrier must be penetrated or if leaving leads to punishment), or the costs of being in the "better" relationships may be made arbitrarily high (e g , the person encounters criticism or derogation)  These characteristics are probably true to some degree of most relationships  a person often knows of some better situations which, out of cost considerations, he dares not enter. But in this chapter we consider the rather extreme case in which the unavailable outcomes are so good and so salient that the person finds his present circumstances to be markedly below CL.°

° A person may, of course, be forced to remain in a situation that yields better outcomes than any of his known alternatives, that is, outcomes well above his CL  A husband may greatly enjoy his marriage, but, at the same time, if he were to attempt to leave it, he would incur heavy financial and social penalties  Because a person would, in this case, voluntarily choose the very relationship to which he

The discussion is no longer restricted to dyads  Rather, we now speak more generally of social situations in which individuals are constrained to below-CL relationships.  For example, this includes children, particularly adolescents, who are both constrained to a familial relationship and excluded from full membership in the adult community  Although the dual elements of *constraint to* and *exclusion from* are usually present, they are not always equally apparent  In some cases, as with prisoners and drafted soldiers, we are inclined to think first of the fact that individuals are constrained to a particular relationship, are prevented from leaving it  In other instances, exemplified by members of ethnic minority groups and the unemployed during an economic depression, the fact of exclusion from a particular relationship—being prevented from joining—is most obvious

To use words like *constraint* and *exclusion* implies the exercise of power by some social agent.  Briefly consider the determinants of power in situations we have characterized as nonvoluntary.  In the case of constraint, this power consists of, say, person A being able to reduce B's outcomes sharply when B tries to leave their relationship  Thus A must have fate control over B which he can exercise (convert) in a selective manner so as to insure A's continued presence in the A–B dyad.  Similar fate control can be exerted by agents outside the dyad who place social or physical barriers against B's leaving, with the effect of reducing B's outcomes when he attempts to leave  Whatever their specific nature, these constraints act to make it unprofitable for B to enter certain of his alternative relationships, the particular ones depending upon how the constraints are enforced  Making certain relationships unavailable moves down B's CL_alt, and the lower the CL_alt, of course, the greater the power others in the relationship have over B

In general, A's power over B will be greater, the stronger the constraints keeping B in the relationship.  Thus the greater the penalties for escape (or attempted escape), the poorer the outcomes that a prisoner can be forced to endure, hence, the greater the distance along the outcome scale through which he can be moved by the prison authorities

The case of exclusion is rather similar in nature  Individual B can be forced to stay in the A–B dyad if the members of better relationships, say C, D, and E, exclude him   By exclusion is meant that they exercise strong fate control to reduce his outcomes when he attempts interaction with them   To put it differently, they convert their fate control to keep B out of interaction with them   These actions have the effect of removing the B–C, B–D, and B–E dyads as alternatives for B and of keeping him in the A–B dyad.   The more such alternatives are removed in this manner and the stronger the exclusion (the greater the fate control they exercise), the more dependent B is upon A or the greater is A's power over him

The reader will note the manner in which a relationship from which B is nonvoluntarily excluded differs from one from which he would exclude himself   In the first case there are good outcomes potentially available in the interaction, but the other member, by virtue of his fate control, is able to prevent B from attaining them   In the second, because of low rewards and/or high costs, none of the outcomes is above CL.   The first is illustrated by a very talented young man who anticipates success in medical school and applies for admission but is not admitted because of his race, the second, by a young man who in premedical work finds his talents are too few or his fears too great for medical school to be very rewarding   Note that a selection committee, reviewing the grades and qualifications of the second man, may exclude him "in his own interests," by preventing him from entering a relationship that is predicted to yield low outcomes for him.

As constraint or exclusion become extreme—as B's alternatives are severely restricted—the determinants of A's power also change in character.   His power becomes more a matter of the punishments he can apply or withhold rather than, as in voluntary relationships, a question of the rewards he can deliver or withhold   In the extreme case, when it is very difficult or impossible for B to leave the relationship, the lower end of the range of satisfaction values through which A can move B is limited only by the instruments A has for inflicting pain and by his scruples about making B suffer   The more unscrupulous A is, the less he is sympathetic and touched by B's suffering, the more fate control he has   Waller and Hill (1951) state this point as their *principle of control*   "That person controls who is most ruthless "   They observe the change in power relations that sometimes occurs as the male-female relationship moves through the courtship stage (when it is more or less voluntary) and into the marriage stage (when the restraints against leaving it become fairly strong)

Often the dominant member is the same person who controlled in courtship, but in marriage both have much to lose, and there may be a shift in control.   In marriage, control often goes to the person who steadily, ruthlessly, and without insight adheres to his own purposes. One dominates by being willing to quarrel before outsiders, by threatening to break up the marriage, by being willing to shatter the rapport and to resist the temptation to be the first to make up, by being a good fighting machine—in short, by being an unstable personality    It is understood that we refer here not to the subtler forms of interpersonal influence but only to the crasser forms of dominance and subordination [p 312]

We now discuss the effects on the individual of being in a nonvoluntary relationship, considering mainly those cases in which the constraints or exclusions are strong, hence in which the deprivation can be rather severe.  These situations are approached from three points of view: (1) the objective deprivations the person can be forced to endure, (2) the frustrations of being below CL, and (3) the fate control to which he can be subjected  Although deprivation, frustration, and subjection to fate control are characteristic to some degree of all nonvoluntary relationships (as we have defined them), they are not always equally important.  For example, an adolescent boy, being allowed to do the things he feels he ought to, may be neither objectively deprived nor frustrated, but he still may chafe under the fact that his outcomes are strictly dependent upon his father's decisions (fate control)  On the other hand, a Negro in a southern community may lead a life of stable reward-cost outcomes, subject to little exercise of fate control, but may be severely deprived in an objective sense  So there is reason to consider separately these three aspects of nonvoluntary relationships by looking at their effects upon the individual and the adjustments or adaptations he might make to them.

## 10 1    Objective Deprivations

When we ask what determines the degree to which the individual experiences his situation as unpleasant, unsatisfactory, or hardship, the first and most obvious answer entails an assessment of the objective punishments and deprivations to which he is submitted.  Brutal treatment in a concentration camp is clearly more unpleasant than the relatively mild restrictions placed upon the member of an ethnic minority group

When we pass beyond the gross hardships contributed by physical punishments, we find other potential sources of unpleasantness that are more subtle and elusive  The unexpectedly powerful effects of sheer reduction of sensory stimulation are illustrated by the recent studies conducted at McGill University (Heron, 1957)

The subjects were male college students, paid $20 a day to participate They lay on a comfortable bed in a lighted cubicle 24 hours a day for as long as they cared to stay, with time out only for meals (which they usually ate sitting on the edge of the bed) and going to the toilet  They wore translucent plastic visors which transmitted diffuse light but prevented pattern vision.  Cotton gloves and cardboard cuffs extending beyond the fingertips restricted perception by touch  Their auditory perception was limited by a U-shaped foam rubber pillow on which their heads lay and by a continuous hum of air-conditioning equipment which masked small sounds [p 53].

The effects of this monotonous experience were ramifying  The subjects found it increasingly difficult to concentrate on anything, many developed vivid hallucinations, and eventually the "whole room appeared to be in motion" [p 54]  As time passed the subjects became "markedly irritable," "felt that the experimenters were against them," and experienced intense spells of restlessness that were described as being "very unpleasant" [p 54]  "In moving about, as when they were led to the toilet, they appeared dazed and confused, and had increasing difficulty in finding their way about the washroom" [p 54]

Not only is the sensory input often limited in nonvoluntary relationships but the kinds of behavior the person may perform may be severely curtailed  With the withdrawal of various inputs and behavioral supports (e g books, radios, tools, writing or drawing materials, and games), the number of behavioral sequences from his repertoire that the person can perform becomes greatly reduced  There is a restriction in what Lewin has called the "space of free movement"  The consequences of this are obvious.  Life becomes empty and monotonous  The necessity for making choices among different behaviors becomes largely eliminated, and, as a result, the ability to make decisions may become dulled  Under these conditions, some individuals make creative and clever use of the resources at hand or resort to complicated fantasy life, others slump into an inactive, stuporous state.

## 10 2  FRUSTRATION

It has often been observed that one can be *objectively deprived* without any corresponding experience of hardship or displeasure.  The range and variety of inputs that are inaccessible to a small child or to a primitive tribesman in the rain-forests of Africa do not ordinarily lead to despondency, to suicide, or to homicidal aggression against the barriers that thwart them

If objective impoverishment is not directly responsible for such experiences resulting from deprivation, what *is*?  The answer lies in the quality of the experienced outcomes in relation to those the person expects or feels he deserves to receive, that is, his CL  As long as the

CL remains anchored in better outcomes, the state of deprivation is also a frustrating one  From the discussion of CL in Chapter 6, the reader will recall that the CL will remain high as long as the unavailable outcomes are regarded as better and as long as there are instigations, external or self-produced, to give them salience

The experienced discontent may be reduced (an adjustment can be made to the frustration) by (1) dropping the CL or (2) finding some means of achieving the unattained outcomes  As (2) would not, strictly speaking, constitute an adjustment to *deprivation* (insofar as it is successful in permitting the person to attain outcomes above his CL), it is considered in a later section.

Lowering the CL requires either (1) devaluating the outcomes believed to exist in the unavailable alternative relationships or (2) decreasing the salience of the good outcomes in these relationships. These two devices are undoubtedly closely related and in some cases difficult to distinguish  An aspect of their relatedness has already been covered in Chapter 6 in our discussion of the problem of *idealization*

In touching on the research of Klein (1954), Atkinson (1953) and Horwitz (1958) we distinguished two extreme personality dispositions: one characterized by low confidence and fear of failure and the other by high confidence and a positive orientation toward success  We related these two illustrative extremes to differences in the perceived range of control, that is, to low perceived control in the first case and high perceived control in the second  The hypothesis was advanced that with increasing perceived control the reward components of unattained outcomes are increasingly instigated and the cost components decreasingly so  Strong instigation from (or high salience of) the reward component and weak instigation from (low salience of) the cost component lead to overvaluation (idealization) of the outcome, and, contrariwise, weak instigation from the reward component and strong instigation from the cost component lead to devaluation of the outcome  In other words, the (mechanism postulated to account for devaluation is decreasing the salience of the reward component and increasing the salience of the cost component)  If a less differentiated analysis is made and the reward and cost components are not separated, then devaluation would occur when the over-all outcome has low salience

Despite the relatedness of these two processes of devaluating the favorable outcomes in alternative relationships and decreasing their salience, it is convenient to consider separately the evidence bearing on them

### 10.2.1 DEVALUATING ALTERNATIVE RELATIONSHIPS

A person (for example, a Negro denied access to the community swimming pool) can devaluate an unattainable relationship either by taking a "sour grapes" attitude toward the rewarding aspects of the interaction ("I don't get much fun out of swimming anyway") or by emphasizing the negative, cost-increasing aspects of it ("It's dangerous and takes a lot of time"). Both of these are greatly facilitated if he can control selectively the information or instigation he receives from the unattained state of affairs, keeping out evidence of pleasures that others receive and letting through evidence of high costs.

Evidence of devaluation tendencies is presented in studies by Solomon (1957) and by Thibaut (1950), described later in this chapter.

A related adjustment may be that of *overcompensation* or supervaluation of the present outcomes. Simpson and Yinger (1953) interpret Negro chauvinism in this way:

> One small phase of the Negro protest movement in the United States is the assertion of the superiority of all things black, best shown in the doctrines of Marcus Garvey. This phenomenon reaches beyond the normal range of ethnocentrism in an attempt to turn what seems to be a handicap (because of the social situation) into an advantage. "I want to be black," some Negroes declare (including many who are most clearly Negro in physical type). This is in part an overcompensation for a strong desire to "be white"—that is, to have the advantages of being white [p. 216].

All of these consequences can be predicted rather well from Festinger's theory of cognitive dissonance (1957). Membership in an underprivileged group is dissonant with knowledge of the good outcomes available in other groups. This dissonance can be reduced by diminishing the value of the unattainable groups or accentuating the virtues of the present one. In addition, the applications of the theory to enforced compliance suggests that the deprived situations will not be dissonant if the forces acting to keep the person there are overwhelmingly strong. On the other hand, if they are just barely strong enough to constrain him to the deprived state, dissonance will be maximal. This suggests the further method of reducing dissonance which consists of magnification of the external constraints which act to keep the person at the low level. This is, in part, involved in the process of reducing salience of the unattainable outcomes by interpreting them as being under external control. This is discussed in the next section.

### 10.2.2 DECREASING THE SALIENCE
### OF ALTERNATIVE RELATIONSHIPS

The CL may also be lowered, and feelings of frustration decreased, by reducing the instigations to the more attractive but unattainable outcomes in alternative relationships. On the avoidance of information and instigation Bettelheim's (1943) observations in a concentration camp are pertinent. He observes that the prisoners who had been in camp a long time " . did not like to be reminded of their families and former friends" and " did not like to mention their former social status . . " Bettelheim comments that, "Old prisoners seemed to have accepted their state of dejection, and to compare it with their former splendor . was probably too depressing" [pp 442–443] Farber (1944) reports that, "Prisoner 24, who had cut off all personal contact with the outside, says, 'I don't do hard time. It's much easier if you get the outside off your mind and just forget about your family, your folks and your wife' For some cases at least, cutting off personal relations with the outside seems to be an effective means of avoiding frustration" [p 176]

The hypothesis in Chapter 6, relating perceived realm of control to the salience of outcomes, would suggest that instigations to the unattainable outcomes can be reduced more readily if they are interpreted as being outside the individual's realm of control. They clearly are so in many instances of nonvoluntary membership, but occasionally the individual is presented with information that works against this interpretation For example, if he is permitted intermittently to enter the prohibited relationships, this not only provides immediate instigations to the outcomes there but also suggests that he has some ability to produce these outcomes for himself Knowing that others, particularly those similar to himself, are permitted to enter the (to him) forbidden relationships has the same effect In general, we would propose the hypothesis that nonvoluntary membership is most frustrating when enforced intermittently or in a highly discriminating manner (i.e., for certain persons but not for certain virtually indistinguishable others)

An aspect of the "brainwashing" technique of the Chinese Communists, as described by Lifton (1956), appears to exploit the effects on frustration of *intermittent enforcement* of the nonvoluntary relationship Lifton reports that an effective device in preparing the prisoner for brainwashing involved a relaxation from time to time of the worse features of confinement, so that intermittently the prisoner experienced better treatment. Another bit of evidence for the effects of intermittent enforcement on frustration comes from the study by Christie (1954) of basic trainees' adjustment to the army   The soldier's contacts with home, through visits, were related to his adjustment to army life as assessed by the Wilkins-Miles Inventory (a measure of *anxiety*)   For unmarried men at least, "     no contact or practically continuous contact leads to the least anxiety" [p 113]   In other words, anxiety was highest for those with intermittent, that is, intermediate degrees of, contact with home   Farber (1944) reports a similar finding in his study of prisoners in a state penitentiary

On the second aspect of the hypothesis, that *enforcement in a discriminating manner* is particularly frustrating, evidence is provided by Stouffer, et al  (1949), in their studies of the American soldier in World War II   In commenting on the relatively high dissatisfaction of married soldiers as compared with single men, they have this to say.

> The very fact that draft boards were more liberal with married than with single men provided numerous examples to the drafted married man of others in his shoes who got relatively better breaks than he did   Comparing himself with his unmarried associates in the Army, he could feel that induction demanded greater sacrifice from him than from them, and comparing himself with his married civilian friends he could feel that he had been called on for sacrifices which they were escaping altogether   Hence the married man, on the average, was more likely than others to come into the Army with reluctance and, possibly, a sense of injustice [p. 125].

An experimental study by Solomon (1957) provides evidence for both types of adjustment to frustration discussed above, namely, devaluating the unattainable outcomes and constricting the perceived realm of own power   In a laboratory experiment each subject played a game against another person who equaled or surpassed the subject in actual power.   Although all subjects thought they were playing against a real person, this "person" was actually a prepared set of plays, programmed to represent to the subject the actions of a person who was apparently motivated to treat the subject in some particular way   For some subjects, the "person" acted benevolently, exercising his fate control to benefit the subject, for other subjects the "person" acted malevolently, exercising his fate control to keep the subject at very low outcomes   The frustration created by the consistent deprivation of the malevolent treatment is well documented by Solomon   Comparing the two treatments, he also found that the subjects exposed to the malevolent treatment attached less importance to doing well in the game, which suggests a process of devaluating the withheld outcomes   Finally, the subjects who were treated malevolently attributed greater "potency" (strength, size, hardness) to the man controlling their fate. This magnification of the power of the agent responsible for the deprivation suggests a tendency to narrow the range of outcomes over which one feels oneself to have control.

## 10 3  THE ENVIRONMENT'S FATE CONTROL

An important aspect of many nonvoluntary relationships is that the social environment exercises massive fate control over the individual. To a greater or lesser degree in all such relationships, the individual's outcomes are determined by the social environment, and in extreme cases the individual cannot respond adaptively, by varying his behavior, to attain the relatively less unfavorable outcomes. Bettelheim (1943) offers an example from his observations of the inmates of a Nazi concentration camp during World War II. He describes the helplessness of the prisoner and his difficulty in remaining "intact as a personality" when he is faced with the arbitrary and overwhelming power of the Gestapo guards. " . . if a prisoner was cursed, slapped, pushed around 'like a child' and if he was, like a child, unable to defend himself, this revived in him behavior patterns and psychological mechanisms which he had developed when a child" [p 436].

The same passive dread of an arbitrary and capricious power has been reported by Jewish college students (Allport, 1954), one of whom writes " 'Anti-Semitism is a constant force in the Jew's life . . . I have encountered at first hand very few overt expressions of anti-Semitism. Nevertheless, I am always aware of its presence off-stage, as it were, ready to come into the act, and I never know what will be the cue to its entrance. I am never quite free of this foreboding of a dim sense of some vaguely impending doom' " [p 144] And Allport adds "In the same series of personal essays written by Jewish students in an eastern university over half mentioned this vague sense of 'impending doom' hovering over themselves as members of their particular ethnic group" [p 144]

The disadvantages in a voluntary relationship of being subjected to fate control without being able to mobilize effective counterpower have been described in Chapter 7. For the person over whom fate control is thus exercised, the severities of deprivation and pain can be ameliorated—an adjustment can be made—if he can somehow have the power converted from fate control to behavior control, for example, by discovering a *behavior-controlling* norm to live by. Consider Lifton's (1956) description of the plight of a certain Bishop C under arrest by the Chinese Communists. Note how strongly the Bishop sought to alter his captors' fate control as the only apparent way of avoiding intolerably extreme outcomes to himself.

> And later an official visited him and spoke in an extremely friendly manner, saying, "The Government doesn't want to kill you It wants to reform you We don't want to punish you at all, we just want to re-educate you " This, for the prisoner, was a meaningful change "It was my first glimmer of hope I felt finally there might be a way out I wasn't feeling so hopelessly alone any more The official had actually shown some human quality "
>
> This shift in tactics invariably has a tremendous effect, it can be a crucial step in the extraction of a confession and in the over-all "reform" The prisoner views it as a potential turning point in his destiny he sees the first hope of a way out of the heretofore insoluble morass of confusion and misery. He feels grateful to the Government for its leniency in stopping the accusatory interrogations, for improving the attitudes of those around him, and for bettering the conditions of his existence He will eagerly do anything that is required of him to avoid a return to his former plight and to work toward his release He will even take the initiative in anticipating his captors' desires and do everything possible to identify with their point of view The prison officials recognize this, and utilize these feelings effectively in stimulating his confession and initiating the organized "re-education" phase They give him friendly advice and books to read, in a new spirit of working together toward a common goal [p. 180]

Invoking the behavior control of a norm, in place of fate control, should also result in an improved adjustment to a state of deprivation In the following observations of Bettelheim (1943), although it is possible that some additional mechanisms are also in effect, the prisoners' attempts to instate norms for regulating their behavior may be interpreted as a means of reducing some of the fateful and arbitrary incursions into their lives

> Often the Gestapo would enforce nonsensical rules, originating in the whims of one of the guards They were usually forgotten as soon as formulated, but there were always some old prisoners who would continue to follow these rules and try to enforce them on others long after the Gestapo had forgotten about them Once, for instance, a guard on inspecting the prisoners' apparel found that the shoes of some of them were dirty on the inside He ordered all prisoners to wash their shoes inside and out with water and soap The heavy shoes treated this way became hard as stone The order was never repeated, and many prisoners did not even execute it when given Nevertheless there were some old prisoners who not only continued to wash the inside of their shoes everyday but cursed all others who did not do so as negligent and dirty [p 450]

Another aspect of the environment's fate control that may afflict the deprived person is related to *time perspective* (Lewin, 1948*b*) Uncertainty about how long an unpleasant state may last is likely to increase conflict, hence costs   That fate control in nonvoluntary relationships entails an indefiniteness about the duration of deprivation is suggested by Cohen's (1953) comment on experiences in German concentration camps   "More serious than one's lack of liberty was that *one did not know how long one was to be imprisoned* and that nothing one did would ever result in shortening the duration of one's imprisonment" [p 128, author's italics].   Bondy (1943) made similar observations on German internment camps in general

> One important factor in the destructive effect of all internment camps is the *"indeterminate sentence"*   I mean by this that the prisoner does not have the slightest idea how long his internment will last.   He always hopes for release   The war prisoners have hopes that an exchange of prisoners will take place, or that the Allies will conquer the country, or that the war will stop soon   Refugees hope that permission for immigration will soon arrive   This uncertainty about the duration of the imprisonment is probably what unnerves the men most   Any other situation, no matter how bad, can be endured better than a disagreeable situation of uncertain duration [p. 464].

Concurring results were obtained by Farber (1944) from his carefully conducted interviews with prisoners in the Iowa State Penitentiary   Again, one of the variables most closely associated with the degree of suffering of a prisoner was the indefiniteness of the prisoner's knowledge about when he would be released.

There appear to be two quite different types of adjustment to this temporal uncertainty   When the probability of ever attaining any improved outcomes is perceived to be quite low (i.e., when own power vis-à-vis external fate control is seen as very low), the least costly adjustment may involve a complex of adaptations such as devaluating the better outcomes and drastically shortening one's time perspective to a moment-to-moment or day-to-day focus   The latter reduces fantasy contemplations of future good, but unattainable, outcomes and along with the devaluation serves to lower the CL and reduce dissatisfaction

However, when the probability that one's outcomes may be improved is perceived to be relatively high, then another kind of adjustment may be possible.   This kind of adjustment entails a lengthening of the time perspective so that the present infra-CL outcomes are perceived to represent only a very small proportion of the total relevant outcomes, many of which, particularly those in the future, are supra-CL.   Making these outcomes salient is apparently not so unpleasant if one feels that the power one can mobilize holds some promise of attaining them

The viability of many oppressed religious and political groups has often been attributed to this evaluation of their present plight "under the aspect of eternity." Lewin (1948b) illustrates this point with his observations on the conduct of the Zionists in Germany shortly after Hitler came to power

> The great majority of Jews in Germany had believed for decades that the pogroms of Czarist Russia "couldn't happen here." When Hitler came to power, therefore, the social ground on which they stood suddenly was swept from under their feet. Naturally, many became desperate and committed suicide, with nothing to stand on, they could see no future life worth living.
>
> The time perspective of the numerically small Zionist group, on the other hand, had been different. Although they too had not considered pogroms in Germany a probability, they had been aware of their possibility. For decades they had tried to study their own sociological problems realistically, advocating and promoting a program that looked far ahead. In other words, they had a time perspective which included a psychological past of surviving adverse conditions for thousands of years and a meaningful and inspiring goal for the future. As the result of such a time perspective, this group showed high morale—despite a present which was judged by them to be no less foreboding than by others. Instead of inactivity and encystment in the face of a difficult situation—a result of such limited time perspective as that characteristic of the unemployed—the Zionists with a long-range and realistic time perspective showed initiative and organized planning. It is worth noticing how much the high morale of this small group contributed to sustaining the morale of a large section of the non-Zionist Jews of Germany. Here, as in many other cases, a small group with high morale became a rallying point for larger masses [pp 104–105]

## 10.4 Attack Upon the Barriers

As noted earlier, the two major means of adapting to deprivation in order to avoid frustration are (1) dropping the CL and (2) finding means of achieving the unattained outcomes. Clearly the relative efficiency of these two kinds of adjustment depend greatly on the objective chances of success in achieving the blocked outcomes. If the objective situation promises a relatively good chance of success in attaining the outcomes, then an aggressive assault on the social barrier might yield both the increased reward of the outcomes and a reduction in frustration costs. This response to frustration occurs so widely and has been documented so frequently (cf particularly the pioneering studies of Dollard, et al, 1939) that we will not dwell on the point, except to mention that the aggression may be strengthened by the creation and maintenance of coalitions, alliances, and the like (Wright, 1943, Pepitone and Reichling, 1955). In his study of American soldiers in Chinese prison camps during the Korean War Schein (1956) describes a number of devices by which the prisoners covertly maintained solidarity and at least symbolic resistance to their captors    One of these devices was the humorous use of esoteric language

> . the prisoners found numerous ways to obey the letter but not the spirit of the Chinese demands    For example, during public self-criticism sessions they would often emphasize the wrong words in the sentence, thus making the whole ritual ridiculous. "I am sorry I called Comrade Wong *a no-good son-of-a-bitch*"   Another favorite device was to promise never to "get caught" committing a certain crime in the future    Such devices were effective because even those Chinese who knew English were not sufficiently acquainted with idiom and slang to detect subtle ridicule [pp. 159–160]

When the aggression and resistance are thus socially shared by members of the deprived group, not only are the chances of achieving the unattained outcomes improved but an additional source of outcomes becomes available  by sharing their hostility toward the oppressors, the members may experience both an increase in affiliative outcomes (mutual respect and affection) and a "rising moral pride" (Rado, 1950) from having repudiated the impulse to give in to their captors   These gratifications may be sufficient to sustain the members even when the objective probabilities of their being able to crash the social barriers (escaping, revolting) are extremely low

There is, however, one negative aspect to attempts to achieve the unattained outcomes.  For the attempts to be undertaken, the outcomes must be brought into focus as the goals of the endeavor   Furthermore, as there is some success, the perceived realm of own and friendly power is extended   Both have the effect of raising CL)  If there is not a corresponding improvement in level of outcomes actually attained there will be an increase, at least temporarily, in frustration  Thus, when there is little success forthcoming, improvement programs may produce greater discontent than ever)  As a reaction to this heightened frustration (and a secondary effect of the unsuccessful program), there is likely to be disillusionment with the power one can mobilize and apathetic reactions to further attempts to do so   This may account for the very high proportion of Negro college students who in the late thirties endorsed the view that, "The trouble with Negro business is that Negroes have never learned to organize or work together" (Davis, 1937)

Thibaut (1950) made an experimental study of the differential consequences of success and failure in attempts to improve the outcomes of an entire group    In each session two groups were created, and one was consistently assigned good tasks while the second performed related but servile ones (e g , holding the target and picking up the bags in a beanbag game). In this situation, in which the deprived persons could hardly avoid instigations from the withheld outcomes, there was a striking increase in the total volume of their communication toward the more privileged group This is tentatively interpreted as serving as a kind of substitute for actual locomotion into the forbidden activities.

After considerable treatment of this sort, each underprivileged group was stimulated to ask the experimenter to improve their conditions In some cases he acquiesced, and in other instances he rejected the request. When a group was successful in "influencing" the experimenter to grant better outcomes, there was a marked increase in the expression of aggression toward the previously favored persons This suggests that successful action causes a general expansion in the perceived area of own control (and friendly power), with a consequent release of hostility that had previously been inhibited [There is considerable evidence that aggressive responses are more restrained, the greater the perceived power of the frustrating agent (e.g , Graham, et al , 1951, Thibaut and Riecken, 1955)]. There is some indication that the unsuccessful deprived group adopted a "sour grapes" attitude toward the outcomes obtained by the more privileged group. At the end of the experiment, the unsuccessful deprived persons reported much less often than the successful ones that they had wanted to be in the favored group because of its good outcomes.

When the *subjective* probability of successful assault upon the restraining barriers becomes near-zero, one common adjustment to deprivation is self-aggression. Indeed, under extreme conditions, such as those described by Bettelheim (1943), in which the slightest aggression toward the prison guards would mean death to the aggressor, a dependable and deeply indurated pattern of self-aggression may be the necessary mode of survival

Even in considerably less extreme situations, for example, that faced by ethnic minorities, what appears to be self-aggression has been observed Lewin (1948c) has discussed this at length in his paper on "Self-hatred among Jews" The phenomenon seems to be prevalent among all ethnic minorities, but particularly intense among Negroes One well-documented result of Negro self-aggression is the development within the Negro community of a prestige-grading by skin shade —the lighter the shade the higher the prestige The Clarks (1952) have shown that this rejection of dark skin begins to develop early in the life of the Negro child. Their data show that even as early as the age of three years the Negro child prefers to play with a white doll instead of a colored one.

To some degree, self-aggression may occur in all frustrating situations (Dollard, et al, 1939) but particularly where direct aggression is inhibited by the status or power of the instigator (Thibaut and Riecken, 1955a) or merely by the absence of a communication channel to the instigator (Thibaut and Coules, 1952)

The circumvention of the social barrier, for instance, in racial "passing," and the discovery of substitute goals may also be forms of adjustment to deprived states  However, for racial passing at least, there are difficulties that attend the adjustment.  As Simpson and Yinger (1953) remark

> There is the danger of "discovery," which might destroy the whole pattern of adjustment that the individual had achieved  There is the problem of relationship to one's old friends and community  To break contact completely is a painful experience.  Sutherland cites the case of a Negro brother and sister who passed, but who were deeply upset when their mother became ill, and later died, and they were unable to visit her for fear of revealing their identity  Some persons who pass develop a sense of guilt that they have deserted "their group"  They cannot completely break off identification with it  Some members of their former community may look with approval and encouragement at their decision (happy that they are avoiding some of the hardships of their former status or glad that they are putting something over on the whites)  Others, however, may strongly disapprove of their action, and so give those who pass a sense of fear or guilt.  Passing is largely limited to urban communities, where one's former status can more readily be hidden.
>
> Despite these difficulties, passing is for a few members of minority groups a decisive way to avoid some of the penalties of their status.  Doubtless many more use it temporarily, for specific purposes, than attempt permanent crossing into the dominant group [p 208].

## 10.5  ADAPTABILITY TO NEW SITUATIONS

The forms of adjustment to deprivation that we outlined earlier may represent the least costly ways of surviving the exigencies of the situation to which the person is constrained  The learning of many of these forms of adjustment (e g , learning to live with fate control, how to lower the CL, how to inhibit aggression) are useful in moving from one nonvoluntary relationship to another  Thus Stouffer, et al (1949), describe the relative ease with which Negro recruits adapted to the army in World War II.  They point out that

> .    entering the Army meant adjusting to a system in which, to a large degree, status (and its accompanying rewards) was "ascribed" rather than "achieved," and in which individuals were subjected to authoritarian

controls which were foreign to their experience and galling to them, and finally a system which many individuals entered at a point relatively lower on the status ladder than their corresponding position in civilian life. Much of this analysis, however, is less applicable to the Negro enlisted man  Negroes were intimately acquainted with a social system in which their position was largely ascribed, where their opportunities for achieving status were sharply limited, and in which they were in many respects subjected to authoritarian control on the part of the group holding the superior ascribed status  On the basis of past civilian experiences, Negro men already knew a set of protective adjustments not too dissimilar from those which white soldiers had to learn.  Moreover, the civilian past of most Negroes was not in such sharp contrast to their Army experiences as to invite unfavorable comparisons as a source of discontent with the Army  For more Negroes than whites, the Army was no worse and often much better than their civilian situation in the type of work it gave them to do, in the economic returns it made, and in the amount of individual status it accorded [p 543].

However, as adaptations to a "free" life in the "outside world," the characteristic adjustments to deprivation are far from ideal  Evaluate the following learning experience in an American prison as training for good citizenship (Hayner and Ash, 1940)

> Deciding to "make the best of it," the new prisoner usually undertakes some form of self-culture  As he adjusts to the dull monotony of prison life, however, there is likely to be a "decline of profitable reflection" and a weakening of the attempts at self-improvement  Daydreaming becomes more frequent  "Prison stupor" or becoming "stir simple" are common end results  As the prisoner grows "con-wise," however, he learns that things denied him by the prison administration may be available through conniving  These *sub rosa* activities provide variety, help break the deteriorating monotony, and constitute another type of accommodation [p 579]

For the prisoner in a concentration camp the adjustments to camp life are even less suitable preparation for adult life in a democracy  Cohen (1953) compares the existence inside the camp with that outside

> In normal life the adult enjoys a certain measure of independence, within the limits set by society he has a considerable measure of liberty  Nobody orders him when and what to eat, where to take up his residence or what to wear, neither to take his rest on Sunday nor when to have his bath, nor when to go to bed  He is not beaten during his work, he need not ask permission to go to the W C , he is not continually kept on the run, he does not feel that the work he is doing is silly or childish, he is not confined behind barbed wire, he is not counted twice a day or more  he is not left unprotected against the actions of his fellow citizens, he looks after his family and the education of the children
> How altogether different was the life of the concentration-camp pris-

oner! What to do during each part of the day was arranged for him, and decisions were made about him from which there was no appeal  He was impotent and suffered from bedwetting, and because of his chronic diarrhea he soiled his underwear  He had not a cent in his pocket  though from time to time he might be given a "premium note" by way of pocket money, and he paid no taxes  His interest did not go beyond the question  How shall I win through? which meant  How shall I obtain more food and get into a tolerable labor group?  This way of life and this attitude toward life cannot, I think, be viewed as anything but regression [pp 173–174]

Of prisoners in similar circumstances, Bettelheim (1943) concludes

They did not admit it directly, but from their talk it was clear that they hardly believed they would ever return to this outer world because they felt that only a cataclysmic event—a world war and world revolution—could free them, and even then they doubted that they would be able to adapt to this new life  They seemed aware of what had happened to them while growing older in the camp  They realized that they had adapted themselves to the life in the camp and that this process was coexistent with a basic change in their personality [pp 437–438].

## SUMMARY

Relationships are said to be *nonvoluntary* when an individual is constrained to a relationship in which his outcomes are relatively poor and/or is excluded from alternative relationships in which his outcomes are relatively good  Furthermore, for the relationship to be nonvoluntary, the outcomes in the alternative relationship must be sufficiently favorable and sufficiently salient so that the individual finds himself below CL

In stating that the individual is constrained to a relationship and/or excluded from alternative ones it is meant that the other persons are able to impose heavy costs on the individual if he tries to abandon his present relationship and/or enter another (more attractive) relationship  In other words, other persons are able to exercise fate control over the individual to enforce a nonvoluntary relationship.  As more and more of the individual's alternatives are made unavailable to him, his CL$_{alt}$ is lowered and consequently the power over him of other persons in the relationship is increased  In the extreme case, when it becomes impossible for the individual to leave the relationship, the other person's power over him is limited only by that person's talents and taste for torture

The effects on the individual of being in a nonvoluntary relationship are discussed from three points of view

(1) In a nonvoluntary relationship the *objective deprivations* may be considerable These deprivations may be relatively gross, as in the brutality of a concentration camp, or relatively subtle, as in the sensory deprivation and loss of "space of free movement" that prisoners may be forced to endure

(2) Objective deprivation does not, however, seem to correspond at all exactly to the degree of experienced displeasure. In order to account for this, it seems necessary to evaluate the person's experienced outcomes in relation to his CL. When the person's CL is anchored in superior outcomes, the state of deprivation is also a state of *frustration* Adjustment to such frustration may be made by lowering the CL, and this may be done by two interrelated means (*a*) by devaluating the outcomes believed to exist in the unavailable alternative relationships or (*b*) by decreasing the salience of the favorable outcomes in these relationships

(3) A third aspect of many nonvoluntary relationships is that the social environment may exercise massive and arbitrary fate control over the individual In an effort to escape this kind of control (the nature of which was described in Chapter 7) the individual may attempt to convert the situation into one in which "behavior-controlling" norms permit him to respond more adaptively

When, in a nonvoluntary relationship, the objective likelihood that the person will be able to achieve the unattained favorable outcomes is low, dropping the CL is probably the most effective means of reducing the frustration On the other hand, when the objective chances of success are good, then an attack on the social barriers that block attainment of the favorable outcomes is clearly an effective adaptation The pooling of power by forming coalitions with other members of the nonvoluntary relationship promotes the success of such an attack, but, if improved outcomes are not attained, frustration will increase, at least temporarily When the subjective probability of successfully assaulting the barriers approaches zero, self-aggression commonly develops

The chapter concludes with a brief discussion of the effects of being subjected to a nonvoluntary relationship on the person's ability to adapt to new situations

PART II

*Complex Relationships*

# 11.

# *Interdependence in Larger Groups*

Although, in Chapter 10, we have already begun to depart from an exclusive focus on the dyad, there has been no attempt to analyze and evaluate the effects of increasing group size on the functioning of groups In the present chapter we have attempted an analysis of some of the complexities introduced into the relationships of interdependence and power among group members when group size increases At the beginning of each of the following two chapters we discuss briefly the effects of increasing size on status relationships (Chapter 12) and on conformity behavior (Chapter 13)

## 11.1 PATTERNS OF INTERDEPENDENCE

We address ourselves to the question· what difference does it make to introduce a third, fourth, or fifth person into the analysis of social interaction? Any answers that we can give to this question will be subjected to this discipline, that they should be derived, insofar as possible, from the concepts and theory developed to this point for the dyad In making the transition from the dyad to larger groups, we have especially considered the *triad*  The consequences of the dyad-to-triad transition are used as a basis for speculating about the effects of increasing size in general

A triad is said to exist when three individuals are observed to interact on successive occasions  These three are seen to come together repeatedly or to be in communication often, conversing, exchanging products, and so on  The repeated coappearance of the three would be perhaps the most convincing evidence of the existence of a triad, but this is not a strictly necessary condition for a triadic relationship

(Person A might converse with B, B with C, and C with A. Cases of this sort are discussed later.)

Like any other group, a triad is viable only if all of its members are dependent upon its continued existence—that is, only if membership in the triad puts each member above his $CL_{alt}$.) It is implicit in this statement that dependence upon the triad means being dependent upon *both* of the other persons—upon their joint actions of "belonging to" the triad. (Any extensive dependence upon either one of them singly will be reflected in the values assigned to the *best available alternative* (since a dyadic subgroup may be a competing alternative relationship to the parent triad) and thus reduce the dependence upon the triad.) Another way of putting this point is to ask who, in a triad, possesses the fate control over person A represented by the difference between his outcomes in the triad and those in the best alternative available to him. The answer is that the other members, B and C, *jointly* possess this power. Any improvement in A's available alternatives or any impairment of the ability of B and C to deliver acceptable outcomes to A may threaten the continued integrity of the triad by a possibly critical reduction in A's dependence on it.

This raises a problem that does not exist in the dyad: when does a given group cease to exist (or become a different group) through loss of members? Clearly, if either person leaves a dyad, the dyad no longer exists. Toward the other end of the size scale, if one person leaves a fifty-man social club, we would not be likely to say that the club has become a different one or that the original one (with him in it) no longer exists. As the group becomes progressively smaller, its identity seems to become increasingly dependent on maintaining each one of its members.

We do not propose to make any serious assault on the classical problem of identity. Let us merely suggest that if the group's resources enable it to withstand the loss of several members, without very dramatic changes in its structure or functioning or in the outcomes achieved by the remaining persons, we might decide to consider this collectivity as maintaining its identity even though there are minor fluctuations in the size and composition of the group. In the case of a triad, for example, if one person, C, is essentially a "hanger-on," to whose presence the other two, A and B, are indifferent, a major portion of the interchange that constitutes this group (i.e., that between A and B) would be unaffected by C's withdrawal. True, the group would no longer be a triad, but for many purposes we would find it reasonable to identify the A–B dyad with the prior A–B–C triad.

## 11 1.1 THE POTENTIALITY OF SUBGROUPINGS

An obvious property of the three-man group is that it may break up into a dyad and the third person, or "isolate" The mathematical possibility of a partition into a pair and an individual is not important, of course, unless there are tendencies toward this state on the part of some of the members of the triad Two rather different cases of this sort may be distinguished (1) member A prefers the dyad A–B to the triad A–B–C, but B does not share this preference (i e., A's choice is not reciprocated), (2) both A and B are indifferent (or nearly so), as between the A–B dyad and the A–B–C triad, and the triad exists only because of C's preference for it over whatever alternative arrangements are available to him (Remember that the triad will not exist if both A and B definitely prefer the A–B dyad ) Both of these cases should be considered in contrast to the situation in which the best alternative relationships for all three members are those involving persons outside the triad

The first case means that the triad contains for one person a potential pair relationship which is highly desirable but from which he is excluded Of course, such relationships may exist for a member of a dyad, but at least the other members of these unattainable relationships are not *immediately present* The triad, then, affords this person a means of associating with someone with whom he would prefer to establish a dyad It would seem that this would complicate interaction within the triad, since the person would act not only out of regard to the three-way relationship but also with an eye toward establishing the pair relationship which he prefers.

The second case raises both theoretical and methodological problems. The members of the mutually attractive pair are likely to fluctuate between preference for the triad and for the dyad ). Accordingly, they may sometimes actively avoid the third person or, even when he is present, engage in an occasional tête-à-tête which rather vividly demonstrates their near-indifference to his contributions It hardly needs emphasizing that being excluded in this fashion has deleterious effects upon the third person's self-regard and conceptions of his power in the relationship. (We note here that this phenomenon is not wholly unknown in dyadic interaction one member of a pair may from time to time prefer solitary activity to the social interaction and may withdraw to this *best alternative*. The wife who finds that her husband occasionally "goes into his shell" can attest to the effect of this upon one's self-regard ) Of course, a person is always likely to encounter exclusion from relationships, but perhaps the main point is that exclusion may be more difficult to tolerate and dismiss when effected by persons with whom one has recently interacted or when there is fluctuation between rejection and acceptance.

Mutually attracted pairs within a triad create a problem in measuring the cohesiveness of the group (how highly interdependent the members are). A triad is, of course, not very cohesive if most of its interdependence derives from the relationship between two of its members. This poses no problem if the interdependence of the triad is measured with each person's best available alternative as a base line. In this case the particular dyad composed of two of the members constitutes their best available alternative, and the triad is cohesive only to the degree that it provides outcomes superior to those obtainable in this dyad.

A problem does arise, however, when cohesiveness is assessed by sociometric methods which require each person to indicate his liking for other *individuals*. It is traditional to assume that a group's cohesiveness will steadily increase as a higher and higher proportion of its sociometric choices are directed to members of the group rather than to nonmembers. This is proper, however, only on the further assumption that the favorable outcomes which underlie each choice can be obtained *only from the group being considered* rather than from alternative relationships. If the outcomes are attainable from alternative relationships, the choice does not reflect the individual's dependence upon the group. When such alternative relationships exist as subgroups within the larger group being considered, the cohesiveness of the larger group may be reduced. Muldoon (1955) provides some evidence for this effect on cohesiveness in his study of forty-two classes of high school students. Sociometric choices were obtained from members of each class. In addition, ratings of the cohesiveness of each class were made by the component members and, independently, by the teachers. The relevant finding for our purpose is that rated cohesiveness declined significantly with increased concentration of sociometric choices. As the choices are restricted to a smaller and smaller subgroup within the total class, the subgroup probably supplants the class as the focus of dependence. Martin, Darley, and Gross (1952) found that indices of mutuality of choice (actual number of reciprocated choices in relation to the number to be expected by chance) were not correlated with indices of cohesiveness based on the proportion of choices directed within the group rather than outside. These authors conjecture that ". . . mutuality, when it reaches a certain level, might reflect divisive rather than cohesive tendencies within a group. . . . Intercommunication breaks down; cliques appear. Instead of a group, there is an agglomeration of discrete sub-groups, the members of each of which may have intimate alliances with persons outside the main group" [p. 551].

This effect has been taken into account by Festinger, Schachter, and Back (1950) in estimating the cohesiveness of student housing groups from sociometric data. They began their analysis by conventionally indexing cohesiveness by the ratio frequency of in-group choices to frequency of total choices. On the grounds that mutual choices may reflect in part a tendency to subgroup formation, they proposed that an improved estimate of cohesiveness should involve a correction to reduce the weight of mutual choices. Lacking an empirical basis for deciding just how large this correction should be, they selected the mid-point between unit weight and no weight at all. This assumes that part of the good outcomes motivating reciprocated choices are not obtainable outside the group (Their revised index then becomes the ratio frequency of nonmutual minus one half frequency of mutual choices within the group *to* frequency of total choices)

Festinger, Schachter, and Back reasoned further that if their revised index represented an improved measure of cohesiveness then its use should enable them to make better predictions of relationships derived from their social theory, namely that in groups of higher cohesiveness there should be manifested greater conformity to group norms. In one housing community (composed of several "courts") they had empirical grounds for believing that there existed group norms about a tenant organization, whereas in an adjacent housing community (composed of several apartment buildings) no such norms appeared to exist. Stated somewhat differently, there was evidence that in the first community the dominant attitudes within each "court" represented a consensus based on prior social communication and influence, whereas in the second community any such dominant attitude about the tenant organization was based on the chance allocation of like-minded persons to the same buildings, each person being relatively uncontaminated by social influence from within the building

Hence the authors predicted a negative correlation between the cohesiveness of "courts" and the percentage of deviates from the dominant attitude within "courts" in the first community and a zero correlation between the corresponding variables in the second community. The obtained rank-order correlations were $-53$ for the first community and $-20$ for the second. When they substituted the revised index for cohesiveness (reducing the weight of mutual choices), the obtained correlations became $-74$ and $-27$, respectively, the first significant at the two per cent level and the second not significant.

### 11.1.2 DIFFERENTIATION OF FUNCTION

In any group it is possible for the various members to make qualitatively different contributions within the group. As group size increases from dyadic to triadic and larger relationships, a number of modes of raising a member's rewards in relation to his costs that are not possible in the dyad begin to appear. Let us consider the triad in some detail to illustrate these emergent possibilities. Again, as in the earlier analysis of the dyad, we begin with the problem of explaining the existence of the A–B–C triad. How is it that any given member, A, can be better off in the A–B–C relationship than in other relationships? The dyads A–B and A–C are especially interesting to consider as alternatives, since the persons involved are the same as those in the triad.

Member A is better off in the A–B–C relationship than in other relationships if his rewards there are higher in relation to the costs he incurs. This applies, for example, if the value of his behaviors to the others is greater in the triad, thus enabling them to return greater rewards to him while still being better off themselves. Similarly, their behaviors, which may be more rewarding to him in the triadic situation, would permit him to return greater rewards to them, or if his costs were somehow reduced by the triad, he would be able to deliver more rewards to them, while enabling them in turn to increase his rewards. Moreover, if their costs were lower in the triad, they could also deliver more rewards to him. Several specific examples may serve to clarify some of the possibilities.

JOINT COST-CUTTING Two persons may be able to cut A's costs when one alone cannot do so. For example, the adolescent girl, conflicted about sex, may be willing to go on dates with two boys but not with one. "Three's a crowd" if she's interested in sexual activities, but "there's safety in numbers" if she wants their company but not their advances.

A similar possibility is that two persons may cut each other's costs enough to enable them to interact with the third one. Two girls may be greatly concerned about visiting a fortune-teller alone but may be willing to do so together.

JOINT CONSUMPTION If A's behavioral products are such that the other members can simultaneously enjoy them without interference, then the total value of his product is increased in relation to his costs, and the others may be able together to provide sufficient rewards in return to make the relationship a viable one. For example, a father may take two children on a picnic with very little more effort than taking one. Or, if he can then get each of them to mow half the lawn, a trading agreement may be possible for the three of them, whereas no pair could have worked one out. A common example is the performer-audience relationship: the performer's jokes or songs may be enjoyed by each member of a large audience. In return, each can applaud or pay an admission fee, the cumulative effects of which may reimburse the performer for his costs. It is possible, of course, that the performer's costs will increase somewhat with the increasing size of his audience,[*] but larger audiences are still desirable if the rate of this increase is less than the rate of increase in total return which increasing size makes possible.

MUTUAL FACILITATION OF ENJOYMENT. A further possibility is that members of the audience (e.g., two persons "consuming" the behavior of a third) may increase each other's enjoyment of the performance by mutual facilitation of appreciative and consummatory responses. The effects of comedy are probably particularly dependent upon social interactions within the audience.

EMERGENT PRODUCTS. The behavioral products of B and C, taken separately, may be of little value to A, but, together, they may be greatly amplified. For example, their respective realms of knowledge may be partial and incomplete but complementary, so that B and C together can provide A with valuable advice and information about problem solutions; or, B's praise of A may be greatly increased in reward value if delivered in the presence of C.

SEQUENTIAL PATTERNS OF INTERDEPENDENCE. A pattern totally unknown in the dyad (hence unique to the triad and larger groups) is one in which A directs his contributions (in provision of rewards or cutting of costs) to one person and receives his outcomes from another. Consider this case: A has a supply of currency which is of value only to B, B has a different currency of value only to C, and C has a third type of currency of value only to A. This sets the conditions for the development of a circular pattern of currency exchange in which A agrees to pass some of his currency to B if B, by passing some of his to C, can induce C to provide some of his to A. Any of these links might, of course, consist of cost cutting rather than the provision of rewards for the next man in the chain. In general, the situation is one in which A is dependent upon C (or potentially so) but has nothing to offer C in return. There does exist, however, a third person who acts as an intermediary. In a sense, this intermediary (or so he appears from A's point of view) is somehow able to transform A's product into something of value to C.

---

[*] Gibb (1951) finds that increasing percentages of group members report feelings of threat or inhibition as the size of the group increases.

In this example the problems of differentiation of function and attribution of responsibility for viability of the triad seem to reach their climax  In most of the earlier examples, as viewed by one person, the other two make fairly similar and equivalent contributions to group viability.  Here, however, A gives to B but receives from C  We suspect the importance of B to the relationship may be seriously underestimated by A  Not having first-hand knowledge of the kinds of contributions B makes to C's continued activity in the relationship, A is likely to have quite inaccurate notions about B's replaceability. It is also intriguing to wonder where A will localize blame for any malfunctioning on C's part—whether with B, whom A pays to guarantee payoffs from C, or with C, who is obviously most directly responsible for the outcomes A receives.

## 11 2   POWER RELATIONS IN LARGER GROUPS

The patterns of interdependence described in the foregoing section will have implications for the amount of power available to the group for exercise over its members  To the degree that outcomes achieved while belonging to the group are superior to those available in the best alternative relationship, the group acquires fate control over its members  However, the patterning of power relationships *within* the group requires further analysis

In any relationship the degree to which there is correspondence between the outcomes of the various members affects the use of their power over one another. (It is unnecessary for the members of a relationship to exercise power if their outcomes are in perfect correspondence over the interaction matrix )  For example, individual A should be indifferent between entering two dyadic relationships which provide equally good outcomes, in both of which there is perfect correspondence between his and the other member's outcomes, even though within these relationships the other member has different degrees of fate control over him  In a relationship in which there is perfect correspondence, one member may have more power than another, hence his actions may be less subject to interpersonal control than those of the other, but in pursuing his own interests the stronger member will maximally benefit the weaker member

On the other hand, (to the degree that there is noncorrespondence of outcomes, the use of interpersonal power enters the scene as a means of maximizing outcomes) that is, as a means available to the possessor of power of obtaining more enactments of the kind of interaction he finds most satisfactory.

In the triad, as in the dyad, it may be true that the best outcomes of all three individuals coincide perfectly, or there may be only partial correspondence of good outcomes or little or no correspondence at all, with no cell in the matrix containing good outcomes for more than one person. We now consider, successively, these three cases of perfect, partial, and low correspondence and examine their consequences for the exercise of power within the relationship. In the subsequent section on coalitions we take up the further case that makes its appearance in the triad and larger groups: high correspondence of outcomes for only a subset of the total group.

### 11.2.1 PERFECT CORRESPONDENCE OF OUTCOMES

In situations of perfect correspondence in the triad all three individuals attain their maximum outcomes from the same joint activities.

TABLE 11-1

AN EXAMPLE OF PERFECT CORRESPONDENCE OF OUTCOMES IN A TRIAD IN
WHICH EACH PERSON CAN EXERCISE BEHAVIOR CONTROL OVER
THE OTHER TWO

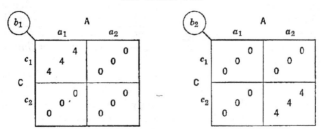

An example is shown in Table 11-1. The outcome matrix for a triad could be represented as a three-dimensional solid, such as that used in Table 9-5. However, for simplicity we use here two two-dimensional matrices, the left one giving the various outcomes when B enacts $b_1$ from his behavioral repertoire and the right one giving the outcomes when he enacts $b_2$. The outcome in the upper right corner of each cell, following our earlier convention, is the one received by the person indicated at the top of the matrix (person A), and the outcome in the lower left corner of each cell is the one received by the person at the side of the matrix (person C). Person B's outcomes are given in the center of each cell. Shown in Table 11-1 is an extreme case of interdependency in which the outcomes of all individuals are dependent upon the actions of all. Each person can exercise behavior control over the remaining two. This might occur when there are strong interference or facilitation effects, for example, when everyone in a group must get into the right mood if any of them is to enjoy the interaction or the experience they happen to be sharing  This would also represent the situation in which a task places alternating conjunctive requirements (section 9 2 1) upon the activities of the various group members, for example, first, they must all pull together, then they must all release together and so forth  In cases of this sort, if any member of the group fails to coordinate his actions with the rest, the entire membership suffers

The problem here is a simple one, since no conflict of interest is involved  All may achieve good outcomes simultaneously, and under optimal conditions all that is required is a decision about what to do first  However, if for any reason there is some likelihood of any individual's not being *able* to coordinate with the others, then increasing the size of the group is a serious matter  If we may assume that on each occasion in which coordination is required there is a certain fixed probability that any given person will fail to coordinate, then with increasing size there will be a direct proportional increase in the frequency of failure of coordination

Inability to make appropriate adjustments may stem from distractions or from strong instigations that evoke inappropriate behavior  This seems to be what Simmel (1902) had in mind when he commented on the heightened difficulty of getting three (as contrasted with two) people to share the same mood

> There is no relationship so complete between three that each individual may not, under certain circumstances, be regarded by the other two as an intruder, even if it is only to the extent of sharing in certain moods, which can develop their concentration and timid tenderness only with undisturbed glance from eye to eye  It may also be observed how extraordinarily rare and difficult it is for three people, even in the case of a visit to a museum or in the presence of a landscape, to come into a really united state of feeling, which, however, may occur with relative ease between two [pp 45–46].

Failure to pay attention, inability to make appropriate discriminations about the behavior of one's colleagues, and failure to grasp the nature of the interdependency can also account for incoordination. Some of these factors seem to help explain the incompetence of groups as compared with individuals in an experiment by McCurdy and Lambert (1952). Twenty-three individuals and thirty-five three-person groups worked at a task set by a modification of the Yerkes multiple-choice apparatus  The apparatus consisted of six two-position switches wired so that a light appeared when the total pattern of switch positions corresponded to that on a master control pattern. Performance was scored on the basis of the number of correct patterns completed within a given time period. Each subject who worked individually was responsible for all six switches, whereas in the three-person groups each subject controlled two switches. The conjunctive task requirements made the group members highly interdependent, since only when the total pattern of positions was correct could the group proceed to a new setting.

The results showed individuals to be significantly more effective ✓ than groups. McCurdy and Lambert attribute this result to the relatively high probability that a group would contain at least one member who was inattentive to the experimental instructions which advised the subjects of the nature of the interdependency among the various switching operations and about an easily committed error of incoordination; and indeed the data show that although only seven of the twenty-three individually tested subjects gave evidence of inattentiveness to the instructions twenty-nine of the thirty-five groups contained at least one member who was inattentive.

Because of the proliferating problems of coordination with increase in size, group norms that specify the behaviors necessary for coordination gain in urgency as groups become larger. At the same time, norms may require more time and effort to achieve as group size increases. Evidence on the slow and arduous process of gaining consensus as group size increases is presented by South (1927) and Hare (1952). A further problem is created when large groups perform tasks requiring a high degree of member coordination. If the member has to make simultaneous adjustments to several other members, his capacities for receiving, processing, and storing relevant information may be seriously overloaded. Sometimes it is possible to reduce such demands on the members by simplifying the communication network: by converting the situation into one with many overlapping dyadic relationships, all of which have one member in common. This enables each person to coordinate his actions with those of only one other person. Examples are the cheerleader and the coxswain.

We should note and emphasize a major exception to the generalization that the greater the number of people, the less likely they are to be able to share the same mood or enter into *synchronized* sets. If the actions of each person are a powerful instigation to a similar (or otherwise appropriate) set for others, then there can be a snowballing effect with increasing tendencies for all members of the collectivity to enact the same behavioral set. The more people who enact a given set, the stronger the instigation to others to adopt the same or related

act. This is a mechanism commonly employed to explain the development of a monomaniacal crowd or mob. (For a summary of this
literature, see Brown, 1954.)

### 11.2.2 PARTIAL CORRESPONDENCE OF OUTCOMES

There are many possible patterns in which there is only partial
correspondence among the various members' best outcomes. Consider
first the case in which there is a circular pattern of *behavior* control:
A has behavior control over B, B over C, and C over A. It is possible,
though not necessary, that in this pattern all individuals attain high
outcomes in the same cell, as shown in Table 11–2. The problems created by this situation do not seem markedly different from those exem-

TABLE 11–2

AN EXAMPLE OF PARTIAL CORRESPONDENCE OF OUTCOMES IN A TRIAD IN
WHICH EACH PERSON CAN EXERCISE BEHAVIOR CONTROL OVER ONE OTHER
PERSON, IN A CIRCULAR PATTERN

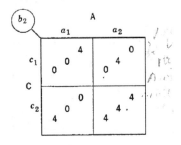

plified in Table 11–1, but it does seem likely that the process of reaching the *dominant* solution (i.e., a cell in which the outcomes are
higher for all three individuals than in other cells) would be more
dependable and straightforward in the present example. The reason
for this lies in the fact that in the earlier case each person's effect upon
one of his colleagues is conditional upon the action of his other colleague. Of his own accord, each man can dependably only *reduce*
another person's outcomes. If A's outcomes are already low, B cannot,
by himself, alter A's outcomes. In contrast, in the situation depicted
in Table 11–2, each individual has behavior control over one other
individual, and this control depends in no way upon the actions of the
third. Each man can always motivate another one to change behavior:
each man is capable of starting the circular process. Consequently,
this pattern should require less prearrangement and discussion for its

solution. It can, so to speak, move to a good cell "on its own steam."

A superficially similar variant is one in which there is a circular pattern of *fate* control: A has fate control over B, B over C, and C over A. (This is the *sequential pattern of interdependence,* described earlier in this chapter.) The matrix is shown in Table 11–3.

Once again, a dominant solution exists in the sense that there is one cell which is at least as good for each and every man as any other cell. However, the process by which the dominant solution is attained may be very different from that characteristic of the cases already considered. Each man can affect the outcomes of the next man but cannot directly affect those of the man in whose hands his own fate lies. However, the possibility does exist for A, for example, to convert his

TABLE 11–3

AN EXAMPLE OF PARTIAL CORRESPONDENCE OF OUTCOMES IN A TRIAD IN WHICH EACH PERSON CAN EXERCISE FATE CONTROL OVER ONE OTHER PERSON, IN A CIRCULAR PATTERN

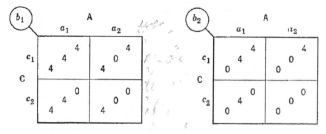

fate control over B by making the delivery of rewards to B conditional on B's appropriate conversion of his fate control over C. In brief, a discussion ensues in which each man says, in effect: "I'll do *this* for you if you will use your power to get him to do *that* for me." Discussion and preagreements are necessary to get the interaction underway, since the operation of each link in the arrangement depends upon the operation of the preceding ones, and, in a sense, the whole operation must start at once unless some persons are to be disadvantaged momentarily. The content of this preliminary discussion can be understood in terms of the conversion of fate control. In the situation depicted in Table 11–3, in which there is high convergence of interest, little resistance to compliance with the converted fate control would be expected. However, as correspondence of outcomes diminishes, acquiescence will become progressively more difficult to achieve.

### 11.2.3  LOW CORRESPONDENCE OF OUTCOMES

An extreme case of low correspondence of favorable outcomes is shown in Table 11-4 for an hypothetical triad. This table might be taken to represent the case of three ladies, each of whom wants only to talk while the other two listen. Obviously, this situation requires alternation in which one individual obtains satisfaction while the others delay theirs. A relationship among these three will be viable only if, with a turn-taking arrangement, everyone can obtain adequate satisfaction within the time available for interaction.

One is reminded by this example of the Mintz (1951) experimental simulation of a panic (see Chapter 9). The matrices for this experiment are identical with those depicted in Table 11-4 if "pull" is substi-

TABLE 11–4

AN EXAMPLE OF LOW CORRESPONDENCE OF FAVORABLE OUTCOMES IN A
TRIAD IN WHICH NO TWO PERSONS CAN SIMULTANEOUSLY ATTAIN
FAVORABLE OUTCOMES

| B talks | | A | |
|---|---|---|---|
| | | Talks | Listens |
| **Talks** | | 0  0  0 | 0  0  0 |
| **C** | | | |
| **Listens** | | 0  0  0 | 0  4  0 |

| B listens | | A | |
|---|---|---|---|
| | | Talks | Listens |
| **Talks** | | 0  0  0 | 0  0  4 |
| **C** | | | |
| **Listens** | | 0  4  0 | 0  0  0 |

tuted for "talk" and "wait" for "listen." The Mintz experiment also requires a turn-taking or queueing-up solution. In addition, however, there is a sharp, though indefinite, time limit imposed because of the impending disaster, hence a strong preference for the front of the queue. As Brown (1954, p. 862) points out in his analysis of the Mintz experiment, the man at the end of the line may have good grounds for believing that he has nothing to gain from cooperation. If several people act upon this strong desire to be first in line and do so simultaneously, there is the further disastrous effect that the whole interaction becomes frozen and unable to move to a different cell. Specifically, a jam-up occurs in the bottleneck, which reduces to zero the ability of the people in the jam to shift back to the alternative behavior.

Less extreme cases, in which correspondence is low but not totally absent (high outcomes for some coincide with moderate ones for others), permit compromise solutions

## 11.3  COALITIONS

Consider the situation in which the outcomes of a subset of the group members correspond perfectly over the matrix but do not correspond with those of others in the group  This sets the stage for the emergence of a *coalition* within the larger group  By coalition we mean two or more persons who act jointly to affect the outcomes of one or more other persons  This joint action is presumably based upon common interest, or, in our technical terms, correspondence of outcomes  Insofar as the outcomes of all the individuals in a given subset are affected in the same way by another individual, the basis exists for their forming a coalition *against* him  The term thus subsumes not only such phenomena as special interest groups within business or political organizations but also such superficially different events as the collaboration of parents in rearing their children and the behavior of an audience in its relationship to a performer  The action of a coalition will usually be "deliberate," although we do not care to insist that they must be so.

The existence of coalitions in larger groups greatly simplifies descriptive analysis of them  For example, suppose that in a triad, the outcomes of two persons (B and C) correspond perfectly but are affected in the same way by the third individual (A) °  This can be described with a simple dyadic model by setting up a matrix with A's repertoire on one side and a repertoire composed of B's and C's joint behaviors along the other side  Several such matrices are presented in Tables 11–5 and 11–6, in which A's outcomes are in the upper right portion of each cell  Either B's or C's outcomes could be placed in the lower left portion, since we are assuming they are perfectly correspondent (or very nearly so) over the matrix

Let us begin our consideration of coalitions by analyzing the various ways in which two persons can mobilize their resources to affect the outcomes of a third  Table 11–5 shows three kinds of *fate* control

---

° If C has no effect on the outcomes of A or B, the analysis is reducible strictly to dyadic terms, regardless of the correspondence between their outcomes  The interdependence of A and B is represented in an A x B matrix to which need be added only indications of C's outcomes for their various joint activities  This is the case marginal between the dyad and the triad in which a third person attaches himself to a pair indifferent to his actions

over A that B and C might exercise jointly. In the first case B and C have separate fate control which by joint action they can accumulate to a large total effect upon A. The other two instances in Table 11–5 illustrate the possibility of fate control being determined by the conjunction of action by B and C. In the first of these conjunctive fate control cases B or C alone can insure A only low outcomes. In the second B or C alone can insure him only high ones. In the first, in other words, either one of the B–C pair can intervene to make certain that the other one does not *improve* A's outcomes. This might occur if each one controlled half of the total equipment which A needs to go on a camping trip. In the second either one may intervene to make sure the other one does not *reduce* A's outcomes. This would be true

### TABLE 11–5

EXAMPLES OF TYPES OF FATE CONTROL THAT THE JOINT ACTION OF TWO
PERSONS CAN EXERCISE OVER A THIRD

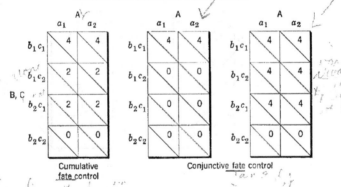

if each one owned the complete set of equipment A needs for his trip.

Table 11–6 gives examples of the joint exercise of behavior control held by B and C over A. In the first case, in which behavior control is cumulative, A can maintain on the average a somewhat higher level of outcome by taking account of the behaviors of either B or C than by disregarding them both. However, he can make maximal adjustments only by watching both B and C. (We assume in this discussion that A has no reason to believe one of the joint responses of B and C is any more likely to occur than another.) In the second case represented in Table 11–6, in which there is conjunctive behavior control, A makes no average gain by simply watching B or C. Both must be monitored if he is to improve his outcomes dependably.

The *two-versus-one* situation we have been considering may be analyzed further in terms of the relationship between the two members of the coalition. A number of problems confront them which require decisions mainly about a division of labor and coordination of behavior in dealing with the third person. Thus, for example, if C exercises behavior control over A and B, at least one of the two must monitor his behavior, and they must in some way make appropriate changes in choice of items from their (joint) behavior repertoire. This may require coordination of their individual behavior changes, accomplished by whatever communication procedures are available. In general, the internal relations of a perfect coalition may be described

TABLE 11–6

EXAMPLES OF TYPES OF BEHAVIOR CONTROL THAT THE JOINT ACTION OF
TWO PERSONS CAN EXERCISE OVER A THIRD

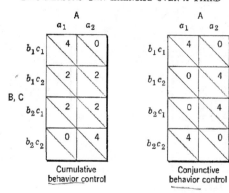

in terms of the *task functions* to be discussed in Chapter 15. These include surveillance of the environment, making action decisions, insuring performance of the proper actions through coordination, and providing instigations to these activities. Insofar as their outcomes do not correspond perfectly, there is also some necessity for performing *group maintenance functions,* such as deciding how to divide up the rewards acquired from the environment, deciding who shall profit first, providing affiliative rewards to those momentarily deprived, and settling status problems.

The principle of simplifying analysis of large groups by classifying all individuals who have high correspondence of outcomes has a further application. In the past many phenomena in large groups have been analyzed in terms of a theory of the relations between the (average) individual member, on the one hand, and the group, on the other. For example, Festinger, Schachter, and Back (1950), in their treatment of cohesiveness and power, discuss the relationship between the individual's attraction to the group and the resultant power of the group over him in terms of what is implicitly a dyadic model. Their generalization, that the higher the individual's attraction to the group the higher the group's power over the individual, is closely related both historically and conceptually to our generalization that the power of B over A is a function of A's dependence upon B, the latter in some cases being equivalent to A's attraction to B.

This type of theoretical analysis now seems legitimate when one may reasonably assume that as any given member varies his behavior the outcomes of the other members of the group co-vary among themselves. The other members will then implicitly form a coalition to affect the particular member's behavior, for example, to make him conform to group norms. Although the conditions for this assumption are approximated in many cases, there seem to be other cases in which the assumption is seriously in error, for example, when A's behaviors affect the others in such diverse ways that they cannot agree on what to try to get A to do. The assumption is clearly reasonable with respect to conformity to norms, since norms by definition consist of widely shared agreements concerning desirable and undesirable behavior. Here the compliance or noncompliance of each member tends (to the degree the norm is shared) to affect the other members in the same way and thus forms the basis for concerted coalition-type action to affect his outcomes.

### 11.3.1 FORMATION OF COALITIONS

Coalitions consist of cooperation among individuals to the end of exercising control over others. We have observed that they form among persons whose interests are the same with respect to an external agent who possesses some degree of power over them. Three factors, then, are promotive of coalition formation between A and B in a triad: (1) correspondence of their outcomes over a section of the A–B–C matrix, this being a section in which (2) C has some control over their outcomes and in which (3) by joint action they can mobilize greater power counter to C's control than by independent action. Item (2) provides the problem to be solved by coalition formation, and item (3) provides the means of solving it. Item (1) insures that it will be possible to reach consensus in the operation of the coalition.

These conditions are illustrated in Table 11–7. A's outcomes are in the upper right-hand corner of each cell. C's are in the lower left, and B's are in the middle. It will be noted that when C enacts $c_2$ neither A nor B obtains positive outcomes. When C does $c_1$, however, both A and B receive an outcome of 5. Either one acting alone can only slightly motivate C to do $c_1$, but (together they have great behavior control in this respect.) Furthermore, because their outcomes are correspondent, both A and B profit as much from the joint action that exerts maximum influence upon C as from any other. Hence there exists a basis for their ready agreement upon the joint action described by cell $a_1 b_1$.

An experimental illustration of the conditions favoring coalition formation is provided by Wright (1943). Pairs of preschool-age children were frustrated by an adult experimenter by his actions in making unavailable to them some highly attractive playthings. Their behavior

TABLE 11-7

An Illustration of the Conditions Promoting the Formation of a Coalition (AB) in the Triad

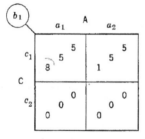 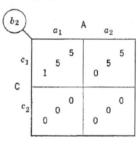

under frustration was compared with that which they had exhibited earlier. Inasmuch as their respective outcomes were being affected in the same way by the experimenter's exercise of his power, the motivation existed for forming a coalition against him. The actions of these coalitions are evidenced in joint attacks and hostile actions directed against the experimenter. Frustration, of course, resulted in a great increase in frequency of such actions, but they continued to be, as in the prefrustration period, predominantly social actions rather than solitary ones. Wright suggests that the children felt more powerful when in contact with each other than when alone. This apparently was particularly true for pairs who were close friends in their daily lives because close friends initiated more hostile actions of all sorts and a great many more direct physical attacks upon the experimenter than did "weak" friends. We may speculate that a close friendship heightens expectations that the coalition will be effective by increasing each person's feeling that he can take for granted or readily induce the other person's support for his actions. It is also likely that close friendship reflects a more complete correspondence of outcomes or commonality of interests. Thus all the power resources of the friendly pair can be mobilized against the frustrating agent without its being necessary to use any to resolve disagreements within the coalition.

The factors involved in forming a coalition against a social agent are also important when two persons are faced with a task and the choice of working on it individually or together. This situation is represented in Table 11-8, where we assume each person gets considerable satisfaction from the task if he solves it by himself, somewhat less if it is solved jointly, and none if the task goes unsolved or is solved by the efforts of someone else. (B's outcomes are in the center and C's are in the lower left portion of each cell.)

The task exercises control over their outcomes, and each one alone has a certain amount of behavior control over it. Together, however, they exert much more. This circumstance, plus the fact that both have fairly high outcomes when they work together to solve it, provides the conditions under which B and C are likely to form a coalition against the task. With the particular values given in Table 11-8, they are likely to do so, inasmuch as their respective expected outcomes (which we will take to be the product of the probability and the outcome values) for working together are higher than for working individually (2.7 versus 2.4 for B and 2.7 versus 1.2 for C).

## 11.3.2   THE STABILITY OF COALITIONS

To begin a discussion of some of the determinants of the stability of coalitions, we will make some simple assumptions about ways in which, by chance, outcomes may differ in degree of correspondence from group to group. For illustrative purposes, we will assume that persons are drawn more or less at random and are assigned to triads, the first three persons forming triad I, the next three persons forming triad II, and so on. By chance, it should be true fairly often that the outcomes of one pair within a given triad correspond to a noticeably greater degree than the outcomes of the other two possible pairs. Such a distribution of correspondence might occur, for example, if one pair of members had quite similar values, similar problem-solving strategies, etc., and the third member has markedly different values.

If a triad of this type began the discussion of a topic relevant to the aforementioned values or strategies, it might be expected that a coalition would begin to form, that is, the two correspondent members would begin to support one another and jointly oppose the other member. Initial tendencies of this sort would be expected to be reinforced and stabilized by the circular causal relationship between positive attitudes or sentiments and rates of interaction or communication, described by Homans (1950) and by Newcomb (1953). (Chapter 5.)

This may suggest a process underlying the findings of Mills (1953), who studied the formation of coalitions in artificially assembled three-man groups of strangers. Forty-eight such groups were presented with

TABLE 11–8

An Illustration of the Conditions Promoting the Formation of a "Coalition" against a Task

|  | | Task | |
|---|---|---|---|
|  | | Solved | Unsolved |
| B and C work together | 3 | 0.90<br>3 | 0.10<br>0<br>0 |
| B, C (joint repertoire) — B works on task alone | 0 | 0.40<br>6 | 0.60<br>0<br>0 |
| C works on task alone | 6 | 0.20<br>0 | 0.80<br>0<br>0 |
| Neither works on task | 0 | 0.00<br>0 | 1.00<br>0<br>0 |

the standard task of constructing a coherent story about three pictures from the TAT series. Using the interactions observed from behind a one-way screen, Mills was able to classify the forty-eight triads into four types, depending on the relationship between the two members in each triad who initiated the most interaction:

*Type 1: Solidary* (or true coalition), in which the two most active members give a high rate of support to one another.

*Type 2: Conflicting*, in which the two most active members give a low rate of support to one another.

*Type 3 and 4: Dominant and contending*, in which the two most active members exchange markedly different rates of support, either the more active of the two giving little and receiving much support (dominant) or the more active giving much and receiving little (contending).

Mills found the solidary pattern to be quite stable internally, both in the sense that the members tend to maintain over time the same rank order in activity rates (initiation of interaction) and in the sense that the mutuality of support within the coalition becomes accentuated over time and the third man becomes more isolated  The other three types of pattern do not show this degree of stability  It seems very possible that, as we have suggested, these various types of pattern may *mutually arise* by a more or less random assignment of persons to triads, as a consequence of the various distributions of correspondence of outcomes that might be expected from chance fluctuations.  The *stability* of the coalition pattern then may be interpreted in the manner suggested by Homans and Newcomb

That the remaining three patterns are unstable is clear from Mills' data, and the process by which such patterns dissolve and get converted into other patterns (principally the solidary one) may also be interpreted along the lines suggested by the theories of interpersonal symmetry of Homans and Newcomb  Our bias, however, is to interpret these events in terms of the implicit conversion of fate control that we used earlier to analyze the Sidowski, Wyckoff, and Tabory (1956) experiment (and which, incidentally, might reflect a process to account for the type of theory advanced by Homans and by Newcomb) Table 11-9 represents the four patterns of support as they appear in an outcome matrix  In the two "unbalanced" cells the most active member, A, gives little support to B, the second member (*dominant* pattern), or receives little support from B (*contending* pattern)  In the implicit conversion of fate control we assume that each partner to the interaction will repeat acts that are rewarded and discontinue acts that are punished  To the extent that reduced support is punishing, A should eventually cease supporting B in the dominant pattern and B should cease supporting A in the contending pattern  Dominance and contention would then shift to the *conflicting* pattern in which A and B inflict mutual punishment  The conflicting pattern is also unstable, and in time both members will be expected (1) to break off interaction, (2) to shift toward exchanging support as in the *solidary* pattern, or (3), as is possible in the triad, either A or B may form a solidary relationship with the third member, thus facilitating an increase in the activity rate of the third member to a degree that a newly composed solidary pattern may come into existence

Mills' data on shifts from pattern to pattern are consistent with our interpretation. (He did not permit his subjects to discontinue their interaction.) Both the dominant and contending patterns are highly unstable, and both tend to shift more frequently into the conflicting pattern than to any other. Although the conflicting pattern appears to be rather more stable than our interpretation would suggest (its tendency to stability does not reach statistical significance, however), it shifts to a solidary pattern more frequently than to either of the remaining patterns. Finally, the solidary pattern is the only one in which

TABLE 11-9

OUTCOME MATRIX SHOWING THE FOUR PATTERNS OF SUPPORT BETWEEN THE TWO MOST ACTIVE MEMBERS IN THE MILLS EXPERIMENT

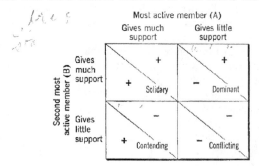

stability reaches statistical significance: initially solidary patterns tend to persist, with more gains than losses.

### 11.3.3 IMPERFECT CORRESPONDENCE WITHIN THE COALITION

With perfect correspondence of outcomes, the relative power of the various coalition members does not matter: each one, in seeking his best outcomes, will help the others attain theirs. Some complexities arise, however, when the outcomes of the potential coalition members are in imperfect correspondence. With imperfect correspondence, some conflict of interest occurs within the coalition, and a person with less power, being less able to influence the actions of the coalition, will be less able to cause the power of the coalition to be used for his own purposes. (Hence he will be expected to prefer coalitions in which he is maximally powerful.) He would be likely also to prefer coalitions which are maximally effective against the social or physical environment.) The joint consequence of these considerations is that he is (likely to prefer a coalition in which both his internal power, that is, his power within the coalition, and the external power of the coalition are maximal ) However, these factors may vary independently Therefore, a person may find it desirable on one occasion to choose a less effective coalition in which he is more powerful and on another occasion, a highly effective one in which he is less powerful

The foregoing principle also governs decisions about entering groups which act upon the environment A person prefers one that is effective and in which he has maximum power. But inasmuch as these factors may vary independently he may be forced to make compromises, for example, by entering a relationship in which he is rather weak simply because its effectiveness in gaining rewards from the environment is very great his lesser share of rewards may still be greater than would be his larger portion from a less effective group.

The effect of differential power within the coalition can be illustrated by reference to Table 11-8 Person B has more power in the coalition by virtue of the fact that he can get more from the task when working individually than can C. (This is according to the principle that the person with the better available alternative to a given relationship has more power in it ) This fact will not make any difference so long as each person inevitably gets three points for the joint solution If, however, their separate rewards for a joint solution are capable of being shared (as would be the case if they were permitted to make side payments in the same or other currency or if they were paid off with a lump sum which they were allowed to divide any way they wanted), then there can be disagreement about a just division of their gains This is essentially a case of noncorrespondence of outcomes: the upper left-hand cell could be described in greater detail, so as to indicate the different positions each person can take with regard to dividing the income Over this portion of the matrix, then, their outcomes would show very low correspondence, hence their relative power becomes important In the case illustrated in Table 11-8, B would be likely to insist on a share of the available six points that is larger than three There is considerable latitude for bargaining in a situation of this sort B might be able to force C to settle for barely more than 1 2 of the six points, but on the other hand, C might be "tough" in his bargaining and hold B down to only slightly more than 2.4 points. They would almost certainly be able to agree upon a mutually acceptable compromise, but it is clear that entering the coalition is no longer so unequivocally desirable from C's point of view In fact, if the coalition were less effective (say the probability value in the upper left cell were only 0.70), B could not expect to be much better off in the coalition than working alone

The main point here is that with noncorrespondence of outcomes the individuals considering the formation of a coalition must take account both of their power relative to that of their prospective colleagues and of the effectiveness of the prospective coalition

We might note that B, in Table 11–8, would appear to contribute more than C to the effectiveness of the coalition, since he is more effective when working alone. In a very real sense B does contribute more, since by joining the coalition he can raise C's outcomes more than C can raise his. Thus, phenomenally at least, power within the coalition is equivalent to the extent of contribution to the effectiveness of the coalition.

### 11.3.4 COALITIONS IN COMPETITIVE SITUATIONS

Coalitions form within triads for the purpose of exercising control over the third person. We have pointed out how this situation parallels the development of two-person "coalitions" against tasks. Let us now consider a situation in which three persons are competing for scarce resources provided by the environment, a task, or a fourth person. The conditions are such that if one person can induce the environment to deliver a reward the other two are thereby deprived of it. The three may differ in their respective abilities to induce the environment to deliver rewards, but they also may form coalitions in order to combine their power over the environment and may share the jointly acquired rewards in any way. However, the environment always applies the rule that "winner takes all," whether the winner is an individual or a coalition. Second best receives nothing.

Since each person wishes as large a share of the rewards as possible, there is a unanimous desire to keep coalitions to the minimum size necessary, each person prefers to win by himself and will ally himself with another person only if absolutely necessary. A three-way coalition is never necessary, since there will always be either a single person or a pair in the triad who can mobilize greater control over the environment than the competitors can. The questions to be considered about this situation are: under what conditions will pairs form coalitions and which pairs will do so? For much of the thought on this problem we are indebted to Caplow's theoretical paper (1956) and an experiment conducted by Vinacke and Arkoff (1957)

Perhaps the problem can best be illustrated by describing the Vinacke and Arkoff experiment. Three subjects play a game in which each

one's counter is advanced along the successive spaces of a path, and
the first one to reach the end of the path is awarded a prize of 100
points. On successive occasions the experimenter rolls a single die,
and each player moves forward a number of spaces equal to the number shown by the die *times* a weight given to him before the game
began. These weights, assigned to the three subjects by chance, are
varied to represent the different types of situations identified by Caplow. Thus, for example, in one case (corresponding to Caplow's Type
IV) player A has a weight of three, player B has a weight of one, and
C, a weight of one. At any time during the game a pair of players can
form a coalition in order to pool their strength. In this event they are
given a single counter which is placed at a position equal to their combined acquired spaces, and then on subsequent rolls they advance according to their combined weights (times the die). Once formed,
coalitions are ruled to be indissoluble for the duration of the game.
Since all players start from the same point and move each time the die
is cast, the person or coalition having the largest weight automatically
wins. Coalition members are permitted to divide the prize in any way
they want to.

Consider first the case in which person A has more power to induce
the environment to deliver a reward than B and C have together
(Caplow's cases IV and VI). In this event he can acquire the rewards
for himself and will do so. He will have no interest in entering a coalition, and there is no point in the others' (B and C) forming one themselves. Vinacke and Arkoff's data bear out this expectation. The
commonest occurrence in these conditions was for no coalition to form;
this supports the general notion that coalitions will form only if
joint action is potentially effective in improving the outcomes of both
persons. Let it also be noted that in these cases each person's initial
weight corresponds to his ultimate power. A's high weight assures him
of getting a high outcome. Thus the power each one has if everyone
acts independently is, in these cases, approximately the same as his
power when coalitions become a possibility.

Consider next the case in which A has more initial power over the
environment than either B or C alone but less than their combined
power (Caplow's Types II and V). Now, each individual's initial
power over the environment is no longer directly related to the power
he has when opportunities exist for coalition formation. Though he
has the highest initial weight, A can obtain some of the rewards only
if B and C do *not* form a coalition. A can prevent this by entering a
coalition with one of them. This accomplished, he might believe that
because of the high weight he brings to the coalition he deserves a

lion's share of the prize (and others might share this belief), but this belief would have no correspondence with the objective facts concerning his power. The variability in A's outcomes is as much controllable by the joint actions of the other two as are the outcomes of either of them each of the three must take zero points if the other two form an alliance Hence, logically speaking (and as Vinacke and Arkoff point out), in cases such as the one described the initial weights do not coincide with the power a person has ultimately in the three-way bargaining situation

In view of this analysis, Vinacke and Arkoff's data are all the more interesting In the Type V case, in which A has a weight of four, B, a weight of three, and C, a weight of two, the most frequent coalition is between B and C. In the Type II case, in which A has a weight of three, B, a weight of two, and C, a weight of two, the most frequent coalition is also between B and C. In the Type III case, in which A has a weight of one, B, a weight of two, and C, a weight of two, A is apparently the most desirable candidate for a coalition, since most of those formed include him.

These results nicely substantiate Caplow's conclusion that "the triadic situation often favors the weak over the strong" In each of the three cases the weakest person (or persons) is most likely to be included in the coalition that receives the prize, but in all cases the weaker ones are weaker only with respect to their initial weight, which signifies merely the power they would possess if everyone acted independently All are equal in the power they possess when coalitions are permitted One wonders, then, why persons with smaller (though sufficient) initial weight are preferred as coalition mates

One speculation is that subjects equate initial weight with ultimate bargaining power They then choose as coalition mate a person whose weight is large enough to decide the balance of power in favor of the coalition but whose power within the coalition (as *perceived*, though not in *fact*) is minimal This is very sensible, except for the confusion between real power and initial weight This confusion would be supported by their experience in other situations in which ability to contribute to the strength of a coalition is in fact relevant to bargaining power within the coalition (Earlier we commented that this association is likely to hold under many circumstances) Subjects may also be encouraged to make the oversimple assumption that initial weights correspond directly to interpersonal power by the fact that the objective relation between weights and power is too complex to be easily understood.

A related difficulty comes from the experimental design, which required each triad to play eighteen games in three series of six games each Within a series each game was an instance of a different Caplowian case Hence cases of Types II III, and V, in which ultimate bargaining power is objectively equal and independent of initial weights, were intermixed with those of Types IV and VI, in which initial weights bear a close relation to ultimate power. This may well constitute an additional source of confusion to the subjects concerning the significance of the initial weights

To counteract these serial effects as well as to simply life cognitively for the subject, it seems desirable to repeat the experiment by exposing each triad to only one class of situation. Types II, III, and V for one set of triads, and Types IV and VI for another set With longer exposure to a single situation, one might expect that sooner or later the true power implications of the situation containing Types II, III and V would become apparent to the subjects For example, in the Type V situation A's high weight immediately threatens to emphasize the "common fate" of B and C, who share the imminent danger of losing the prize According to our general principle that correspondence of outcomes in an area controlled by a third person provides the basis for coalition formation, the very assignment of weights is likely to suggest to B and C the desirability of forming a coalition Thus the B–C coalition has a kind of salience from the beginning Vinacke and Arkoff imply this in their comment that ". . . the weaker members can immediately understand the necessity for forming a coalition, whereas the stronger member must go through more complex reasoning to do so" [p. 408].

If B and C do coalesce, of course, A's initial "power advantage" in the Type V or similar situation is lost If A is repeatedly excluded and defeated, he might be expected to learn that his initial advantage is more apparent than real and that in the bargaining for admittance to a coalition he has no more power than the others He should, then, be able to approach the others on an equal footing and ultimately to enter as many coalitions as either of them At this point, the three possible coalitions should be observed to form equally often, this eventuality reflecting the true power relations among the three

An experiment by Hoffman, Festinger, and Lawrence (1954), although performed for a rather different purpose, seems to substantiate some of our general points about the formation of coalitions within triads under competitive conditions. Each member of a number of three-man groups was working to make as many points as possible toward his individual score on what was supposedly an intelligence test The second part of the "intelligence test" was presented as a bargaining situation which measured the ability to interact with other people. Although the rules emphasized that each person's objective was to earn as many points as possible, the bargaining character of the situation carried the strong implication that the subjects should assume a competitive orientation. At the outset of the critical test situation, by prearrangement, one subject (a confederate of the experimenter) gained a large initial advantage in points. From that time on it was possible for a subject to score further points only by entering a coalition with one other subject. The experiment yielded data on how often the confederate was able, following a standard bargaining procedure, to enter a coalition with one of the other subjects.

By his initial success, the confederate threatened to defeat the other two subjects, so their respective fates were similarly affected (or threatened) by his actions. Thus a coalition would be expected to develop between the two genuine subjects. The data indicate that this was the case: the confederate was less often included in a coalition and had to accept a relatively small number of points in order to be included at all. Furthermore, the tendency for the genuine subjects to form a coalition was strongest when the magnitude of the confederate's threatened effect was greatest (operationally, when the alleged intelligence-test scores were believed to have high validity, hence were of great importance to the subjects) and when the genuine subjects' joint effectiveness against his threat was perceived to be high (operationally, when he was believed to be equal rather than superior to them in ability). Thus the general factors in coalition formation outlined earlier (being subjected to a common fate by an agent against whom joint action holds some promise of being effective) seem to apply in a competitive situation. There are also some data from this experiment which suggest that when coalition formation tendencies are strong, even in a generally competitive context, cooperative attitudes develop *within* the coalition. At least with respect to the factor of relative ability of the subjects, the authors report that when the factor favored coalition formation (i.e., when the confederate was equal to the others in ability) the coalitions formed more often included an agreement to share *equally* the rewards received than did those coalitions formed under conditions less promotive of coalition formation (i.e., when the confederate was perceived as greatly superior in ability).

## SUMMARY

In this chapter groups larger than the dyad are dealt with explicitly and the effects of increasing group size on interdependence and power are evaluated. Most of this analysis is focused on the triad and extended to larger groups mainly by implication and occasional illustration.

As in any group, the triad is viable only to the degree that each member is above his $CL_{alt}$; each member is thus dependent on *both* of the others. To the extent that a member becomes dependent on only one of the others, a dyadic subgroup becomes an increasingly attractive alternative relationship, thus reducing dependence on the triad.

Two cases are discussed in which a tendency exists for the triad to break into a dyad and a third person, or "isolate." (1) Member A may prefer the A–B dyad to the A–B–C triad, but B does not share this preference. (2) Both A and B are indifferent as between the A–B dyad and the full triad, and the triad continues to exist only because C prefers it. The second case raises problems about the measurement of group cohesiveness, since subgroupings (mutual choices) may compete with attraction to the total group.

As group size increases from two to three, new ways emerge by which a member's rewards can be raised in relation to his costs. Several examples are cited: joint cost cutting (two persons may be able to cut A's costs better than one); joint consumption of rewards (A can produce rewards which B and C can simultaneously enjoy without interference); mutual facilitation of enjoyment (audience interaction heightens their rewards); emergent products (B and C may create products which taken separately are of little value to A but which jointly are of great value); sequential patterns of interdependence (when a circular pattern of fate control exists).

As outcomes of various members come to correspond more and more closely over the cells of the matrix, the use of power to attain superior outcomes becomes progressively less possible and necessary. Three cases are considered as they affect the exercise of power within the relationship.

(1) *Perfect correspondence of outcomes.* Since no conflict of interest is involved, the problem is mainly one of synchronization (e.g., all must pull together and release together). A difficulty may arise, however, if a member is not *able* to coordinate his activities with those of the others, and this difficulty frequently becomes serious as group size increases.

(2) *Partial correspondence of outcomes.* Although there exist many possible patterns in which members' outcomes correspond only partially, two are chosen for discussion. A circular pattern of *behavior control* appears to have the advantage that each member is able in-

dependently to move the process to the *dominant* solution in which all three members simultaneously attain good outcomes. To attain the dominant solution in a circular pattern of *fate control*, it seems necessary for preliminary discussion to take place in which all members of the triad agree to convert their fate control simultaneously.

(3) *Low correspondence of outcomes.* In the extreme case only one member at a time can attain a favorable outcome, and alternation becomes necessary if the triad is to be viable. As group size increases and/or time limits become briefer, taking one's turn early becomes more and more desirable. This may lead to competition for a position at the front of the queue and a resulting "jamming" of the turn-taking process.

*Coalitions* are likely to form when outcomes correspond perfectly within a subset of members but not between this subset and the remaining members. A coalition exists when two or more persons act jointly to affect the outcomes of one or more other persons. The analysis of coalitions is begun by considering some of the ways in which two persons can exercise their joint power over a third. Various cases of cumulative and conjunctive fate and behavior control are discussed. The analysis is then extended to a further consideration of the conditions under which coalitions are likely to form both against persons and tasks.

If triads are created by random assignment, the outcomes of one of the three possible pairs within a triad will often, by chance, correspond much better than those of the other two possible pairs. This initial tendency toward coalition formation is likely to be reinforced and stabilized as the two members of the highly correspondent pair implicitly convert their fate control over each other, the result being a dependable pattern of mutual support.

When correspondence of outcomes within the coalition is imperfect, the coalition member having inferior power will be less well able to insure that the power of the coalition is used in his interest. Therefore, the person will prefer a coalition in which both his power within the coalition and the power of the coalition over its social environment are maximal. This is, of course, not always possible.

The foregoing analysis is used to interpret the results of experiments in coalition formation and to discuss related writings.

# 12.

# *Status*

A person's evaluation of a group depends upon how well the outcomes he attains there compare with his CL when the CL reflects the outcomes in other relationships which are salient for him. A person may also evaluate his outcomes in relation to those he perceives other members of the group to be attaining) The result of this evaluation we refer to as *subjective status* A person has high subjective status when he is above the level of outcomes that he attributes to his colleagues and low subjective status when he is below this level)

In general, we view status phenomena as stemming from the tendency to evaluate our own outcomes by comparing them with those of others  Subjective status refers to that component of the evaluations of our outcomes that is affected by comparison with others within the same group. The consequences of high or low status are very similar to those of above-CL or below-CL positions in general  For these reasons, the present analysis relies heavily upon the theory and hypotheses presented in Chapter 6 and elaborated in Chapter 10

Although status has no necessary relation to attraction to the group, the common dependence of these two factors upon the outcomes attained in the relationship suggests that they will usually be positively correlated to some degree.  This will definitely be true when the outcomes of the other members are the only ones instigated (in which case the level of outcomes attributed to others is equivalent to the CL discussed in earlier chapters) or when for any other reasons all members have the same CL for the relationship  With different CL's, it is possible for a high-status member to be little attracted to the relationship or for a low-status one to be much attracted

In larger groups, particularly those incorporating well-defined sub-groups, an individual may evaluate his position differently with respect to different sets of his colleagues. For example, he may believe himself to be better off than some but worse off than others. In these circumstances, when there are middle statuses, it might be possible to identify several comparison levels, each based upon the outcomes perceived to be attained by a specific class of members. Although not excluding this case, for simplicity we have limited our discussion largely to the two-status case.

The foregoing comments present status as an individual subjective matter, and, indeed, the first part of this chapter deals with the factors that encourage the individual to make status evaluations. However, status evaluations are often a matter of social consensus. The subjective comparisons made by various group members are sometimes consistent with one another by virtue of the operation of common, intercommunicated standards for evaluation. When for this reason there exists a considerable amount of consensus about the status of each member (or subgroup or set of role occupants), a *status system* may be said to exist in the group. Each individual then has a *social status* which, depending upon his acceptance of the consensus, more or less corresponds to his *subjective* status. The second part of this chapter discusses the function of the status system and the circumstances favoring its emergence.

Our focus is, of course, upon status phenomena in small groups. Although there have been many empirical studies of stratification, social class, and mobility in larger social structures, very little research has been done on status systems (as here defined) in primary groups. Therefore, the documentation in this chapter is necessarily rather sparse. At this point in the development of social theory it seems unwise to rely too heavily upon social stratification as a model for small group status systems or to test hypotheses about these systems by reference to evidence from larger aggregates [*]

## 12.1 Conditions Favoring Status Evaluations

For many reasons one person in a group may attain better outcomes than another. he may have a higher $CL_{alt}$, he may enjoy the joint ac-

---

[*] It might be in order to note that the present use of status to refer to an evaluative dimension is much more limited than that of Linton (1945) and others who use the term to refer to a position or location in a social system. Our use refers to the invidious value attached to a person or position and therefore is more closely akin to such terms as prestige, esteem, and rank.

tivities more, or he may be more proficient at them.  Given that differences in outcomes do exist, say as detected by an omniscient observer,
when will they be reflected in subjective status evaluations?  The general answer to this, suggested by the conception of CL in Chapter 6, is
that for each person the outcomes of other members must be known
and highly salient.

Consider first the question of how one person can know another's
outcomes.  This question was glossed over in Chapter 6 because there
we considered mainly the individual's own outcomes in other relationships.  It seems quite reasonable to assume that a person can compare
and "scale" his present outcomes with those experienced in the past or
anticipated for the future.  But in the present context the problem of
interpersonal comparisons looms large.  Can one person compare his
outcomes with those of another?  We believe the answer to be "yes"
and base this belief primarily upon what people seem to do.  They do
in fact compare their pleasures, their income, their circumstances, etc.,
with those of others.  This is not to say they make these comparisons
accurately nor that there are always consistencies among various persons' evaluations of the same comparison.  The possibility certainly
exists for disagreement between A and B as to their relative statuses.
Person A may be of the opinion that his own outcomes are poorer than
B's, which implies that B's status is higher than his own, whereas at the
same time B may feel that his status is lower than A's.  However, there
are available to each member a number of different cues relevant to an
assessment of the other's outcomes: (1) direct evidence about the rewards the other is receiving and the costs he must pay, (2) expressions
of pleasure and displeasure associated with the experiencing of various
outcomes, (3) the alacrity (latency) with which the other approaches
or avoids the various outcomes, and (4) manifestations of status evaluations in behavior and conversation.  Although these types of cues will
differ in their validity, taken together they afford the possibility of
evaluating the goodness of the other's outcomes.  They also afford the
basis for agreement about relative statuses, but this is left for the next
section.

Both knowledge of outcomes (or the kinds of evidence above) and
their continued salience are greatly promoted by face-to-face contacts
among the group members.  The same is true of other conditions (e.g.,
lack of privacy) which bring the consumption of rewards and the incurrence of costs out into the open.  The contributions to salience
from perceptions of own power have been discussed at length elsewhere.  It is sufficient here to note that when all of the members of a
group are seen to have the same power in relation to outside agents of

control the collective totality of outcomes will tend to be salient for each member. If, however, the range of outcomes is too great, the salience of those extremely divergent from the individual's own outcomes will tend to be low, as extremity of outcome is taken as a sign of different realms of power.

In short, status evaluations will be most likely when members of a face-to-face group interact frequently with few opportunities for privacy, when they obviously have pretty much the same realms of power, and when their outcomes cover a not-too-wide range. These attributes characterize quite well certain nonvoluntary groups, hence we would expect status evaluations to appear quite markedly in these cases (e.g., men in prison, ethnic groups living in segregated "ghetto" areas). Individuals subjected to a common powerful fate control, restricted to one another in their contacts, and denied opportunities for covert consumption of rewards become extremely concerned about how they stand in comparison with their fellows. Under deprived conditions, of course, a "good" status position may have much greater value to the person than in better times. One might also argue that the heightened tendency toward status comparisons in such deprived circumstances occurs largely because the common dependence of such subordinated persons on a powerful authority serves to reinstate old status comparisons among siblings in childhood. But this merely re-states the problem, since one then has to account for sibling rivalry. The present suggestion is that tendencies to make status evaluations under circumstances such as those described are in part an epiphenomenon of a special set of conditions which act together to make highly salient for each person the outcomes of his fellows.

Conditions similar to the foregoing may prevail for a limited set of persons within a group, specifically any subgroup whose members have similar power in relation to the larger group and are constrained to frequent interaction. The prime example would be the children in a family, but equally familiar examples would be such subgroups as the graduate students in an academic department, the tellers in a bank, or the junior executives in a large corporation. Carolyn and Muzafer Sherif note some interesting anecdotes on this intra-organization comparison tendency, reported in *Time*:

> A few years ago, a Dallas company set up a new subsidiary with five brand-new vice presidents installed in identical offices. Everything was peaceful until one used his expense account to replace his single-pen set with a two-pen set. Within four days all five worked their way up to three-pen sets. . . . A big Chicago oil company caused a major crisis a few years ago when it bought a new type of posture chair to test on a few

of its executives   Those left out were so miserable that one man to save
face, bought a chair with his own money and smuggled it into the office
(Sherif and Sherif, 1956, p 621)

In these examples the thing possessed is not important so much for
its own sake as for the fact that it symbolizes one person's having more
than another

These examples also raise the question of the comparability of outcomes received by different individuals.  For example, it is true that
a husband can evaluate how much he gets out of the marriage in relation to what his wife enjoys from it, but this comparison is likely to be
a difficult one to make   The interdependence upon which such relationships are founded usually means that there is some sort of barter-
ing wherein the kinds of contributions A makes to B are *qualitatively*
different from those B makes to A   Hence comparisons of A's and B's
outcomes are difficult to make   How can the value to the husband of
the wife's performance of household chores, child supervision, and
other wifely activities be compared with the value to her of his performance on his job, washing the car, completing the income tax
forms, etc ?  We would hypothesize, then, that a sharp differentiation
in activity between the members of a dyad would minimize status comparisons and the various problems such comparisons create.  As the
role of husband and wife merge, as some observers of modern trends
suggest they are doing, at least in American life, the question of who is
better off in the relationship becomes a meaningful one

With the triad and larger groups, status comparisons may be quite
important, for it becomes possible for two (or more) persons to be
receiving much the same kinds of rewards or cost cutting from a third
person   The prime example, of course, is that of sibling rivalry.
When two children require and receive pretty much the same sort of
treatment from a parent, any difference in the quantity of rewards received will be highly visible   If the parent is to avoid sibling jealousy
and being charged with favoritism, either he must be scrupulously
equitable or he must create some sort of noncomparability between
the children's outcomes by providing them with different kinds of rewards   If the two children are quite similar, the first is possible; if they
are quite dissimilar, the second is possible   Sewall's (1930) data on
jealousy as affected by age difference between siblings is consistent
with this analysis, although not conclusive because of small numbers
of cases   Jealousy was found to be greater for intermediate age differences than for very small or large ones.  On the other hand, a difference between the children often renders one of them more attractive to the adults, with the consequence that he is favored over the sib

Koch (1956) reports that among first-born children the wish to change places with the younger sibling increases with the age difference between them. She comments that, "The sib who is two to four years younger than a five- or six-year-old is at that adorable one-to-four-year age when it will probably be showered with attention and affection by adults, both in and out of the family" [p. 31]. We suspect a similar explanation accounts for Smalley's (1930) finding that relationships between siblings are more frequently characterized by jealousy, the larger the difference between their intelligence quotients.

### 12.1.1 ACCEPTANCE OF DIFFERENCE IN OUTCOMES

The phenomena discussed above can be considered from a different point of view. Specifically, one may ask when, given objective differences among group members in their outcomes, will there not be subjective feelings of status and all the attendant consequences. The reader can probably anticipate the answers we would give, so we have indicated them without preamble. Objective differences will be accepted and not reflected in subjective status evaluations under conditions such as the following:

(1) The activities of each member are largely hidden from the view of others so that covert consumption is the prevailing mode.

(2) Sharp differences in power are perceived between those receiving high and low outcomes.

(3) There is a large gap in outcomes between those who are better off and those worse off.

Under the second and third conditions, even though a person may readily admit he is less well off than another, he does not ordinarily compare himself with that other person, hence the superiority of the other's outcomes does not afford grounds for dissatisfaction with his own fate.

### 12.1.2 COMPETITION AND RIVALRY

The notion of evaluating one's outcomes in relation to those of another person leads directly into the problems of competition and rivalry. We have noted earlier that when there is noncorrespondence between A's and B's outcomes over their matrix (one person's high outcomes derive from interactions which yield low outcomes to the other) they are in a sense in competition with each other. This conforms closely to the notion of competition described by Katz and Schanck (1938): each person is simply seeking to satisfy his own desires, and the situation happens to be structured so that as one attains success in increasing his outcomes, the other one suffers a reduction in his.

Consider now the case in which the two persons are interdependent with respect to their CL's, that is, in which each one's CL is totally dependent upon the other's outcomes. Because of this fact, each one's satisfaction varies inversely with the other one's outcomes and, therefore, with the other's satisfaction. This is the relationship characterized by Katz and Schanck as one of rivalry. each one seeks not only to improve his outcomes but to defeat the other person.

What is the relation between competition and rivalry? Katz and Schanck suggest that because of early learning experiences competitive situations usually arouse attitudes of rivalry. Such attitudes appear in the form of personal intentions that go beyond merely doing well in the competition and involve the goal of hurting the other person, perhaps going out of one's way to do so.

Can there be rivalry (interdependent CL's) when the necessary conditions for competition (namely, noncorrespondence of outcomes) do not exist? Suppose there is high correspondence of outcomes and, for some reason, each person attempts to surpass the other. As each one manages to attain higher outcomes, his CL rises at the same time, since his 'rival's' outcomes have also increased. For rivalry to occur, then, there must be some noncorrespondence of outcomes as well as the rather complete anchorage of each CL in the other's outcomes. From this reasoning, we would expect rivalry to be less "satisfying" between persons whose outcomes correspond rather closely, for example, between friends. A bit of evidence on this point comes from a study by Philp (1940) in which pairs of friends and pairs of strangers (all kindergarten children) played a cooperative and a competitive version of the same game. If we assume that some rivalry was aroused by the competitive version of the game, a less satisfactory interaction setting should have been provided for the friends than for the strangers. That this was so is indicated by the children's subsequent choices as to which game to repeat. The strange pairs more frequently chose the competitive game and the friendly pairs, the cooperative one.

We have claimed that mutual rivalry exists between two persons when each one's outcomes are the sole determiners of the other's CL. An earlier discussion of control and salience of outcomes (Chapter 6) suggests that this will be true only when the two persons view their respective realms of power as being equivalent or nearly so. It is also to be expected that persons who perceive their own power to be extensive will more frequently develop attitudes of rivalry toward others they encounter. In general, individual differences in subjective estimates of own potency and control will affect the tendency to make status evaluations, hence will affect the feelings and strivings that accompany these evaluations

Some of Deutsch's (1957) work suggests that there is a tendency for rivalry to beget more rivalry  If one person acts to reduce another's outcomes, the latter tends to react in a way that has the same or a worse effect upon the first person  In an experimental study of tendencies to reciprocate and take revenge Deutsch compared person A's reactions to different treatments by B, a stranger with whom A had had no prior contact  The two relevant conditions are those in which (1) person B, in the course of maximizing his own score, caused A to receive a score of zero, and (2) person B acted in a manner that yielded himself the same score as in the first case but also caused A to suffer a sizable loss in score  From similar comparisons made by Solomon (1957), it is apparent that in condition (2) A perceives B as being motivated by malevolence (to make A lose as much as possible) or rivalry (to win more than A does). Treatment (1) is usually perceived simply as reflecting B's desire to win as much as he can for himself  Of relevance here is the fact that A's reaction to the second treatment much more frequently indicates a strong attitude of rivalry and often consists of a behavior that causes B to lose even more points than B forced A to lose.

## 12.2  STATUS SYSTEMS

A status system exists when there is general agreement, or consensus, as to the status of each group member.  For a consensus to exist, the members must make status evaluations reflecting a uniformity among them in the degree to which the various outcomes are instigated and valued.  For reasons given in section 12 1, it is to be expected that under certain conditions (e g, overt consumption, close contact, etc.) there will be some consistency among group members in the salience and valuation of outcomes, hence in their status judgments  Needless to say, however, these conditions for uniformity do not always prevail

Furthermore, persons in low-status positions can to some degree alleviate the negative consequences (dissatisfaction, etc ) of their positions by selectively controlling the instigations from various classes of outcomes  They can overlook outcomes not available to them, or they can give special weight to the particular kinds of rewards they are able to attain  These processes are suggested by a study of status perceptions in a southern community, reported by Davis, Gardner, and Gardner (1952), although "status" in studies of this sort is a much broader concept than here used    The screening of instigations to better outcomes is suggested by the finding that ". . . individuals visualize class groups above them less clearly than those below them, they tend to minimize the social differentiations between themselves and those above" [p 287]    Selective instigation from different reward dimensions is indicated by the tendency for the basis of status distinctions to be interpreted differently by persons at various status levels. For example, upper middle-class persons report that wealth (of which they have an adequate supply) should be an important criterion of status, whereas they acknowledge only with reluctance the generally high status accorded the "old aristocracy" whose outcomes include heavy contributions from family prestige and, at least in the eyes of the upper middle-class, "immoral behavior"    This example shows that in spite of some agreement about the statuses of various people this consensus is not totally shared by those persons who have kinds of outcomes given low value.    The main point for present purposes, however, is that persons in inferior status positions may be motivated to instigate selectively their own and other's rewards and costs.    The effect is to reduce the degree to which a consensus about status can be achieved and maintained

Despite the situational and personal hindrances to attaining it, consensus about status does appear to develop in most groups that exist for any length of time, and it also appears that the consensus is supported by social norms.    Not only are there similar evaluations, but these are widely intercommunicated and informally taught

Perhaps the most remarkable aspect of these norms is the degree to which low-status members endorse them, thereby (so it would seem) penalizing themselves    More often than one might expect, they acknowledge the value of rewards received by high-status persons and manifest this acknowledgment by expressions of admiration and attempts at upward mobility, even though in this process the instigations from better outcomes will assuredly put them below CL

The reasons for this acceptance of evaluative norms are probably various    In part, low-status persons permit themselves to consider better outcomes because they entertain some prospects of eventually achieving them)    Also, the low-status person is obliged to acknowledge the value of certain kinds of rewards when variations in them are very important in his day-to-day life)    For example, the poor man can hardly dissent to the value of money or food, though he may be able to deny the immediate value of mink stoles or high-fidelity records

Status consensus has one further consequence which may also furnish part of the low-status person's motivation to accept it    When the low-status person acknowledges the value of the high-status person's position and in some way communicates this to him, the very value of the position is increased. This is an example of the general principle that value-support is in itself rewarding (Chapter 3). The value that the high-status person places on his privileges and rewards is validated by the low-status person's strivings, admiration, etc., and in this manner the rewards attained by the high-status person are increased. (The consensus may yield some increment of reward for the low-status person, too, but presumably this will be much smaller, since the matter is of less direct importance to him.) In general, then, some of the positive outcomes to high-status members seem to depend on a wide consensus that their activities are valuable. Low-status members are asked, in effect, to subsidize the outcomes to high-status members by assenting to the value of activities, many of which are exclusively the province of the highs. *The effect of this assent is to give low-status persons some power over the higher ones.*

As is often true, high status reflects a power advantage that has been used to attain superior outcomes. To the degree that consensus improves the outcomes to high-status persons, it tends to exhaust their initial power advantage. In a sense, then, the status consensus helps to "pay off" the person who enters the group with a power advantage, and the result is to keep unused power differences at a minimum. The high-status person who held great initial power is no longer able to make sharp demands if by virtue of the status awarded him he is already reaping the rewards that are due him. Life within the group is thereby made more stable and predictable for those of lower initial power: they need have less fear of arbitrary intrusions from the more powerful.

We would not claim that this function of status consensus is explicitly understood by group members nor that their according high status to the more powerful is a deliberate strategy to reduce the unused power extant among the members (Chapter 7). However, as status systems are found to have this functional utility, their acceptance probably meets with lowered resistance and becomes reflected in the folklore in the form of such sayings as "Give credit where credit is due." [*] This value of status systems is also implicit in the common observation that an important social function of the status hierarchy is that it provides a set of rewards for members who contribute to the

---

[*] This principle seems partially acknowledged in the Constitution of the USSR: "From each according to his ability, to each according to his work." This gains meaning by comparison with Karl Marx's parallel statement which concludes ". . . to each according to his need."

\)group and incentives to spur others to do likewise. The status system constitutes a form of currency with which members upon whom the group is highly dependent may be paid off  And let it be noted that when a consensus exists about status this currency has a dependable, common value, being regarded in very much the same way by each member and thus having high interpersonal comparability

The above analysis suggests that consensus can be most readily achieved when there is a power hierarchy to which the status system can be fitted  It also suggests that status and power will generally be positively correlated  The person who is accorded high status will tend also to have great responsibility for variations in other members' outcomes  Remember, however, an earlier point· if power differentials are too great at the outset, status evaluations will not be made, and although there will be a consensus about power a status consensus will never be at issue  This would be true, for example, in an old-fashioned family in which the father's power is so great that none of the children compare their privileges with his, hence questions of relative status never arise, at least not until the children gain power through maturity.

If it is true that a status consensus tends to reduce differences in unused power potentials, then we might expect high-power persons to refuse to some degree to accept the consensus  This is based upon the assumption that some unexploited power has advantages for the possessor, which, for example, enable him to insure an even level of good outcomes for himself in the future even though circumstances change. It is also likely that power in and of itself will have acquired reward value by virtue of its instrumental values  So just as the high-power person may attempt to maintain social distance from his subordinates in order to avoid power reduction through excessive friendliness (Chapter 7), he may try to disguise his status  It is a common observation that high officials of organizations emphasize the costs associated with their jobs and attempt to conceal their rewards from their underlings  Perhaps this serves to reduce the envy arising from unfavorable status comparisons, but it may also serve to maintain the ability to make demands upon the less powerful  An alternative strategy, perhaps, is for the powerful person to make it perfectly clear that he intends to employ his unused power in the best interests of the other members.  This will reduce their desire to attenuate his power and enable him in fact to keep a freer hand than he might otherwise  This explanation may underlie the frequently given admonition that the successful leader must maintain clear identification as a good group member by careful conformity to the norms most central to the group and most symbolic of its identity.  (As discussed in Chapter 13, there are other reasons why a leader might prefer to conform to these norms or why especially close conformity might be required of him.)

### 12.2.1 STATUS CONGRUENCY

Adams (1953) describes an investigation of status congruency that is highly relevant to the present discussion. By status congruency he means the degree to which the various members of a group have the same rank order on a variety of dimensions related to status. In fifty-two eleven-man aircrews Adams determined each man's standing on the following variables: amount of flight time, age, education, length of service, military rank, importance of position in the crew, combat time, popularity, and reputed ability. Each crew was given an index of its congruency, essentially based on the average intercorrelations among the nine variables within the crew. These indices were then compared with measures of crew performance and of interpersonal relations, with some very interesting results emerging. As congruency increases, the crews show higher friendship ratings, greater mutual trust, greater intimacy, and (most remarkably) *less* perception of rank differences within the crew. Crew performance (as measured by bombing scores, instructors' ratings, and crew ratings) shows a curvilinear relation to congruency, the moderately congruent performing better than either extreme.

Adams' interpretation of the first effect is worth quoting: "The individual who considers himself appropriately placed within the group will be less subject to discontent or compensatory behaviors which may disrupt relationships with crew mates. The crew mates in turn will regard him without feelings of threat, envy, or contempt" [p. 21]. This comment suggests that the higher the congruency, the more the status system is accepted, even to the point (so the data indicate) at which the crew is seen ". . . as less sharply divided by status differentiation" [p. 19]. From the preceding discussion, two reasons can be drawn as to why this might be so.

(1) In highly congruent crews the power differences associated with different statuses are great in magnitude and are in close correspondence with the status hierarchy. Therefore, others' outcomes are little instigated for each person, and there is little interpersonal comparison with the attendant feelings of dissatisfaction, envy, etc.

(2) Each man is rewarded in terms of his contributions (or ability to contribute) in the highly congruent crews. Therefore, there is little unused power left in the hands of the initially more powerful members, and this serves to make the crew more comfortable for everyone.

Additional explanations can certainly be adduced. For example, congruency as measured in this study means that different kinds of rewards are delivered in a consistent way to each person· the one who gets high pay also gets high military prestige, high social approval (popularity), etc  This reduces the possibility of lower status persons becoming disillusioned with the hierarchy because it fails to acknowledge some type of outcome they happen to receive in quantity

The second interpretation (2) may be viewed as partly explaining Adams' second finding, that moderately congruent crews perform better than those having high or low congruency  The deleterious effects of very low congruency are not difficult to imagine  If potential for contribution goes unrewarded, crewmen will hardly be motivated to improve their performance  At the other extreme are the highly congruent crews  Consider the possible consequences when the high-power members have, so to speak, used up all of their power by the status rewards they have accepted  In the Air Force situation the officers have not only all of the formal prestige and economic rewards on their side but in the highly congruent crews they also have let themselves be flattered by popularity and rewarded by personal intimacy  This may serve to temper the social climate in the crew, but the officers have given up their last reserves of power, hence their ability to make more than routine demands  As Adams puts it  "   .  leaders may become more considerate, with a resultant loss in willingness to organize and structure activity" [p 21]  Once again, alternative interpretations may be made of the data and Adams suggests several, but in Chapter 15 we return to the present one with further evidence.

## 12.3  CONSEQUENCES OF STATUS POSITION

Throughout the preceding discussion allusions have been made to the consequences of various status positions  Here, they are· considered more systematically as we survey some empirical studies in which status has been the independent variable

In Chapter 6 we noted that although better outcomes are always welcomed by the person he especially strives to achieve the level represented by his CL  Because his CL is heavily determined by the better outcomes of his colleagues, the low-status man by definition finds himself below it. (However, we would expect him to try to improve his level of outcomes) or, what could have the same effect, to reduce the outcomes of those better off than he)

What of the man whose outcomes fall somewhere in the middle of the group distribution? May we expect any improvement efforts from him? For the following reasons, we would expect many such middle-status persons to be below CL, hence to exhibit upward mobility attempts. *First*, we find it reasonable to assume that such a person has experienced and continues to experience (at least prototypes of) all of the types or dimensions of rewards and costs known at lower levels. In other words, middle-status persons have sampled and continue to sample the various types of rewards and costs associated with lower status activities. Moreover, the higher statuses include additional activities which have not been sampled by lower status persons. In other words, the activities included in various status levels tend to constitute a Guttman scale. This would not hold, of course, in a strict caste system in which there are proscriptions against performance of low-caste activities by high-caste persons. (It might be possible, incidentally, to derive a Guttman scale from the further assumption that for any given type or dimension of reward there are diminishing returns in terms of experienced reward as the quantity of the rewarding product increases. Hence, in order to continue to move upward on the reward-cost continuum, a person would have to seek new kinds of rewards rather than merely adding more and more of the same kind.) *Second*, in Chapters 6 and 10 we have advanced the hypothesis that unattained outcomes will be overestimated by relatively "confident" persons and will be underestimated by "unconfident" or "failure-fearing" persons. The condition assumed here is that at least some middle-status members will be the confident type and will, therefore, overestimate the unattained outcomes. To the extent that the foregoing conditions are met, middle-status persons will be motivated to move upward in the status hierarchy. By the first condition, the only unattained outcomes are those upward, and, by the second, these outcomes are overestimated by at least some persons. This overestimation of upward outcomes would lead to a skewing of the outcome distribution: higher outcomes are perceived to be farther above one's own position than lower outcomes are below it. Hence certain (confident, optimistic) persons objectively in the middle of the group in terms of their outcomes will tend to be below CL. In addition, the higher status persons will have a greater effect on their CL's than will lower status persons. It is as though the CL's were displaced upward, with resultant lowered satisfaction with the obtained outcomes and attempts to attain better ones.

Improvement attempts can manifest themselves in too many ways for us to detail them here. For example, a person may associate with those who have most control over the supply of rewards, attempting by

formal or informal means to place himself in a position in which further
rewards can be expected or demanded  Assuming that to express liking for a person constitutes an informal means to this end, we would
expect such expression to be directed to more powerful persons  (For
further coverage of this point, the reader is referred to a discussion of
power strategies in Chapter 7 )  A similar prediction could be made
about such behavior as expressing agreement with the high-power
person's opinions, interest in his activities, or admiration for his possessions  A great variety of evidence is consistent with this assertion, all
of it showing a tendency for sociometric choices and expressions of
liking to be directed from low-prestige (low status and power) levels
to higher ones, this to a greater degree than from high prestige to low
For example, Lundberg and Steele (1938) and Dodd (1935) report
this for two quite different communities, Riley, Cohn, Toby, and Riley
(1954) observed it among ninth- and tenth-grade school children,
Vreeland (1942), among fraternity brothers, Masling, Greer, and Gilmore (1955), within military units, and Hurwitz, Zander, and Hymovitch (1953), among community mental-health workers.

What if attempts to improve one's outcomes are blocked?  When
instigations to the better outcomes remain strong, behavioral accom-
paniments of fantasy about the high-status position might be observed
For example, in an experiment in which group members were differentiated only on the basis of the attractiveness of their jobs Kelley
(1951) found that low-status persons who had a strong desire to improve their status communicated frequent conjectures about the nature of the high-status task.  Some confirmatory evidence is provided
by Cohen (1958)  It has also been proposed that association with and
communication to persons of high status serve as substitutes for
blocked upward mobility and enable the low-status person to enjoy
vicariously the advantages of the higher position  This interpretation
was made of Thibaut's (1950) finding that as experimentally induced
discrimination proceeded in favor of members having higher status
(but equal power) the underprivileged members increased their total
volume of communication and decreased the proportion of it that contained signs of aggression

One might also expect immobilized low-status persons to avoid, if
possible, instigations from the higher status outcomes  Some evidence
on this is provided by Kelley (1951) and by Cohen (1958)  Persons
permanently relegated to an undesirable position were found to initiate a large volume of communication irrelevant to the situation  It
may be suggested that this irrelevant content affords an escape or diver-
sion from the unpleasantness of the low-status position

Another means for the low-status person to adapt to his deprived state is to bring about a reduction in the outcomes of the higher status persons. Their rewards and privileges may be devaluated and they themselves regarded with an attitude of scorn rather than envy. Although no evidence appears to bear directly on this point, there are some indications that, at least under conditions in which instigations from high status are strong, permanent low-status persons are relatively unfriendly toward higher ones (Kelley, 1951; Cohen, 1958). Kelley found a similar tendency for high-status persons whose positions were threatened. The latter manifested little friendliness toward persons at the lower levels who were their competitors for high status. The unfriendliness exhibited by immobile low-status persons toward those of high status is in sharp contrast to the previously mentioned tendency for sociometric choices to be directed upward rather than downward. As implied earlier, our speculation is that the upward-choice tendency appears in situations in which upward mobility is possible and in which it is controlled largely by persons in high-status positions.

# SUMMARY

A person's *subjective status* refers to his evaluations of how his outcomes compare with those attained by other members of the group. When his colleagues' outcomes are known to a person and are highly salient, they define a special CL in terms of which he appraises his own outcomes. If the comparison is favorable, he may be said to have high subjective status, and, if unfavorable, low. The consequences of such evaluations are similar to those of being above or below the more general CL discussed in Chapter 6.

Status evaluations are encouraged by factors that render publicly visible the consumption of rewards and incurrence of costs, that put persons in positions in which they receive qualitatively comparable outcomes, and that lead people to believe they have comparable realms of power. The speculation is advanced that outcomes vastly different from one's own or attributable to marked differences in domains of power are ordinarily not salient in the determination of one's status CL and, therefore, play little role in one's subjective feelings of status.

A state of rivalry exists between two persons when each one's CL is highly dependent upon the other one's outcomes. This is to be distinguished from a competitive relationship in which the situation happens to be such that one person obtains his low outcomes when the other one obtains his high ones, and vice versa

A status system exists within a group when there is general consensus as to the status of each member A person's *social status*, then, refers to the commonly held opinions about how his outcomes compare with those of other group members Although it might be expected that persons attributed low positions by a status consensus would refuse to endorse the consensus (since to do so tends to put them below CL), in many cases low-status persons do in fact support the status system they are in Several reasons can be given for this phenomenon Emphasized here is the interpretation that the low-status person's acknowledgment of the value of the high-status individual's position tends to give the low some power over the high To the degree that consensus improves the outcomes attained by high-status persons, it reduces any initial power advantage they may have had This interpretation has several important implications

(1) Consensus about status will be most readily attained when status differences reflect initial differences in power

(2) The status system provides a common "currency" with which members may be compensated in proportion to the importance of their contribution to the group

(3) The greater the extent to which initial power differences are reduced by corresponding differences in status rewards, the less will high-power persons be able to exert effective control over the behavior of other members. This will make more comfortable the circumstances of low-power persons but may reduce the effectiveness of the group with respect to its tasks Suggestive evidence on the latter points comes from an investigation of status congruency

The chapter concludes with a consideration of the consequences of occupying low- and middle-status positions When there is some possibility of status improvement, there is commonly observed a tendency for lower-status persons to express liking for high-status ones When upward status locomotion is impossible but instigations to the better outcomes are high, there is some tendency to enjoy the higher position vicariously and in fantasy, but there are also tendencies to avoid thinking about the higher position and to reject its occupants

# 13.

# *Conformity to Norms*

A norm exists when there are (1) agreements, or consen-
suses, about the behaviors group members should or
should not enact and (2) social processes to produce adherence to
these agreements

In an earlier chapter (Chapter 8) we discussed the nature of these
agreements, their typical course of development, and some of the functional values they have for groups and individual members.  Now we
shall consider the formal properties of the social processes which
produce conformity to norms and the various factors affecting the extent of this conformity  As we move from a discussion of norms in
the dyad to the ways in which they operate in larger and more complex groups, the functional contributions of norms become progressively
greater  As the size of the group increases, the costs in time and difficulty of attaining consensus grow greater and greater (South, 1927,
Hare, 1952)  Hence, as groups become larger, it becomes increasingly
important that regularized and dependable agreements supplant the
informal process of attaining consensus *ad hoc* each time a new issue
arises  Furthermore, as noted earlier, when the number of members
increases, there is an associated increase in the likelihood that interferences in response-sets will occur, leading to higher costs and lowered rewards.  Finally, with increasing group size there is frequent
increase in the division of labor or specialization of function among
the members, and this development leads to new problems of control
and coordination of behavior (Chapter 15)  The solution to all of
these problems is aided by the emergence of a complex of norms and
by provisions for insuring a degree of conformity to them.

239

## 13.1   NORM-SENDING PROCESSES

In general, it may be said that norms develop under circumstances in which individuals would not regularly behave in a certain manner of their own accord. The behavior or mode of behavior specified by a norm is not that which all individuals would consistently perform because of its intrinsic value to them. These are not, then, behaviors that a group can predictably elicit by exercising its behavior control, but rather they are behaviors whose performance can be insured only by the exercise of converted fate control over the individual. Therefore, the process of transmitting and enforcing norms (we use Rommetveit's term, "norm sending") always involves in some degree and

### TABLE 13-1

GROUP DEPENDS ON MEMBER FOR A BEHAVIOR HE PREFERS NOT TO DO

|  |  | Group | | |
|---|---|---|---|---|
|  |  | $g_1$<br>Praise member | $g_2$<br>(other behavior) | $g_3$<br>Reject member<br>from group |
| Member | $m_1$<br>Prepare<br>minutes | 2<br>4 | 2<br>1 | 0<br>0 |
|  | $m_2$<br>(other<br>behavior) | 1<br>6 | 1<br>3 | 0<br>0 |

in some way the operations or activities necessary for the exercise of converted fate control.

Consider, for example, the case in which a group is dependent upon one of its members for the occasional performance of a special service (e.g., preparing the minutes of their regular meetings). The matrix of relevant outcomes regarding this behavior might be represented as in Table 13-1. Taking the minutes and typing them up is not a task from which most people derive rewards, so the outcomes from this task are poorer than those associated with other typical behaviors member M might perform. On the other hand, the group has fate control over M and can convert this to insure (or at least to make it highly probable) that M will prepare the minutes.

As noted in Chapter 7, converting fate control in order to get a person to perform a specific behavior requires three different kinds of activities: (1) *stating a rule* as to the desired behavior and the consequences (of doing it or not), (2) *maintaining surveillance* over the person (especially if reduction of outcomes is to be the consequence of noncompliance) and evaluating the degree to which his behavior meets the normative criterion, and (3) *applying sanctions* to produce the predicted consequences In the illustration above, the group can convert its fate control in any one of several ways; for example, by rejecting the member from the group if he fails to prepare the minutes and by withholding rejection if he prepares them This matching rule (that $g_3$ will be matched with $m_2$ and $g_1$ or $g_2$ with $m_1$) can be conveyed to M verbally or by actually exercising it To enforce M's performance of the desired behavior, $m_1$, the group must monitor his activities and then enact or not enact $g_3$ to produce the predicted contingencies between M's behaviors and his outcomes

These various activities required in norm sending—stating a rule, maintaining surveillance, and applying sanctions—may be performed in many different ways All three norm-sending functions may be performed by the same agents of the group or they may be divided among different agents For example, the police maintain surveillance and the judges apply the sanctions, or, a mother may state the rules to her children, keep her eye on them, and then report to their father, who delivers any punishments or rewards that may be necessary

Some of these functions may also be performed by agents outside the immediate group For example, punishments may be delivered by aunts or uncles. This has the advantage that aggression aroused by punishment will be directed toward the outside agent and not toward other in-group members, with a possible loss in group cohesiveness

It is but one step further to turn over some of these norm-sending activities to imaginary outside agents (e g, witches, bogey-men, "laws" of nature) Stating rules would still ordinarily be done by agents within the group, but surveillance and application of sanctions may be handled by external agents, either personal or impersonal. Since these agents perform the same norm-sending functions that parents perform early in a person's life, there is probably a strong tendency to personalize them ghosts and witches are the agents among the Navaho, the "Tchitchi man" among the Sioux, and ghosts and the Japanese among the Papago (Thompson, 1951)

The effectiveness of these imaginary outside agents depends on the acceptance of the in-group depiction of their action and power This is the kind of socially supported belief a person is loath to test, especially if the possible penalties for going against the rule are severe—hence beliefs about the actions of these agents are likely to be self-perpetuating Even though from the vantage point of another cultural background it can be asserted that these external agents are unreal, for persons subject to them they may have considerable reality

The ultimate development away from personal control by in-group agents is achieved when the norm is internalized and the norm-sending functions are taken over by the individual himself    It is the ultimate end-state of the socialization process, which constitutes training in conformity by repeated enactment of the norm-sending processes, to produce internalization of these activities    The end product is that the individual cues himself to appropriate behavioral rules (or in some cases responds to timing signals from the norm sender), that he applies them to his own behavior, and that he feels rewarded or punished (morally elated or guilty) according to his adherence to them

Hence socialization requires the various norm-sending activities of stating a rule, maintaining surveillance, and applying sanctions    The repeated operation of these functions may yield substitute mechanisms of self-surveillance and self-delivery of sanctions    However, the original social processes are probably always latent in a continuing group, ready to be mobilized in support of the internalized processes should their control be threatened    In fact, if conformity is *totally* governed by internalized values and norm-sending processes are not activated in the absence of conformity, it is questionable as to whether a *norm* should be said to exist    We are inclined to follow Homans (1950) on this point and insist that the term *norm* be applied only when these processes are instated following nonadherence to a rule

### 13.1.1   THREE TYPES OF SOCIAL INFLUENCE

We have introduced the general process by which norms are transmitted to group members.    Let us now turn to three types of social influence that in varying degrees may operate to induce conformity to norms    For illustrative purposes these three types of influence are treated as discrete cases, which, however, can be arranged on a continuum representing the degree to which the social influence depends on the active presence of the agent of influence, the agent may be either a group or an individual.    The cases are taken up in their order of dependence on the agent's presence, from most dependent to least    We refer throughout to the agent as A and to the recipient of the influence attempt as B.

*Case 1*    The type of social influence in which conformity to the norm is most dependent on the active presence of A is that in which B's conformity is contingent on A's surveillance    As we have noted in

Chapter 7, A's active surveillance is necessary only if his influence is based on converted fate control with enforcement by the application of at least some degree of negative sanction (reduction of outcomes) for nonconformity, and our emphasis on surveillance in the present chapter rests on the assumption that some punishment for nonconformity is characteristic of normative processes. The first case to be considered, then, is the extreme one in which converted fate control depends for its effectiveness entirely on negative sanctions. A must actively monitor B's behavior and mete out punishment (withdrawal of rewards or intrusion of costs) for nonconformity. Since B's outcomes in the matrix contain only reduced outcomes (for nonconformity) and no increments (for conformity), it is to be expected that B's outcomes will generally fall below CL and that his available alternatives are not good—that, in brief, his relationship to A is *nonvoluntary* (Chapter 10).

If the negative sanctions available to A are sufficiently strong, the likelihood is high that B will acquiesce, at least as long as he is under A's surveillance. Although this *public* compliance is the most general and dependable consequence in Case 1—and the one we wish to emphasize—it is also likely that under certain conditions public compliance may be accompanied by *private* acceptance (Festinger, 1957).

*Case 2* When, in converting his fate control, the agent employs only positive sanctions (*augmentation of outcomes through increased rewards or reduced costs*), the situation changes. The agent is still actively involved in the influence process, since B's conforming behavior depends on A's presence. But A need not monitor B's behavior. B can be counted on to present evidence of his conformity to A in order to obtain positive sanctions, assuming that they are large enough to be worth having. If A continues dependably to provide rewards for B's conforming behavior, then, by the principle of association described in Chapter 7, A's behavior and ultimately A himself will acquire reward value to B. B will begin to value what A values and to disvalue what A disvalues. A correspondence of outcomes begins to develop throughout the matrix. Consensus begins to form and norms to emerge, and from these norms a stable role relationship can be elaborated.

*Case 3* The third case to be considered is that in which B's dependence on the agent A is quite different. In this case B is under behavior control from a task (Chapter 9) and B's rewards and costs derive from the task attaining truth or validity, being correct, etc. The function of the agent is that of an expert or a trainer who helps B to make appropriate matchings of items from his repertorie with states of the task. A is influential to the degree that he is a credible intermediary

The three cases above correspond fairly closely to Kelman's (1956) three types of social influence compliance, identification, and internalization Kelman describes these three processes very carefully and systematically by specifying for each process its necessary antecedent conditions, the details of the intervening process, and its differential consequents Although our brief summary cannot hope to do full justice to his complete account, the following paraphrases may be made.

COMPLIANCE The critical antecedents specify that compliance exists if the agent A is able to induce conformity behavior in B by controlling the means by which B can achieve a "favorable social effect" An important differential consequent specifies that the induced response of conforming will occur if B can be kept under surveillance by A.

In Kelman's description compliance may be enforced by either positive or negative sanctions But since he specifies that A's surveillance of B is a condition for the performance of the induced response and since we have shown that only when the threat of reduction in outcomes is used to enforce conformity is A's surveillance required, it is difficult to see how positive sanctions alone can satisfy the conditions of his definition of this process

With the proviso, then, that reduction is required for enforcement, Kelman's description of compliance seems to be interpretable as converted fate control, as summarized in our Case 1

IDENTIFICATION The antecedents specify that identification exists if through A's "attractiveness" B is able to maintain a satisfying "self-defining" relationship The induced response will occur when the relationship to the agent is highly salient. Kelman intends to describe this process broadly enough to include the classical identification by which B models (takes on the attributes and matches the behavior of) the agent A as well as the reciprocal role relationships by which B "defines" himself in relation to A B's behavior then may be either modeling or complementary Kelman also intends that the agent may be either a person or a group within which B has a specified role.

We suggest that this process of identification may be interpreted as originating in the conversion of fate control in which enforcement relies primarily on augmentation, as described in our Case 2. By repeatedly rewarding B for conforming behavior, A's behaviors become "autonomously" rewarding, and, as B's outcomes begin to correspond more and more closely with A's, the basis is laid for the development of noimative agieements out of which can be elaboiated B's role ielationship to A, either as one of reciprocality or of "behavioi matchmg"

5 INTERNALIZATION. The antecedents specify that internalization exists if by virtue of his "credibility" A can provide the means to B's acquir- ing "useful content," that is, right, true, valid, or meanmgful outcomes The induced iesponse of confoiming to A's message will occui when the content of A's message is "relcvant to the issues" A's surveillance is not necessaiy to elicit the response.[*]

Internalization thus appeais to be readily interpretable in terms of the task's behavior control over B, wheie A figuies only as a moie or less credible inteimediary His influence is a function of his validity and ieliability as an instrument mediating the states of the task and B's repeitoiie, as desciibed in Case 3.

For analytic puiposes we have dealt sepaiately with each of these processes. Howevei, in any actual instance in which a group eveits social influence to gam conformity to a norm all three piocesses are very likely to be involved at least to some degiee. Let us ieturn again to the example of the group's efforts to induce membei M to piepaie the minutes of its meetings (Table 13-1) Initially, the gioup's noim sending is likely to involve both augmentation (praising M) for con- foiming and thieats, at least, of ieduction (rejecting M) foi not con- forming As the membei's confoiming behavior is iepeated fiom meet- ing to meetmg, it may acquire stability both thiough "identification" and "inteinalization" To some degiee he may come to depend for his "self-definition" on his role ielationship to the group, and con- formity would be elicited when the salience of this valuable role rela- tionship is high But, also to some degree, he may come to inteinalize the noim so that in any gioup meeting his piepaiation of the minutes would depend only on a sign that the setting is appiopiiate and the be- havioi is ielevant. Internalization is likely to occur if he finds that in

---

[*] In fact, the very act of surveillance may suggest to the agent that B is merely complying (ie., avoiding negative sanctions) rather than identifying with A or internalizing the norm Strickland (1958) has performed an expeiiment which in- dicates this effect Each subject supervised two subordinates who woiked at a monotonous task and over whom the subject supervisor held the power of ad- mmistering a "fine" for slow work By experimental aiiangements, one subordi- nate's productivity could be iather continuously monitored and the other s could not At the end of the woik period both subordinates had completed about the same amount of work and at a satisfactory rate of speed The iesults of the ex- periment showed that subject supervisors attributed to the monitored subordinate less trustworthiness and reliability as a worker than they attributed to the un- monitored one.

other situations this same note-taking behavior is successful in attaining favorable outcomes, for example, the note-taking skill facilitates his library research Eventually then an autonomous motive will be expected to develop under a wide variety of conditions

## 13 2  FACTORS IN CONFORMITY

We may now consider some of the various specific factors that determine how much conformity to a given norm will be exhibited by a given member of a group   The factors are numerous and interrelated in rather complicated ways, so the following analysis is necessarily somewhat oversimplified   It may also seem redundant at times because the same factors can be looked at from two points of view. that of the norm-sending group and that of the norm-receiving individual member

### 13.2.1  EFFECTIVENESS OF NORM SENDING

Conformity obviously depends in the first place upon the efficacy of the norm-sending processes that are mobilized in the group with respect to a given norm   We may begin by considering the factors that affect the group's *potential* for norm-sending activities and then take up factors determining the extent to which these processes are actually mobilized

Certain limits are placed upon the norm-sending processes in a group by the general properties of that group   For example, the ease with which communication is possible among members determines how accurately the norm can be transmitted to various members   Wood (1948) presents some evidence suggesting that consensus is more accurately perceived in better integrated more coherent groups which might be expected to have more intragroup communication   Similarly, the greater the extent to which all the actions of members are open to view the more thoroughly can surveillance be maintained   If behavior can be practiced in privacy, the real impact of the norm may be greatly reduced   This may yield a state of *pluralistic ignorance* in which the common ideas about the amount of conformity to the norm are greatly at variance with the actual facts of conformity   In the classical study of this problem Schanck (1932) found that although the citizens of Elm Hollow publicly expressed both strong disapproval of card playing and the conviction that no one in their community would approve of such a thing the actual fact was that surreptitious card playing was common throughout the community.

Even if public evidence of nonconformity exists, unless the group can identify the particular recalcitrants sanctions cannot be applied to produce conformity. That this is so seems to be indicated by Mouton, Blake, and Olmstead (1956), who report that yielding to a group norm about the number of metronome clicks heard was less when the judgments were made anonymously than when the subject's personal identity was revealed. This generalization must be qualified, though, when retaliation can be made against an entire group or subgroup for violations committed against a norm by any of its members. The Nazis were able to maintain at least some degree of normative control by applying massive sanctions for sabotage to hostages or to entire communities. And in the laboratory Festinger (1947) found that, as contrasted with Roman Catholic girls, Jewish girls (for whom the application of group-wide sanctions was presumably a more salient possibility) required more convincing evidence of their *group's* anonymity before they would express private opinions.

If a group is to apply sanctions, it must, of course, have fate control over its members. Relevant to this point are the studies relating conformity behavior to attraction to the group, if it is assumed that in the groups under investigation dependency of the members on the group is roughly approximated by the members' attraction to the group. These studies show that the more the members are, on the average, attracted to a group (or the greater the group cohesiveness), the greater is their conformity to its norms (Festinger, Schachter, and Back, 1950, Kelley and Volkart, 1952). A different set of factors becomes important when the source of sanctions is shifted to an agent (real or imaginary) outside the group. Under these circumstances, the power (real or imagined) of the agent over the members, as well as the credibility of the group as a predictor of how the agent will exercise his power, becomes relevant.

The norm-sending processes are also limited by the nature of the norm. For example, some rules apply to behavior under virtually all circumstances. These are often referred to as *universalistic* norms. Others, *particularistic* norms, apply only under certain conditions. The particularistic norms, being more complex to state, are probably more difficult to transmit accurately.

Given that a group has the necessary potentialities for norm sending, the next question is: to what extent are these communication and control resources mobilized with respect to a specific norm? For example, in Table 13–1 the group may move the member over a sizable range of outcomes (from zero to four or six) or, by using other behaviors not shown, may move him over a more limited range   What factors determine how much of the potential fate control is used to produce conformity?

The first factor that suggests itself is the importance of the behavior to the group.  Norms about behavior that are highly important to the life and success of the group will be more thoroughly publicized, more carefully monitored, and more strongly enforced than norms about behavior of little importance   Some evidence on this point is provided by an experiment by Schachter (1951) and a later replication by Emerson (1954)   In some groups the question being discussed was highly relevant to the purposes of the group, and in others it was tangential   In the first groups there appeared to be greater pressure toward uniformity, as evidenced by the fact that greater influence was exerted upon persons with deviant opinions   Also, the sanction of denying group membership (indicated by rejections on sociometric questions) to persons who continued to resist the conformity pressures was more often applied in the groups to which the issue was important

Another factor affecting the exertion of conformity pressures comes from the heterogeneity of the group.  In voluntary relationships heterogeneity of attitude may be expected to lead simply to subgroup formation (Festinger and Thibaut, 1951), but, when the costs of leaving the group are high and the members are thereby constrained to membership, for example in national states, the greater the heterogeneity among the members the more forcefully will conformity sanctions have to be exerted in order to achieve an operating consensus, too much diversity thus yielding the opposite of freedom

It may not, of course, be equally important for all members to exhibit conforming behavior   For example, it has been suggested that conformity to certain central norms of a group is especially required of leaders or members who represent the group to the external world, presumably because of the important symbolic value of their conformity

On the other hand, if a person is very valuable to the group (i e , the group is highly dependent upon him), maximal sanctions may not be applied to him for fear of driving him out of the group   The only evidence bearing on this point is provided by anecdotes from work groups   Hughes (1946) describes how newcomers to a work group are expected to conform more closely to its production norms than workers who have been there a long time   It is not unreasonable to believe that the group has become quite attached to the old timers, hence more dependent upon them than upon newcomers

## 13.2.2 THE INDIVIDUAL'S REACTIONS TO THE NORM

Just as the factors affecting the norm-sending processes can be considered in terms of those affecting the potentialities and those affecting the processes actually mobilized, so can we consider the individual's reactions to a norm in terms of what he is able to do potentially and what he is motivated to do.

An individual usually has various means at his disposal for avoiding conformity to a norm. He may act to defeat or ameliorate the effectiveness of any or all of the norm-sending functions. For example, he may avoid being exposed to a statement of the rule, or he may misconstrue or misinterpret it to make it more consistent with his personal preferences. These are, of course, highly unrealistic maneuvers if the rule is actually enforced. The group may overlook some nonconformity if the person pleads ignorance and can give some reason for not having been aware of what is required of him. But, generally, "ignorance of the law is no excuse," especially if the rule has been stated or illustrated frequently and clearly.

Rank and file members may be particularly prone to this source of nonconformity, since there is some evidence that as compared with leaders they are less well informed about group opinion, hence about norms. Chowdhry and Newcomb (1952) report this result and interpret it as signifying that members who are especially sensitive to group opinion tend to gain leadership positions. An alternative interpretation—and one acknowledged by Chowdhry and Newcomb as a possibility—is that the leader's "centrality" in the group's communication network accounts for his superior knowledge of group opinion. Hites and Campbell (1950) report results inconsistent with those stated above. They found no differences among appointed leaders, elected leaders, and followers in ability to estimate group opinion. However, within their groups there seems to have been a greater homogeneity of opinion and a higher rate of communication than obtained in the Chowdhry and Newcomb groups. Hence in the groups studied by Hites and Campbell all of the members may have been so fully aware of group opinion that the leaders' advantages in the communication network are undetectable.

A person may also resist a norm by avoiding surveillance. Ability to do this seems to require having some sort of control over the physical environment in the sense of having access to regions of privacy or of being able to block off contact with other persons (see Orwell's *1984*). The point to be made here is that the exercise of converted fate control can be partially thwarted when the lower power person has these kinds of control over the physical environment

Perhaps the most obvious countermeasure to norm sending an individual can take is to use his counterpower to render the enforcer's power unusable _ The potentiality here depends, of course, upon how much power he has over the group, this is determined by the value of his contributions to the group and how readily he can be replaced— in short, how far above its $CL_{alt}$ for him does his behavior put the group     For example, in his study of staff experts in labor unions Wilensky (1956) found that those with high influence in their unions had more frequently received other job offers and had more frequently developed contacts that made them unreplaceable than had uninfluential staff men    On the importance of knowing that one's contribution to the group is valued, one of Wilensky's staff experts says "The greater degree of independence a top man can feel the better—he can speak up and offer his honest independent judgment   There's much too little of that   Staff people are too dependent on their jobs.   The ideal situation is when you have staff people who know they're wanted and are in demand.   They can then have security and be independent. Too great a dependence on the officer affects your judgment—no question about it" [pp 228-230]

Further data on this relationship between attitudinal independence and acceptance by the group are provided both by laboratory and by field studies.   In a laboratory experiment with college undergraduates Dittes and Kelley (1956) found that in making both simple perceptual judgments and more complex social judgments subjects who were not quite fully accepted by their groups adhered to group norms more closely than did fully accepted subjects.   This heightened conformity of marginally accepted subjects was observed not only for judgments made in public but extended even to conditions of privacy   High conformity in public judgments also occurred among subjects least accepted by their groups, presumably because these subjects perceived overt conformity as a means of preventing total rejection by the group Further confirmation of this last result comes from a field study by Menzel (1957)   Data were obtained from a sample of medical doctors which appeared to support the inference that a norm of "up-to-dateness" existed in the medical community with respect to the use of drugs   Doctors who were least accepted by other doctors (as measured sociometrically) showed more public conformity to the norm of being up-to-date than did doctors who were highly accepted

Similar results are reported in a laboratory experiment by Jackson and Saltzstein (1958) who demonstrate that the public judgments of members who are not accepted by the group are more highly influenced by majority opinion than are those of fully accepted members. Although the authors entertain the possibility that such public conformity may derive from a "need for social reassurance" [p. 23], they also point to another factor—that members who are not accepted undergo a loss of confidence in their ability to make the required judgments, hence depend disproportionately on "social reality" as a basis for making such judgments. In any case, from the preceding three studies it seems clear that those members who are most highly valued in the group and are most secure in their membership are better able to deviate from the norms of the group than are those less valued and less secure.

If we assume that a person would be able, if he wished, to frustrate the norm-sending process, it would then become important to determine the circumstances under which he would exercise this potentiality.

First, consider the intrinsic value of the behavior designated by the norm. When it is costly or punishing, the individual would be expected to use whatever countermeasures are at his disposal. On the other hand, if the designated behavior is intrinsically rewarding to the person, he would not be expected to deviate from the norm no matter what his capacities for doing so. The "intrinsic value" referred to here may be that associated with the behavior before its connection with a norm (i.e., by a prior process of internalization), or it may be the value built up by an identification process in the particular group. The general point to be made is that norms develop because *some* group members cannot be counted on to act in the designated way; this does not mean, however, that the action is undesirable for *all* members. Some may prefer it and may appear to be conforming when in reality they are merely acting in accord with their own private preferences. This is particularly important when a given member (perhaps a leader or a member having high power) has had an exceptionally strong voice in determining the norm and has been able to see to it that the norm specifies a style of behavior consistent with his personal desires. For example, Talland (1954) presents evidence that leaders are disproportionately influential in determining the formation of group opinion. For such persons for whom the designated behavior is intrinsically desirable, what may appear to be conformity behavior will be exhibited whether or not the norm-sending processes are effective.

Finally, there is the important consideration of the individual's dependence on the group. (This is simply viewing the power of the group from the point of view of the individual.) If the rewards for conformity are sufficiently important to the individual, he will not avail himself of his opportunities for counteracting the norm. This would be the case when the individual strongly desires status within the group and conformity is a condition (though perhaps only a minimal one) for attaining status. In this connection Sherif (1951) describes how less popular boys in his camp groups exhibited overconformity in an apparent effort to increase their acceptance. Conformity may be rewarding to others, hence, in a sense, may be a way of increasing one's value to them. This is consistent with various sets of evidence which show a positive relation between popularity and conformity (Newcomb, 1943, Kelley and Volkart, 1952).

### 13.3   Changing the Group Norm

When the group controls all three of the norm-sending functions (rule statement, surveillance, and sanction application), it is able to establish the conditions under which the member will be rewarded for conforming. (The member will find it advantageous to buy rewards (approbation, security, etc.) at the cost of conformity. To the extent that the member's conformity is important to the group (i.e., to the other members) for any reason (e.g., for maintaining all members above CL by sharing values), then the group is rewarded by the member's conformity, and the result is a high correspondence of group and member outcomes; that is, good reward-cost positions are attained by both in the same cells of a matrix such as that in Table 13–1. In this case both the member and the group gain rewards when the member conforms.

However, when the group controls only the statement of the rule and when monitoring and the application of sanctions are under the control of "nature" (e.g., when the member is working on an impersonal task), there is the possibility that some noncorrespondence of group and member outcomes will occur. In the group's history norms may have been developed which, although perhaps once believed to be functional in dealing with the problem environment, are no longer so when put to more sophisticated test. However, these norms may be retained because many of the group members are in no position to test them against task demands and also because the members continue to be rewarded by sharing these beliefs. For example, the group may assert the rule that one should believe the earth to be flat. However, nature (i.e., the problem in the external environment) may be thought of as monitoring the member's behavior and offering a reward for a problem-solution that corresponds to a different rule (belief that the earth is round) Here there would be a conflict between the two sources of sanctions that delivered by the group, which is striving to achieve a perfect sharing of values and attitudes, and that delivered by nature or external reality The resulting noncorrespondence of group and member outcomes will lead to *resistance* on the part of the member and therefore a lowered likelihood of his conforming to the group norm

To repeat, we assume that the sharing of values or achieving consensus of attitude may be rewarding in itself. But, the correspondence of outcomes between any given member and the rest of the group that is required for continuing consensus can occur in only two ways (1) if the group is insulated from the external world or if the problems posed by the external world are sufficiently ambiguous or difficult in relation to the skills of the group members (Chapter 9), (2) if the shared value is changed all at once to correspond to the problem demands of the environment The first of these ways is decreasingly possible in the kind of rapidly changing and technologically sophisticated world in which we live, but the second way may provide some answers to problems of culture change and the assimilation of innovations This second way is essentially that proposed by Lewin (1947) in his analysis of the problem of changing group standards. He suggested that piecemeal attempts to change individual attitudes and values would meet with the kinds of difficulties that we have summarized under noncorrespondence of outcomes and recommended that surer success in changing standards would require a rather sudden and concerted change in the standard itself.

The beginnings of an understanding of how this might be done are illustrated in the studies of group decision and the "self-survey" process conducted by Lewin and his associates. As an example, we might cite a study by Marrow and French (1945) Managerial personnel of a sewing factory were found to cling to the view that older women were less efficient workers than younger ones, even in face of contradictory evidence presented by experts However, when the managers participated in planning and conducting their own study of this question, their beliefs changed in line with their findings (identical with the earlier evidence) The implication is that shared beliefs can be changed if all the members are required to interact, so to speak, with the environment, that is, if they all submit themselves to the behavior control of the external task.

## SUMMARY

As groups grow larger, norms become increasingly important, both because consensus is so difficult to attain and (without norms) interferences in response-sets are so likely to occur. Norms develop to insure that members will perform behaviors that they would not perform in the absence of norm enforcement. These norm-prescribed behaviors, then, are enforced by the group's converting its fate control over its members. To effect this conversion of fate control, the group must (1) state a rule, (2) maintain surveillance over the members, and (3) apply sanctions. These norm-sending activities may be divided among various agents of the group, or they may be performed by agents (real or imaginary) outside the group. Ultimately they may become so internalized that the individual member will apply them to himself without the necessity of external enforcement.

Three types of social influence, arranged in order of their dependence on the presence of a social agent, are discussed. Case 1 is that in which person B's conformity is contingent on A's surveillance; hence A's converts his fate control by applying negative sanctions (reduction) when B fails to conform. This appears to correspond to Kelman's *compliance*. In Case 2 A again converts his fate control but now applies positive sanctions (augmentation) for conformity. Under these conditions, B can be expected to present evidence of his conformity to A in order to receive his reward, hence A need not monitor B's behavior. This case generally corresponds to Kelman's *identification*. Case 3 involves quite different processes. In this case the task exercises behavior control over B, and A's influence depends on his ability as an expert or trainer in mediating between states of the task and B's repertoire. This case corresponds fairly closely to Kelman's *internalization*.

The factors that appear to affect the degree to which members conform to group norms are discussed from two points of view: first, from that of the norm-sending group and then from that of the norm-receiving individual.

The group's potential for effective norm sending is increased as good communication within the group permits more accurate transmission of the norm. Good communication is essential, especially if the norm is particularistic and therefore complex to state. Similarly, for surveillance to be effective, the behavior of the members must be open to view and individually identifiable, although in extreme instances sanctions are applied to whole groups when any nonconformity is detected. For sanctions to be applied, the group must have fate control over its members: they must be dependent on the group.

Assuming that the group has the necessary potential for norm sending, the degree to which it will mobilize such resources will depend in the first place on the relevance or importance of the behavior to the group. Also, with increasing heterogeneity of attitude in the group, if the members are constrained to membership, more forceful sanctions must be applied to attain an operating consensus. It is not likely that uniform pressure to conform will be exerted on all members: although it is important that leaders conform, for the symbolic value of it, if for no other reason, still members who are highly valued by the group are usually not threatened with sanctions strong enough to drive them out of the group.

From the point of view of the norm-receiving individual, his potential for avoiding conformity is in the first place partly determined by his aptitude for avoiding exposure to the rule or misinterpreting it. Although this strategy is generally so unrealistic as to be ineffective, it may be tolerated among the rank and file members of the group. Sometimes a more successful strategy is that of avoiding surveillance. But the most dependable leverage for the individual is his counterpower, his value to the group, which he may use to render the group's power unusable.

Given that the individual member has the potential to frustrate norm sending, his exercise of this potential will depend largely on two factors. The less the "intrinsic value" of the normative behavior, the less will the individual be motivated to perform it. On the other hand, if the individual has managed to build his own preferences into the content of norms, he will perform the behavior even in the absence of enforcement. The member's motivation to perform the normative behavior will be greatly affected by his dependence on the group: to the degree that the group can give him what he most wants (status, acceptance), he will be likely to conform.

The chapter concludes with a discussion of some of the problems involved in changing a group norm. When at least part of the sanctions are under the control of nature and these are at variance with the group's stated rule or norm, noncorrespondence of member outcomes can be expected to occur. However, this can perhaps be avoided by a sudden and concerted changing of the norm, accomplished by arranging that all of the members respond to the behavior control of nature.

# 14.

## *Group Goals*

On frequent occasions the members of a group decide together to take some action. For example, the members may decide to raise funds for a new clubhouse, to launch a membership drive, or to learn how to play chess In all of these cases the members define some end-state toward which they will work.

Because these end-states resemble the goals of the individual, they have often been called group goals Like an individual goal, a group goal designates that some action will be taken toward putting a given task in a particular state (Chapter 9) The selection of this task and state will be a joint function of the individual's or the group's assessment of its power over the task (i e , its competence) and the quality of the outcomes expected to be attained. More pointedly, if the individual or group, given the range of behaviors in its repertoire estimates that there is an acceptably high probability that the task will take a certain state and if the probable outcomes to the group or individual are acceptably high, then that particular state will be selected as the goal.

Individual and group goals cease to resemble one another when the inquiry is pressed further The obvious difference is that group goals are social matters and require at least some degree of consensus before they can be prosecuted by enough of the members to warrant their being called group goals Consensus in this context means that a considerable number of the group members accept (or act as if they accept) the desirability of attempting to put a certain task into the specified state It is probably idle to speculate about just what degree of consensus is required before group goals can be said to exist, it is more profitable to regard individual and group goals as lying on a continuum, at one end of which each member is pursuing his own individual aims and at the other the group has attained perfect consensus Another problem regarding degree of consensus is how much is necessary for a given group to achieve a specific state of the task Suffice it to say here that the answer to this depends on the nature of the task (e g , whether it has conjunctive or disjunctive requirements) or, alternatively, upon the power of the various members over the task

In this respect, that a degree of consensus is required, group goals bear a strong resemblance to norms There are distinct differences, of course, mainly in that group goals may be developed for specific purposes which do not necessarily recur, whereas norms generally persist through time and are more or less continuously operative Further, group goals perhaps more often than norms are devised by deliberate acts of decision, whereas norms tend usually to be imported from other relationships or developed by gradual and implicit processes, with codification into formal law, if it occurs at all, often being only the formalization of procedures that had existed informally for some time However, in spite of these differences, by virtue of their common dependence on consensus, norms and group goals are very similar, sometimes (as in recurrent production "goals") being virtually indistinguishable

So we can say that group goals represent an operating consensus about a desirable state of a given task) Our discussion is concentrated first on the processes by which consensus about goals is attained, and some attention is given to the role of group discussion in achieving the acceptance of goals Then we discuss briefly group problem solving from the point of view of the group's attempting to discover behaviors that will put the task in the state designated by goal decisions

## 14.1 PROCESSES OF GAINING CONSENSUS

The processes of attaining consensus about goals are basically the same as those in norm sending As with norms, it is probably necessary that this consensus rest largely on the *acceptance* of these goals by a relatively large number, possibly a majority, of the group members. By the(acceptance of a group goal is meant that the individual believes he will attain good outcomes when the task is put into the state designated by the goal ) And for consensus to be based upon acceptance, there must be correspondence among the members in this respect each must believe he will attain good outcomes in the portion of the matrix associated with the goal task state As with the acceptance of norms, acceptance of goals implies that the person is dependably ready to enact the behavior thought to put the task in the goal state even in the *absence* of enforcement by the techniques of gaining compliance surveillance and sanctioning

From these comments it is also clear that when the group goal is accepted by a member he is motivated for the group to achieve the goal and is satisfied when it does so. Indirect evidence of this is given by Horwitz (1954) in an experiment which shows that the typical group member recalls more of the tasks interrupted by the experimenter than tasks completed by the group Horwitz interprets this to mean that the typical member has a "tension system" directed toward the group's completing the task and that this remains active or in tension until the task is completed by the group There are no manifestations of a tension system if the group vote is against completing a task Lewis (1944) and Lewis and Franklin (1944) had previously done experiments which they interpreted in a similar way when a task with disjunctive requirements is undertaken by a pair of persons, the tension system of any given individual member will be reduced by completion of the task, whether this is accomplished by the joint efforts of the pair or by the efforts of his partner alone

Horwitz' analysis of his data also showed that the existence of member motives to attain the group goal does not depend upon whether the individual voted for the group to attempt it Even though initially he may vote not to undertake a task, he may subsequently accept the group's decision to do so and become motivated to see the group complete it This can be explained by the fact that each of the groups in Horwitz' experiment was composed of girls from the same college sorority and the experiment was introduced as a test of how well the group could perform in representing its sorority Under these conditions, member acceptance of group goals would be expected to be high Members of organized groups under such conditions are likely to "identify" with the group and "internalize" its goals

In his study of cooperation and competition Deutsch (1949*b*) created high acceptance of group goals in his cooperative condition by arranging that the outcomes to the individual members of previously unorganized groups would have high correspondence· individual outcomes were made to depend on the effectiveness of group performance with the consequence that there was strong individual motivation to complete the group task In his competitive condition individual outcomes in each group were made negatively correspondent, so that it is not reasonable to refer to *group* goals in this condition As compared with the competitive groups, the cooperative ones showed greater division of labor but greater coordination of their efforts, more

effective intermember communication with greater acceptance of each
other's ideas and fewer difficulties in understanding each other, and
greater intermember friendliness and desire to win one another's respect  Perhaps most significant is the fact that the cooperatively
organized groups were more productive_ They solved puzzles more
rapidly and wrote longer and better recommendations on human relations problems.  The members were generally more satisfied with the
group and its products

Although it is likely, as we have said, that consensus about goals
must rest on a base of widespread acceptance, it is also likely that to
operate effectively a group must have a consensus even wider than that
yielded by initial acceptance  To attain this, some of those members
who initially do not accept the goal must be caused, if not to accept
the goal, then at least to comply by acting as if they accepted it (e g ,
by announcing their support or by working for its attainment)  This
means that the majority group members may have to exercise whatever
power they have in order to attempt to gain an operating consensus

Since their members are highly interdependent, highly cohesive
groups should have a relatively great amount of fate control to convert
for the purpose of gaining compliance from deviate members who do
not accept the goal of the majority  Schachter (1951) shows that
highly cohesive groups do direct more communication toward the
deviate than do less cohesive groups and that, furthermore, highly
cohesive groups more emphatically reject the deviate when he fails to
join the consensus.

Because of its fate control, a highly cohesive group should be able
to insure a high degree of behavior in accordance with any type of
group goal.  Schachter, et al. (1951), advance the hypothesis that, as
compared with less cohesive groups, highly cohesive groups will attain
more conformity to work goals, whether these are directed toward
restricting output or toward increasing it.  In their experiment to test
this hypothesis Schachter, et al , obtained support for the hypothesized
relationship only when the work goal was to restrict output  However, Berkowitz's (1954) variation on the earlier experiment appears to
support both parts of the hypothesis  Seashore (1954) extended this
line of investigation to industrial work groups and has obtained confirmation of the relationship between cohesiveness of the group and
conformity to production goals, both when the goal is toward lower
and when it is toward higher productivity  Seashore has also thrown
light on a determinant of the level of the production goal set by the
group.  When the group members perceive the company as providing
a "supportive setting" for the group, the goal that is set is toward higher

pioductivity, and when the company is perceived as not providing a suppoitive setting the goal tends to be toward iestricting pioduction

We have said that with increased cohesiveness of the group its members can moie dependably be made to behave, at least superficially, as if they accepted the group goal, but cohesiveness may also have moie subtle effects which facilitate genuine acceptance  High cohesiveness both ieflects and pioduces a widespiead shaiing of values Since these values affect the selection of goals, there is also likely to be found in such groups a relatively widespiead consensus based on acceptance  It would seem to follow from this ieasoning that the costs of monitoring compliance and applying sanctions for noncompliance must in the main be boine by gioups whose lack of cohesiveness makes such cociion all the less dependable

Consensus about goals may not require that influence attempts be actually communicated from the majority to the undecided oi unaccepting minority  It is possible that the minority member will acquiesce if he peiceives that the goal is accepted by a nearly unanimous majoiity  In hei expeiiment on the relative effectiveness of vaiious aspects of the group-decision piocess Bennett (1955) found this to be so, and, moreover, it appeared to be a major determinant of the acceptance of gioup decisions  In situations like those arranged by Bennett, in which each gioup member publicly declares his opinion about the goal, suiveillance by the majority is automatic, and it is likely that various subtle sanctions are transmitted directly and/or by promise

## 14 2  GROUP DISCUSSION AND GOAL ACCEPTANCE

A member may resist accepting a goal for a variety of reasons, many of which appear to deiive from unclaiity about such matteis as what is the most desirable state of the task?  What will his outcomes be if the specified task is put into the designated state?  Do his inteiests in this matter coiiespond with those of the other membeis?  Is it possible to get the task into a ceitain desirable state?

That such unclarities have ramifying effects which include a contribution to the member's resistance to goal acceptance is indicated by an expeiiment conducted by Raven and Rietsema (1957)  Their statement on this point is worth quoting

> As a gioup member, the subject who had a cleai pictuie of his group goal and group path expeiienced greatei feelings of group-belongingness, particulaily as manifested in an involvement with the group goal and in sympathy with group emotions  He was also      moie willing to accept influence fiom his gioup, than subjects who weie uncleai about the goals and paths of their gioup [p. 42].

They also report that the subject with clear understanding of the group goal was more interested in his goal-related task

The general speculation may be hazarded that, over-all, much of the unclarity that members have about prospective goals may be reduced by group discussion, with a maximum of participation throughout the group Studies by Bavelas (reported in Maier, 1946) and Coch and French (1948) indicate that new production standards for work groups are more readily accepted when the individual participates in setting them than when they are introduced by managerial fiat or with exhortations and assurances from above

Willerman's early investigation of the *group-decision* method (1943) indicates that the same general principle applies to producing member acceptance of group goals The problem studied was that of increasing the consumption of whole-wheat bread in college dormitories during World War II In some cases the groups were asked to decide how much they would increase their consumption for the following week, and in other cases a specific goal was set for them and they were requested to try to meet it The result was that the members felt more eager to reach the goals they had decided upon themselves (even though these were no less difficult than the goals given the other groups) and whole-wheat consumption tended to be greater in the decision groups The exception to this trend was one decision group in which a high goal was set by a bare majority of the members The minority was quite dissatisfied with this goal, and the general level of motivation to achieve this goal was lower in this group than any other one.

This incident raises again the question of perceived amount of support for the group goal, mentioned earlier in connection with Bennett's study (1955) In the situation studied by Willerman this factor may have an important bearing on the person's confidence that the group will be able to achieve the goal Even if a person would like to see a certain task state effected, he is not likely to support the attempt to do so if he judges the group's power over the task to be inadequate However, in many cases, as in Willerman's, the group's power depends upon how uniformly members can be induced to take necessary actions Amount of consensus, then, will have a circular effect Only the rasher members will much favor the goal unless many persons do, so a consensus may be slow in developing But, once some threshold degree of consensus is reached, there will be a snowballing of support as with increasing consensus the less and less confident members become convinced that the group will be able to mobilize sufficient power.

A further important finding by Willerman was that in the decision groups eagerness to achieve the group goal had no relation to the individual's own preference for whole-wheat as compared with white bread  In the request groups, on the other hand, these two variables were correlated, persons liking whole-wheat bread were more eager to see the group's consumption increased  This finding suggests again, as did Horwitz', that in organized groups members may set aside their personal preferences in favor of the group decision  This is probably explained by the existence of rather generalized identification relationships (i e., a correspondence of outcomes) among the members of such groups. if some fail to achieve what they set out to do, the outcomes of the others are reduced as well, but with success for some all members' outcomes are increased

Although it is true that evidence from Bennett's carefully analytic experiment (1955) suggests that the discussion aspect of the group-decision procedure might be dispensed with, in other settings this may be an important (though admittedly unanalyzed) factor  For example, the sequence of events by which a given member will profit from attainment of the group goal is often long and tenuous, particularly in large groups. (On this point, the reader is referred to the earlier discussion in Chapter 11 of complex patterns of interdependency and control in large groups )  In such instances it is certainly possible for group discussion to contribute to acceptance of group decisions by reducing concern about compensation for working to attain the goal. Of course, some members of the group may be convinced that the role they have been assigned or are likely to be assigned in pursuing a given group goal may involve too much of the cost and too little of the reward due to them in the light of their CL's. For such a person, group discussion may afford an occasion for a kind of artificial and temporary correspondence of outcomes to be generated  Explicitly or implicitly, he can place a price upon his cooperation, thereby inducing the other members to convert their fate control in an augmentative fashion  By this means, a person who otherwise stands to gain little or even to suffer a loss from the attainment of the goal can be assured an improvement in his outcomes should that event occur.

In discussing the advantages of group discussion and participation procedures, we should not overemphasize their function merely to clarify for the various members the value and attainability of the group goal  An equally important fact may be that, as compared with other methods of goal setting, these procedures lead to the selection of goals that are in fact more acceptable to a larger proportion of the members) This would tend to be the case if the participation procedure heightened the likelihood that the values most widely shared among the members are reflected in the goals finally selected There may also be (actual changes of opinion about the value or attainability of the goal, and as the individuals exchange their information about it these changes are likely to be convergent, with a resulting increase in the degree to which the members' outcomes actually correspond )

Particularly in groups that do not voluntarily assemble (Chapter 10) there may be members who exist chronically below CL by virtue of the fact that their outcomes cannot ever be correspondent with those of the majority of the group These individuals would be inclined to resist and obstruct any consensus about group goals Fouriezos, Hutt, and Guetzkow (1950) have studied phenomena which suggest this effect. Evaluations were made of the amount of ego-related or "self-oriented" behavior exhibited in decision-making groups. This behavior exemplifies the kind of activity which results from lack of goal acceptance because, as the authors define it, self-oriented behavior shows no regard for the attainment of the group goal or the solution of the group's problem Groups showing a high incidence of self-oriented behavior were found to express less satisfaction with their meetings and their decisions, to perceive themselves as less unified, and to meet for longer times while completing fewer agenda items.

We have already mentioned that resistance to consensus may come from strong doubts about the likelihood that the state of the task designated by the group goal can be attained with the group's range of skills An experiment by Rosenthal and Cofer (1948) demonstrates that as the group goal begins to appear increasingly unattainable the members turn more and more to their own individual goals The implication would seem to be that these members would gradually begin to show "self-oriented" behavior as exhibited by the members of the groups studied by Fouriezos, et al On the other hand, Berkowitz and Levy (1956) show that when members learn that their group is doing well their motivation regarding the task increases, as indicated by a high amount of task-oriented discussion during a "break" between work periods

## 14 3 Goal Attainment (Group Problem Solving)

In this section we assume that a certain group goal has already been accepted by most members and we consider the processes by which actions are chosen as means of attaining that goal It should be emphasized that the processes of goal setting and means selection cannot usually be clearly distinguished in natural situations. As noted in the

preceding section, acceptance of goals often depends upon a prior
determination of the availability of means adequate to their attainment
The justification for the separate consideration here of means-selection
processes is that a great deal of research has been conducted in which
an investigator dictates a goal for a given group and in which the
incentives are such that all or most of the members may be assumed
to have accepted it    In the many studies on group problem solving,
for example, some sort of puzzle or problem is given the group and the
interest is in how the members arrive at a means for solving it

Earlier in this chapter group goal is defined as a certain state of a
particular task that the members regard as yielding them, in one way
or another, favorable outcomes.   The means to attaining these outcomes may consist of behaviors effective in putting the task into the
desired state (in the case of a variable-state task over which the
members have control) and, in any case, consist of the behaviors yielding the high outcomes for the given state    Reaching a proper decision
about these behaviors involves all of the psychological processes
specified in Chapter 9. discrimination of the various task states, knowing what items in the behavioral repertoire yield high outcomes for
different task states, and enacting the appropriate behaviors    The
problems assigned to groups in problem-solving research always involve these processes, but often, because of the investigator's interest
in one particular process, the requirements with respect to the others
are made very *easy*   For example, in an investigation of perceptual
discrimination the subjects are instructed to use a simple set of responses that they have already mastered, and the question of which
of these responses yields high outcomes (i.e , which is correct) for
each state of the presented stimuli is either obvious or readily learned
The only problem, then, is to distinguish the various states    Or the
problem may require the group to learn which combinations of task
states and behaviors yield good outcomes, the various possibilities
in each set being quite distinguishable and the responses easily
performed

In any case, the situation is always one in which each member of the
group can make judgments as to the states of the task, has an opportunity to determine which are the optimal matchings of states and actions, and can control part of the action necessary to put the task into
desired states °   The social processes by which a group attains a goal

° In Chapter 15 we consider situations in which there is a division of labor or
specialization with respect to these processes, by virtue of situational restraints
(e g  different channels of information are available to different members) or
social roles (some members are given special responsibility for certain processes,
and other members are more or less excluded from them)

always rely upon these individual behaviors of judging, thinking, acting, etc For example, a group decision as to which of several means to employ in order to reach a goal is always based upon an analysis of the situation by one or more members It would not be appropriate here to go into the details of the basic psychological processes themselves, but we are interested in how the social processes in group problem solving *affect* and *utilize* the judgments, ideas, and abilities of the individuals For example, a member's analysis of a problem may be improved by the information he gains from discussing it with others, but, then, when he thinks he has a good approach to the problem, he may not be able to get his colleagues to listen to it A characterization of the social aspects of group-goal attainment can be derived from investigation of (1) how his ideas are affected (if at all) and (2) how they are incorporated into the group decision (if at all) For the first part of this it is useful to compare the performance of persons acting as group members with their performance while working as individuals in isolation For the second part it is necessary to examine the group-decision process and its products in terms of the utilization of the ideas and contributions of the various members *

### 14 3 1 EFFECTS ON INDIVIDUAL PERFORMANCE

There are many indications in the research literature that the face-to-face social setting which typically characterizes group problem solving has marked effects on the individuals' judgments, thought processes, and actions In Chapter 4 we have already mentioned the effects of working side-by-side with other people the increased quantity and intensity of action (at least when there are no norms to restrict action), the distractions and interference effects where intellectual activities or concentration are concerned, the inhibition or control of certain responses, etc These effects may appear without there being any discussion or communication among the members. For example, with regard to judgmental operations, Allport (1924) found that subjects making (unannounced) judgments in each others' presence showed greater moderation, that is less tendency to give extreme judgments than when the judgments were made alone Allport suggests that when acting *with* other persons one tends in part to respond as if one were reacting *to* them There is certainly overwhelming evidence that when people react to each other, for example, when discussion is permitted, there are strong tendencies toward uniformity

* Elsewhere (Kelley and Thibaut, 1954) we have provided a rather detailed summary of the literature on these points, so the present one will be quite brief.

of behavior, reflecting both mere compliance and genuine changes in outlook, depending upon the factors discussed in Chapter 13

When members' judgments are communicated within a group, there is probably some increase in the range of possible answers each person considers, especially if the communication occurs under conditions (e g , of anonymity) which minimize the uniformity tendencies mentioned above     Dashiell (1935) has suggested that the greater the variety of judgments of others a person is cognizant of, the more likely he is to make a correct one himself     Evidence consistent with this has been presented by Jenness (1932), who found a greater increase in accuracy of individual judgments when a discussion group incorporated a large range of opinions than when it included only a narrow range     Along similar lines, Ziller (1955) found judgments decided upon by groups to be better when there was greater variability among the initially announced individual judgments     On this point, Ziller says, "Since the decision reached must emerge from the scale of judgment developed by the group, the probability is greater that the most superior decision will be included in a relatively heterogeneous range of alternatives than in a relatively homogeneous range of alternatives" [p 153]

There are several indications of the considerable ability of a group to gather and retain a wide range of information—an attribute most authorities would agree to be important for intelligent decision making     For example, several studies indicate that, as compared with individuals, groups are superior at framing the questions to ask in order to obtain information necessary for problem solution.     Lorge, et al (1955), found that the members of groups asked more questions, hence had more information to work with     The groups also seemed to construct many more fruitful hypotheses about the solution     Taylor and Faust (1952), employing the game "Twenty Questions," found that groups required fewer questions to attain the answers     This result may reflect the greater pool of knowledge potentially available in groups or possibly the greater ability of groups to keep active the information that has already been acquired     In other studies the considerable *memory* capacity of groups is indicated by their more rapid learning, as compared with individuals (Gurnee, 1937a, Perlmutter and de Montmollin, 1952)     A very simple interpretation of this, specifically that remembering is usually in the nature of a disjunctive task, can be made  if one person recalls an item, the others need not     If the memory pools of various members do not overlap too much, the total pool of items that can be made available to the group is sizable     Disjunctivity will hold, of course, only as long as there is general acceptance of recalled items    Later, we have more to say on this aspect of tasks

The quality of the ideas produced by persons working in groups is a rather controversial issue at the moment    The early work by Allport (1924) indicates that the effect of the sheer "together" situation is to reduce the likelihood of idiosyncratic associations (on a free association task) and of high quality arguments (on a task of writing arguments against didactic materials)    Allport concluded from his researches that under the stimulus of co-workers, "The *intellectual* or *implicit responses* of thought are hampered rather than facilitated" [p. 274].

Lorge et al (1953), found evidence that group discussions produce novel ideas, that is, ideas none of the group members had mentioned in the individual protocols obtained earlier.    One third of the ideas incorporated in group decisions were original in this sense, but this proportion by itself is difficult to interpret, depending as it must upon the task, amount of time allowed for individual work, and so forth

The recent experiences of Osborn (1957) and others with the discussion procedure known as "brainstorming" leads them to believe that persons can generate many more creative ideas when working together under brainstorming rules than when working alone.    However, Taylor, et al (1958), dissent sharply from this view.    They find that the procedure produces fewer ideas and less original and good ones    However this inconsistency may be resolved eventually, the theory underlying brainstorming seems, in the light of available evidence, to be sound    The general purpose is to produce intercommunication of as wide a range of ideas as possible    The main procedural rule is that criticism and evaluation of both one's own ideas and those of others are to be withheld (until some later time).    A "free-wheeling" attitude is encouraged, as is also "taking off" from other persons' ideas    Taylor's experience suggests that, at least with his college-student subjects, these rules do not have the desired effect    the individual does not feel completely free of criticism in the group situation, and the discussion tends to get everyone into the same "groove" rather than to produce greater variety of approach    One would expect that the success of brainstorming (or of group problem solving in general) would depend a great deal upon the relations among the members, the type of leadership, the nature of the problem, and so on.    For example, we know that highly cohesive groups can mobilize powerful conformity pressures, but Bovard (1951) has evidence suggesting that such groups may develop a clear differentiation between realms of conformity and nonconformity which permits members to feel exceptionally

free in certain areas  This_and similar studies_lead one_to_wonder
whether it may not be possible for a rather small, intimate group to
establish a problem-solving process that capitalizes upon the total pool
of information and provides for great interstimulation of ideas without
any loss of innovative creativity due to social restraints.

## 14.3.2  UTILIZATION OF INDIVIDUAL PRODUCTS

The judgments, ideas, etc, of various members are often utilized by
the group in highly discriminatory ways, some being given little or no
consideration and others, a great deal of consideration.  In part, this
is a matter of *self-weighting*, in which a person voluntarily supports a
point of view that differs from his private one or expresses no opinion
at all  Self-weighting has_been observed to occur particularly in the
case of persons who have little confidence in their own independently
achieved opinions  For example, Gurnee (1937*b*) required groups
to use an acclamation voting procedure to select a single answer and
found that the correct members responded more quickly, hence carried more weight, than the ones with incorrect ideas, this effect presumably being mediated by differences in confidence.  Several studies
find the more correct subjects to be the more confident ones, but it
seems hardly likely that this is always the case.

An effect of this sort is not possible, of course, if there is the strictly
conjunctive task requirement.that every member_must_independently
reach the appropriate decision if the group is to succeed at all  But
with a less stringent conjunctivity requirement (e g , a majority rule
which requires only that a majority be correct for the group to succeed) a minority may withhold its decision each time.  This self-
weighting is advantageous only if the minority consists of those persons
with poor opinions on the issue  That this need not be so is suggested
by Maier and Solem's (1952) evidence that at least on certain problems
a leader can improve the quality of group decisions by making sure
that the members initially in the minority have an opportunity to present their views  Lorge, et al (1953), present evidence that has similar implications  At the beginning of a training course in staff procedures small groups were found to lose a large proportion of the ideas
their constituent members had for solving some problems.  After the
training the group decisions were found to be greatly improved, even
though the individual performances of the same personnel were no
better  The indicated conclusion is that the groups learned how to
retain and use a larger percentage of the ideas possessed by their
members  The same investigators found that the likelihood that an
idea would be reflected in the group decision is directly related to how

many people have the idea before the meeting, but this may mean either that the commoner ideas are the better ones or that an idea has little chance unless several persons support it

Even if there is a strict conjunctivity requirement, the more confident persons' views may carry more weight For example, an experimenter will often make the requirement that all members must agree to a given answer before he will accept it as the "group solution " If discussion is then permitted, members with more conviction in their answers can induce the others, by persuasion or coercion, to act in accord with them It goes without saying that the danger then lies in an agreement being reached through coercion under circumstances in which members with greatest power are not those who possess superior insight into the problem at hand This has not been illustrated in experimental studies, perhaps because power differences within the groups studied have been rather minimal Most investigations into the question have found that group solutions achieved with opportunities for discussion and exertion of pressure are more correct than they would have been otherwise (e g , Thorndike, 1938a, Timmons, 1942) In brief, the controlled studies indicate that in group discussions the right answer tends to win out, but one wonders how true this is in groups in which differences in power are large and not correlated with differences in competency

Shaw (1932) describes some of the social influence processes by which various suggestions and ideas are incorporated into the group solution or rejected She concluded that the more frequent correct solutions attained by her groups (as compared with individuals working on the same problems) can be attributed to the high frequency with which incorrect suggestions are rejected, particularly by someone other than their originators Marquart (1955) essentially replicated Shaw's study and concluded that the observed superiority of groups is due merely to the fact that their performance tends to reflect that of the most capable group member This is, of course, implied by Shaw's description of the *corrective* processes in the group discussion It has the practical implication that, *if* one knew beforehand who the most capable individuals were, it would be more economical from the point of view of getting good answers to assign them problems individually than to employ groups in which a broad range of ability is represented

Certain tasks lend themselves to a division of labor, enabling each person to specialize his activities. In some cases this makes possible rapid learning of the necessary activities and efficient performance through focusing of attention and mechanization of responses (e g , Lorenz, reported on p 1112 in Dashiell, 1935) Specialization also often requires close coordination among the various activities, for example, in an assembly line in which each person's actions depend upon those of the men ahead of him. If only a *temporal* coordination is required, a group work tempo tends to develop which is ordinarily faster than that of the slower individuals but slow enough that some of the faster workers have to drop below their individual tempos The problems of division of labor become much more serious when a *qualitative* coordination is necessary, each person having to adjust what he does to what his colleagues do This is well illustrated in Thorndike's (1938b) experience with groups working on the task of constructing a crossword puzzle. Using other tasks, he found evidence that groups do especially well when the solution of the problem permits of many alternative solutions rather than of only a limited number In the task of constructing a crossword puzzle, however, groups did very poorly, even though an innumerable set of alternative solutions existed. The reader probably can imagine the difficulties that arise when several people work simultaneously on this task As Thorndike points out, the suggestions from different individuals tend to follow diverging lines and are very difficult to fit together. Because all parts of the puzzle are intimately interrelated, yet there are so many different ways to begin, the contributions of various individuals tend not to be very cumulative.

Perhaps the most obvious example of a task requiring coordination is one in which the various members have literally to pull together. Studies of the pulling power of groups indicate that, at least up to sizes of eight or ten, the power per person tends to decrease as group size increases (Dashiell, 1935, p. 1113). Thus two men exert slightly less than twice as much force as that exerted by an individual, and three men, considerably less than three times as much. Presumably, the difficulty indicated by these results revolves around the problem of obtaining adequate coordination of their pulling efforts when several persons work together.

## SUMMARY

Group goals resemble individual goals in that action is taken in both cases to put a task in a particular state, but group goals are more nearly like norms in their dependence on at least some degree of consensus among the members In fact, group goals and norms are frequently difficult to distinguish, the differences resting mainly in the tendency of the group goals to be developed for specific and often nonrecurring purposes and to involve deliberate and planful decisions.

By *acceptance* of a group goal is meant that the group member believes that his outcomes will be improved when the task is in the state designated by the goal. Acceptance of group goals is likely to be high in organized groups and is increased as member outcomes tend to correspond. By virtue of their available fate control, highly interdependent (cohesive) groups are able to gain compliance from initially nonaccepting members (strongly rejecting persistently resistive deviates) regardless of the nature of the goal, that is, whether a production goal calls for restricted or for heightened output.

A member may resist accepting a group goal because of unclarity about the most desirable state of the task; or the resistance may be due to the member's perception that the group has insufficient consensus and/or power to achieve the goal. A further source of a member's resistance may be his concern about whether compensations will ultimately reward him for lengthy and arduous participation. In all of these cases group discussion may provide information and reassurance which reduce the member's resistance to accepting the goal.

Assuming that a given group goal has been accepted by a majority of the members, the processes by which actions are selected as means of attaining the goal are analyzed. These processes may be studied by inquiring into the ways in which the individual member's ideas are affected by them and the ways in which his contributions are incorporated into the group solution. The evidence on group problem solving and group action is shot through with contradictions and inconsistencies. This probably signifies that the problem-solving and goal-attainment processes in groups entail both positive and negative factors. As we have seen, the social setting may inhibit the individual and narrow his perspective, *or* it may stimulate him with a broad realm of information and provide him with a liberating diversity of ideas. In reaching decisions, a group may discourage the person from mentioning an unusual idea, or quickly override him when he does suggest it, *or* it may insure that every suggestion is heard and considered. In brief, the social setting may be constrictive and inhibiting, or it may be provocative and supportive.

As to what makes it one way or the other—what variations in group size, organization, routine, or leadership—the existing evidence furnishes only a number of suggestive leads. These conditions must be identified if we are ever to make intelligent decisions about when to rely on the individual for productive thinking and when to resort to what is sardonically termed "group think." Even if group problem solving proves to be rather limited in its effectiveness in producing high quality decisions, it is hardly likely that decision making can be turned over entirely to individuals. The reasons are implied in the earlier sections of this chapter but may be worth repeating briefly. As long as group members are interdependent in attaining their goals, there must be wide acceptance of the chosen means as well as of the goals themselves. Indeed, as we have noted before, goal acceptance often hinges upon knowledge that an adequate means is available. Furthermore, the coordinated joint action of many members that is necessary to reach certain goals requires widespread understanding of the nature of the chosen means (If general participation in developing and planning a means heightens understanding of it and commitment to it, the group problem-solving process may be more economical in the long run than one that begins with the most expert thought and advice.)

# 15.

## *Functional Analysis of Roles*

From the group-wide uniformities that may derive from conformity to norms and goals, we now turn to a discussion of the special behaviors that each group member may adopt as various roles become differentiated in the group. We present a functional analysis of roles of the type suggested in Chapter 8. There the possibility was raised of determining the roles that should be prescribed and enacted in a group if it is to be successful. If these functionally requisite roles can be identified, even approximately, they afford a kind of model against which the roles actually prescribed and/or enacted may be evaluated and from which implications can be drawn for modifying the group structure in the interests of a better satisfied and more effective membership. This analysis also provides a framework within which we discuss some of the complex problems of leadership.

The reader will recall that by a (prescribed) role we mean the class of one or more norms that applies to a person's behavior with regard to a specific external problem or in his relations with a special class of other group members. Similarly, an enacted role would refer to the actual behaviors that a person exhibits with regard to some problem or class of people. With this as our starting point, the determination of the roles that should be prescribed or enacted in a group involves answering several questions: what are the major external tasks and problems of internal relations confronting the group? In view of these tasks and problems, what specific functions (i.e., required activities) and general classes of function should be performed by some (one or more) of the members of the group? And, finally, how should these

273

functions be organized into roles? That is, what functions or required activities should each group member perform?

These questions are considered in turn in the following two sections

## 15.1 Maintenance and Task Functions

In order to answer the questions posed above, we must have some basis for knowing what is required or desirable for the welfare of a group    Several points of view may be taken here    Some are internal to the group, looking at the question of "desirability" in terms of its shared values (norms) or goals (what behaviors promote the central values of the group?) What behaviors promote the attainment of its goals?

Another possible point of view is an external, more objective one. As an outside observer, one can take into consideration the long-term survival of the group—a point of view that does not necessarily accept the group values or goals as criteria    With this stance, the norms and goals may themselves be subjected to evaluation    The latter point of view is the one to be taken here

We begin with a conception of a typical group which has both internal problems of the relations among its members and external problems of dealing with tasks in its environment °   For a group of this kind to survive, the ultimate requirement is that it must hold its members, that is, keep each one consistently above his current CL$_{alt}$ This means that for each member adequate rewards must be provided and costs of participation in the group must be kept down to reasonable levels,

Since some of the rewards available to members of a group in interaction with a task environment come from that environment, the group must operate successfully upon that environment in order to provide adequate rewards to its members    Thus a family must have adequate financial income or sufficient provision of food and materials from its land, a baseball team must have financial and moral support from its fans    Hence one general problem that confronts this generalized type of group is that of controlling its social and physical environments so that they will yield high outcomes for its members) The activities

° Our analysis owes much to Homans' (1950) distinction between internal and external systems    The following development would not be entirely applicable to either of the extreme types of groups described by Jennings (1950) *psyche-groups*, in which the relations among members constitute in and of themselves the major object of membership and the central purpose of the group, in contrast with *sociogroups*, in which member interaction exists only as required for working together on a common external problem required to do this will be referred to as *task functions*. The adequacy of the performance of task functions determines how much usable power the group has over its social or physical environments and how appropriately this power is exercised. This usable power may be that derived from either fate or behavior control over a social environment or that derived from behavior control over a physical environment (impersonal task).

From Chapters 7 and 9 we can state that the amount of usable power available to the group will be a positive function of the ability of the group (1) to alter the state of a variable-state task or (2) to affect the outcomes to the social environment and will be inversely related to (1) the degree to which the group's outcomes are adversely affected by using its power or (2) the degree to which the power of the group can be resisted by the counterpower of the (personal or impersonal) task.

In general, the greater the usable power available to the group, the better the reward-cost positions that the group can obtain from its environment. If the group's usable power is low, the rewards to be distributed among the group members will be low, and if the group is to survive (i.e., remain intact) then measures will have to be taken to insure that each member is above his $CL_{alt}$. Even if usable power is relatively high, various circumstances may intervene to make group survival problematic in the absence of special measures to insure it. First, the scheme for allocating rewards within the group may be such as to place some members perilously close to $CL_{alt}$. Second, in task activities, as in any activities, costs are involved, and these generally are incurred before rewards are forthcoming. Moreover, certain members may incur unusually heavy costs. And, finally, in many task activities the rewards are fed back to the group only after a considerable time delay. Hence, while awaiting the reward feedback, the group members may be in the neighborhood of $CL_{alt}$, no matter how much usable power the group commands.

In short, to the degree that (1) the group suffers from inadequate usable power, (2) inequities exist in the allocation of rewards among group members, or (3) the latency of rewards fed back to the group is long, then special measures are required to keep all members above $CL_{alt}$. This maintenance of positions above $CL_{alt}$ for all members turns out to be equivalent to maintaining the degree of interdependence in the group. We refer to these activities by which the interdependence of the members is maintained (and, therefore, by which each member maintains his position above $CL_{alt}$) as the *maintenance functions* of the group.

The task functions are those that have to do with controlling the external environment in such a manner as to yield high-reward (or cost-cutting) inputs to the group. In terms of our earlier analysis of tasks, some of the specific processes or activities that would be included under task functions are the following

(1) making discriminations about the present state of the task (perceiving and diagnosing the problem),

(2) changing the state of the task or holding it steady (readying the task for group action),

(3) making predictions about the favorableness of the outcomes for various combinations of actions and task states (concept attainment),

(4) adding behavioral items to the group repertoire (training the members, expertising),

(5) performing the work that produces rewards or cuts costs for the social environment,

(6) fending off interference from the environment,

(7) trading with the social environment.

Whereas the task functions *indirectly* affect the outcomes available to the group members, the maintenance functions are those having to do *directly* with the problem of insuring that each person is kept above his $CL_{alt}$ With a given level of reward or cost-cutting input from the environment, the more effectively the maintenance functions are performed, the higher the general level of satisfaction with the group Under maintenance functions the following might be included.

(1) perceiving and assessing the reward-cost positions of the various members,

(2) allocating the rewards to the various members,

(3) synchronizing reward allocation with cost peaks,

(4) smoothing out fluctuations of rewards by *saving* so that regular payoffs are provided for members, even though the group's intake from the environment is irregular (the treasurer, banker, or investor functions),

(5) creating new rewards for the members, particularly affiliative ones,

(6) cutting costs by reducing anxieties, etc,

(7) cutting costs by improved communication,

(8) lowering both the CL and the $CL_{alt}$ for the various members, for example, by censoring favorable information about available alternative relationships

### 15 1.1 GROUP FUNCTIONS AND INDIVIDUAL INTENTIONS

A word should be said about the concept of *function* as used above In speaking of function we are referring, of course, to the behavior of individual group members, but the level of analysis or the framework from which behavior is viewed is different from that previously used In discussing *sets* we analyzed behavior from the point of view of the individual performing it—his intentions, his immediate goals, etc Therefore, *set* refers to a behavioral sequence that exhibits organization and direction from the viewpoint of the actor On the other hand, the analysis of behavior in terms of group function is made from the point of view of the group· a function is a sequence of behaviors which belong together—exhibit organization and direction—in terms of serving some purpose for the group )

This purpose served by a behavior sequence need not necessarily be reflected in the intentions, conscious or otherwise, of the actor, but it may be It seems reasonable to suppose that if a person is aware of the functional significance of his behavior, he will make a greater contribution to the group's success, assuming he is concerned about it, than otherwise Furthermore, if his personal intentions correspond to functional values, his contribution is likely to be greater than if they are related only to the achievement of purely personal goals Some evidence on this point is provided by the study of Fouriezos, Hutt, and Guetzkow (1950), referred to in Chapter 14 Observations were made of a large number of decision-making groups (boards of directors, planning committees, etc.). Each group was evaluated in terms of the extent to which the behavior of the members was directed toward the satisfaction of ego-related or "self-oriented" needs without concern for its effects upon the solution of the problem facing the group. Groups rated low on amount of self-oriented need, as compared with those given high ratings, were found to move more rapidly through a large number of the items on their agendas

## 15.2 ORGANIZATION OF FUNCTIONS INTO ROLES

The specific processes and functions listed above may be organized and carried out in various ways Generally, there tends to be at least a minimal degree of regularity about which processes are carried out by which people, that is, norms begin to develop and stability of expectation and behavior ensues. Then when the performance of particular processes becomes regularized by norms applying to specific persons, role differentiation has begun.

In keeping with our earlier general definition of role, we may define (prescribed) *functional role* to mean the class of one or more functions that a person is expected to perform in relation to some specific external problem or in relation to a special class of other group members. Given this definition, let us now consider the question of the organization of the various functions into roles. Are there any principles relating to the best division of the various functions among the members of a group?

The first considerations have to do with the abilities of the individuals performing the roles. It is fairly apparent that no person should perform a role that overloads his perceptual or motor capacities. This is ultimately a matter of minimizing costs, since these costs probably rise sharply as the limits of a person's abilities are approached. Functions should also be combined with a view to the organization of abilities within individuals. For example, some functions require mental skills (cognitive and concept-formation skills), whereas others require social skills (sensitivity to other's outcomes and ability to reassure and praise). We might expect that a factor-analytic study would reveal that these various abilities comprise several orthogonal factors. If this proved to be true, it would then be reasonable to assign to a person with high concept-formation skill all those functions requiring this ability and to another person with high social skill, a set of functions appropriate to *his* ability.

A different consideration, one that might cut across the above, is the compatibility of the various sets a person is required to assume in order to perform his assigned functions. Functions should be grouped that involve sets characterized by little mutual interference (praising others, reducing their inhibitions, and assessing their affective states are probably compatible) or in which the incompatible sets are unlikely to be activated simultaneously.

Functions may also be organized with an eye to minimizing communication or synchronization costs. For example, referring back to norm-sending functions, it is simpler, as well as perhaps more effective, to have the same person maintain surveillance and apply sanctions than to have different persons do this. In general, when functions must be coordinated, then within the limits of compatibility and work load they should be performed by the same person.

### 15.2.1 SEPARATION OF TASK AND MAINTENANCE ROLES

One basic question is whether the task and maintenance functions should be performed by the same persons. R. F. Bales has suggested that the most primitive and widespread role differentiation in small groups is the emergence of a task specialist and a social-emotional specialist, the latter performing most of what we have termed maintenance functions. Bales and Slater (1955) comment that,

> The appearance of a differentiation between a person who symbolizes the demands of task accomplishment and a person who symbolizes the demands of social and emotional needs is implicit in the very existence of a social system responsive to an environment Any such system has both an "inside" and an "outside" aspect and a need to build a common culture which deals with both The tendency toward this fundamental differentiation holds whether there are age and sex differences between members or not In the small decision-making group it appears as the difference between the task specialist and the best liked man, in spite of the absence of differences in age and sex. In the marital couple it appears as the difference between the role of husband and wife, according to the sex difference, with age usually about the same or irrelevant In the parent-child relation it appears along the age or generation axis, and holds whatever the sex of the parent or child [pp. 303–304]

Zelditch (1955) examined data from fifty-six societies on role differentiation in the nuclear family. He concludes that although there are some methodological problems in the classification of cases the families in these fifty-six societies show a differentiation into a task specialist and a maintenance specialist, and, further, for families consisting of just one male adult, one female adult, and their immediate children, it is the male adult who is the task specialist and the female adult who is the maintenance specialist.

Bales' account of the basic events that lead to this simple differentiation may be paraphrased in our terms as follows when any newly formed group is confronted with a task or problem, the members of the group begin to incur costs as they set about working at the task These task-related or problem-solving behaviors are instigated by one of the members who is at least temporarily the task specialist (or task leader) and who is identified simply by virtue of his initiating the largest number of task-relevant interactions (We are not concerned at the moment with whether he is a "good" or competent leader ) The task leader's role thus induces increased costs in the other members Unless the task quickly yields compensating rewards, the result is that the other members tend to drop below CL. The annoyance and aggression that the group members develop from this below-CL experience may be in part directed toward the task specialist who instigated the cost-incurring behaviors. If this process continues so that the members' outcomes begin to fall toward $CL_{alt}$, the group may begin to disrupt if special action is not taken, and it is here that, for groups that survive, the maintenance (or social-emotional) specialist enters His contribution is to increase the rewards to members, by warm supportive behavior toward them, and/or to reduce their costs, by such behavior as making jokes that release tension and, in general, by reducing their anxieties

As to why it is desirable that these roles be performed by different persons, several possible reasons may be offered First is the possibility that the abilities required by the two roles are fairly independent. If there is little or no correlation between the two sets of abilities and if the two persons most suited for the roles actually enact them, then the most probable pattern will be that two different persons will perform the two roles There may also be an actual incompatibility between the two roles, one requires arousing other members out of their quiescent states and instigating them to work on the task at hand, the other requires reassuring and rewarding behavior that in some degree operates to return them to a relaxed, satisfied state These roles also tend to produce quite different reactions among the other members, the task specialist evoking at least a bit of hostility and the maintenance specialist very positive sentiments (the latter is usually the most popular person in the group). If these roles were assumed by the same person, the remaining group members would have strong ambivalence toward him The costs created by this conflict can be reduced by splitting the roles and thereby splitting the ambivalence, that is, by permitting other members to express at least some hostility* toward one person and totally positive feelings toward another

Evidence to document the hypothesis that task and maintenance functions cannot effectively be incorporated in one leadership role comes from Fiedler (1958) His data on leadership and group effectiveness in basketball teams, surveying parties, bomber crews, tank crews, and open-hearth crews in a steel mill may be interpreted to mean that the addition of maintenance functions to the leader's role may seriously interfere with his ability to carry out his task functions With good consistency through the diverse groups studied two main findings emerge from Fiedler's research when groups that perform effectively are compared with those less effective.

(1) For a group to be effective its leader must be accepted Operationally, acceptance means that group members will rank him well

* We do not wish to exaggerate the intensity of this hostility Countering the development of hostility toward the task specialist will be an appreciation of his instrumental worth, and in any case there will usually be some external social restraints as well as internalized ones against any extreme and overt manifestations of hostility.

up on the list in response to the question "Who is your most preferred co-worker?"

(2) For a group to be effective, its leader must maintain a certain degree of social distance from his followers This social distance is manifested by the fact that the leader is critical of incompetent followers, sharply differentiating them from the more competent ones.

In Fiedler's words. The leader

. . must be willing to reject co-workers who do not adequately perform their jobs This requires emotional independence and detachment from others The person who readily forms deep emotional ties with his subordinates, who needs to be liked and supported by his men, will find it difficult to discipline or to discharge them, since this may decrease his popularity or cause him to lose their friendship. . .

This requires a reinterpretation of the social barriers which by custom and tradition separate officers from enlisted men in the armed services, and executives from other employees in business and industry These barriers cannot be adequately explained in terms of the "familiarity-breeds-contempt" notion that one must prevent subordinates from becoming too familiar with their leader Rather, the main function of the barriers seems to consist of preventing the leader from becoming too familiar with his men . In the presence of such social barriers, the leader is less likely to form deep emotional attachments or close friendship with subordinates, which could lead to favoritism toward some and poor discipline among all the men in his unit [p 44]

And, recalling the discussion of power strategies in Chapter 7, we might add that this resultant "poor discipline" may derive in part from the leader's loss of power if he comes to depend too much on his 3) followers for friendship If the performance of maintenance functions tends to have this effect by reducing social distance between leader and followers, then the task leader should specialize in task functions and leave maintenance activities to others

Although differentiation may be desirable in a small group between the person who performs the task functions and the one who acts as maintenance specialist, there is some evidence suggesting that the continued effectiveness of the group is contingent upon the development were that for groups which show these two specialists to be in conflict of a coalition or at last a modus vivendi between these two Heinicke and Bales (1953) report a study of developmental trends in small problem-solving groups observed over four sessions Their findings for example, when the task specialist attempts to displace the maintenance specialist, the task performance of the group deteriorates It may be supposed that both persons have considerable power in the

group by virtue of their role performances   The placing in opposition
of their power must have repercussions throughout the group, interfering with the effective performance of their respective roles and
bringing confusion to the other members as to where responsibility for
various functions resides

An example of a successful coalition is provided by the technique of
group therapy often used at the Tavistock Institute in London ( Sutherland and Menzies, 1947 )   The technique takes off from the assumption
that the group members are initially ambivalent toward any authority
Rather than deplore or combat this ambivalence, the therapeutic
strategy attempts to exploit it   Two therapists are assigned to the
group.   One of these deliberately makes a series of very bald interpretations of member behavior and attitudes—interpretations calculated
to get ( hostile ) feelings and defenses out in the open   Eventually, the
second moves in to use the positive feelings that the members have for
him  to initiate integrative processes that re-establish a relationship between the first therapist and the group

The dichotomous separation of task and maintenance roles may not
be necessary under all conditions   From the foregoing analysis, we
would expect the separation to be especially desirable ( whenever the
use of personal influence is required for getting others to work on the
task, ) as in groups in which norms about task performance do not exist )
If, however, there are clear norms as to what each person should do on
the common task and when he should do it  instigations to conform to
these norms may come from many members, and no person will need
to generate much hostility toward himself if he uses the norm as the
basis for urging others to task efforts   This is an important part of the
pattern of behavior referred to as "democratic" leadership.   The
democratic leader encourages the members to influence one another
in their work on the task, thereby avoiding the risk of antagonizing
them by personal and direct pressures   By group decision and participation procedures, he attempts to distribute many of the task functions among the membership at large, and in this manner is enabled
to perform a maintenance role himself   Lippitt and White (1952)
found that democratic leadership resulted in a high frequency of member suggestions for group action, low dependency on the leader, and
little member discontent about their relations with the leader   It may
be, however, that the obviously superior knowledge and power of the
adult leader in these studies also acted to reduce the necessity for his
maintaining social distance from the other members ( eleven-year-old
boys )

### 15.2.2    ALLOCATION OF "LEADERSHIP" FUNCTIONS

One common question that arises in connection with the organization of functions into roles has to do with the allocation of certain *leadership* functions, such as those involving planning, making decisions, and coordinating the activities of the members  Is it desirable for these functions to be performed by one specific person or is it better for them to be distributed through the group?  In other words, should there be a leader whose role is unique, different from that of the other members?

There are a number of different opinions about this issue (Chapter 36 in Cartwright and Zander, 1953)   Some authorities believe that differentiation of a leader role results in greater efficiency.  Other authorities, pointing to the group-decision studies and the experimental comparisons of authoritarian and democratic leadership styles, contend that the motivation of members is higher the more they are permitted to participate in the performance of some of the leadership functions The present evidence does not afford a basis for answering the question precisely, but it does suggest that under many circumstances *both* differentiation of the leader role, with respect to some functions, *and* distribution of other functions are desirable (The question then seems to be which functions should be concentrated in a leader role and which should be performed by many members )

Perhaps the most extensive evidence on this problem comes from a series of studies of work-group supervisors and foremen conducted by the Survey Research Center at the University of Michigan and reported by Kahn and Katz (1953).  In a number of different businesses and industries work groups were separated into those of high and low productivity  The members of each group were interviewed about the activities of the various members and especially about the person designated as supervisor  With fairly high consistency across the different kinds of work groups and organizations, supervisors of the high productivity groups were found to play a more differentiated role than the supervisors of groups with poor production records  They spent more time planning, providing materials, doing special skilled tasks, and "supervising", they devoted less time to the tasks which the other men themselves were doing  This differentiation was also associated with high morale.  On the other hand, although the high productivity supervisors gave more time to supervisory functions, they did not supervise so closely and they delegated authority to a greater degree than the low-production supervisors, checking up on the employees less frequently, giving work instructions less frequently, and letting the subordinates have more freedom to do their work at their own pace and in their own way

These results suggest, then, that at least in a situation in which there is a formally designated leader it is advantageous if he plays a role somewhat different from that of the other members, but this differentiation does not preclude his delegating some functions to the other members  This conclusion is quite in keeping with most of the studies of democratic and "participatory" leadership   For example, in the Lippitt and White (1952) experiment, the adult leader permitted the boys to perform such functions as setting goals and assigning jobs, but the leader always assumed responsibility for keeping the boys informed of the general steps to their goal and for proposing possible solutions to problems that arose.  This study is especially important in showing dramatically the different consequences of explicit delegation of functions (as in the democratic groups) as opposed to dispersion of functions through default of the leader (as in the "laissez-faire" groups)

Perhaps, then, the question is not whether there should be differentiation but what the particular functions should be that distinguish the leader  The answer to this undoubtedly depends upon the particular work and organizational setting within which the group operates  Group goals are often prescribed, as in work groups, but there is usually some need for planning and coordination of activities   Only in the extreme instance in which each person's activities are totally prescribed does it seem likely that there will be no need for some sort of special supervisory role

Many different explanations may be given for the finding that the supervisory role should be somewhat differentiated   In work groups, such as those reported on by Kahn and Katz, some of the planning and coordinating functions are likely to go by the board if the designated supervisor defaults on them  But, beyond this, there may be an advantage in focusing the responsibility for these functions in order to maximize the motivation for their performance  There may also be certain functions that are more effectively performed by a single person for reasons of insuring coordination, particularly if that person is especially competent

It may also be desirable to fulfill members' expectations about a special leadership role, as illustrated by a pair of studies of decision-making conference groups in business, industry, and government   In the first of these Berkowitz (1953) shows that members tend to be less satisfied with the conference when persons other than the designated chairman perform leadership functions.  This sharing of leadership is indicated by the designated chairman's exerting little control over the group process and being little differentiated from the other members in the functions he performs Berkowitz concludes that " there appears to be an expectancy of role differentiation between the designated leader and the group members with each performing somewhat unique functions" [p 238] However, these expectations can apparently be set aside and sharing of leadership, accepted, if the problem under discussion is an urgent one that members are strongly motivated to solve. Berkowitz reports that the differentiation between chairman and other members is correlated with satisfaction only when the problem is not a pressing one

As to what the functions expected of the designated conference chairman might be, Crockett (1955) provides some evidence in a further report on the same groups He describes how persons other than the designated chairman take over leadership when the chairman is inadequate in establishing goals, outlining the problems entailed in achieving these goals, asking for information, encouraging clarification of members' contributions, and proposing solutions to the problems These functions, then, are evidently those which the designated chairman is expected to perform If he fails to do so, other members will perform them in his place

One further finding reported by Kahn and Katz is noteworthy Consistently, the foremen or supervisors of productive work groups were characterized by the workers as taking a personal interest in them, even in their off-the-job problems Kahn and Katz describe these supervisors as being employee-oriented rather than production-oriented or institution-oriented They have good communication with their men, help them out with problems, and provide special training when necessary Thus the differentiation of the supervisory role in the effective groups was not found to require an impersonal relationship or social distance between the supervisor and his men

These findings seem to contradict those of Fiedler (1958) who, it will be recalled, came to the conclusion that an effective leader must maintain some social distance from his followers Yet the contradiction may be only superficial The objective evaluative attitude which Fiedler states is necessary for an effective leader to maintain need not be compromised by his expressing an interest in his men or giving them help and support on the job, for these activities do not necessarily render the supervisor emotionally dependent upon his subordinates. Indeed, we would ordinarily expect such activities to increase *their* dependency upon him Only if the nature of the personal contact is such as to cause the supervisor to become personally attached to the men is

it likely to interfere with his ability to evaluate and discipline them
Careful investigation of the exact nature of the interaction between
supervisors and men, along with an analysis of the emotional needs
various supervisors bring to the work group, is indicated.

## 15 3  FACTORS AFFECTING THE FUNCTIONAL
ROLE ORGANIZATION

After the foregoing consideration of how functional roles *should be*
organized, note should be taken of certain factors that affect the way
in which they *actually are* organized, whether this is the best organization from a functional viewpoint or not

One important factor in determining organization is that(expectations and perceptual readinesses about "natural" patterns or combinations of functions)are imported into any new group, and these expectations tend to conform to the member's past experiences with the cus-
tomary behavior of important role occupants, for example, his mother
and his father   The separation of the task and maintenance roles in
small informal groups, observed by Bales, may importantly reflect (as
Bales himself realizes) the modeling of the role-structure after the
mother-father role differentiation in the family—a small group in
which all persons have had earlier experiences   This importation of
the family role models *may have* little or nothing to do with the role
differentiation that would be most desirable for the welfare of the
group   For a small group that exists within a larger organization, role
models may be provided by other groups or levels of the organization
For example, Kahn and Katz (1953) found that a lower level supervisor tends to exhibit a style of supervision similar to that he experiences from his own supervisor.  The foreman who is allowed little authority or freedom by his boss in turn delegates little authority to his
own subordinates   This probably reflects not only a "modeling" process but the sheer limitations on the functions over which the foreman
has any sort of control

Preconceptions about role organization may also operate with respect to what is generally referred to as "status "   If group members
differ in their general social status, there may be tendencies to organize
and assign roles that are "fitting," in the common cultural stereotypes,
for each status   Thus decision-making and leadership functions are
likely to be sought by high-status persons.  If, in the external social
organization, these persons have power, lower status persons may
acquiesce to this role differentiation   For example, Bass and Wurster

(1953) present evidence that high officials in a company exhibit more leadership in temporary, initially leaderless, discussion groups than do officials of lower rank. Crockett (1955), in a study mentioned earlier, also found that emergent leaders had relatively high positions in the larger organizations within which the small decision-making groups were operating Crockett presents evidence that the persons taking over the leadership functions tend to be those who are most ego-involved in the discussion and the ensuing group decision Thus various motivational factors, such as those reflected in concern about the task and executing group decisions, have an effect upon which members perform which functions.

Sheer size may have an effect upon organization of roles. Hemphill 3 ) (1950) presents evidence from a broad-scale questionnaire study that in larger groups there is greater tolerance for "leader-centered" direction of group activities and greater demands are made with respect to functions the leader is expected to perform Thus one might expect greater differentiation between the leader and follower roles in larger groups than in smaller ones Consistent with this is the evidence that as a group increases in size from three to seven there is increasing differentiation between the one or two most active members and the rest (Bales, et al., 1951, Stephan and Mishler, 1952, and Bass and Norton, 1951)

Considerable role differentiation may be *dictated* by the super- 4 ordinate social environment, for example, when the plant manager or industrial engineer distributes regular work assignments to specific employees and designs a communication network to control social interaction, or when the experimenter in a psychological laboratory induces a particular behavior set in his subjects or manipulates the possibilities for communication among the subjects.

The effects of experimentally created communication networks) on 5 the assignment of roles and related aspects of small-group functioning have been well documented in recent years The impetus to this work was given largely by Bavelas (1948, 1950), who extended and refined some ideas of Lewin (1941) In addition, Bavelas pointedly illustrated the possibility of studying interpersonal organization with concepts that Lewin had used primarily for analyzing intrapersonal organization With a rigor uncommon in social psychology, Bavelas developed the beginnings of a language for describing patterned structures within which positions are linked by communication channels With these concepts, it is possible to describe and measure with some precision the relative centrality of positions within a structure (the most central position being that separated from all of the others by the lewest communication links or channels) as well as differences between structures in terms of their degree of centralization.

Research deriving from these concepts has been done mainly with four- and five-man groups arranged so that each member is assigned a position in the structure which permits him to communicate only to the other positions specified by that structure. For example, in a five-man "wheel" structure or network the most central man can communicate to each of the other four, each of whom can communicate only to him. Another network—a "decentralized" one—is the "circle" in which each man can communicate with the two men on either side of him and a message can return to its initiator by transmission around the circle, passing once through each of the others. Thus in the circle all positions are equally central. These two networks illustrate the extremes of centralization of the seven or eight networks that have been studied.

Typically, in this research each man in the network is given an equal amount of information and the group task is to assemble the information into a solution. Although a number of kinds of dependent variables have been studied, we mention here only those relevant to role differentiation. These results demonstrate quite dramatically the effects of central location in a communication network on one's role and one's satisfaction with that role. Numerous studies (e g., Leavitt, 1951, Shaw, 1954, Gilchrist, et al , 1954, Goldberg, 1955) have shown that the likelihood of being nominated as leader of the group is an increasing function of centrality of the position in the network. Moreover, satisfaction with one's position, individual morale, is similarly related to centrality of position (Leavitt, 1951, Shaw, 1954, Gilchrist, et al , 1954). Leavitt has suggested that morale is increased by positional centrality because the more central the position, the greater the possibilities for independent action. As the position becomes less central, the individual's alternative possibilities for sending and receiving information become more and more restricted. Leavitt assumes this to be the source of dissatisfaction. Shaw points to an additional possible explanation those in more central positions spend less time per message than those less centrally located, the former are busier and less likely to get bored.

## 15.4  Leadership

At various points throughout this book and particularly in the last sections we have considered problems and evidence that pertain to leadership. We do not attempt here to survey the extensive research literature on the topic but merely present some general evaluative comments   As an introduction to the voluminous literature, the interested reader may wish to consult the summary provided by Gibb (1954)

Not much smaller than the bibliography on leadership is the diversity of views on the topic   Many of the studies essentially ask what do people mean when they speak of a leader?   Other studies begin with a conceptual or empirical definition of leadership and then proceed to determine the correlates or consequences of leadership so defined   Even a cursory review of these investigations shows that leadership means many different things to different people .  Far from being a unitary concept or simple dimension, it is probably one of the most complex phenomena social psychology confronts

Yet, among the complex aspects of leadership, there do not seem to be any properties unique to the phenomena   In virtually all cases leadership seems to be analyzable in terms of other, simpler concepts For example, the leader often emerges as a possessor of power which enables him to initiate changes in the behavior of other persons or to introduce innovations   In other instances, the leader appears as a person who performs certain functions for the group   A related view is that the leader performs the broad organizing functions of assigning members to roles and insuring coordination and communication among various roles.   Yet other emphasis is upon the leader as a norm sender, where he is evaluated with regard to the vividness and accuracy with which he symbolizes the group norms

These views by no means exhaust the different emphases nor are they mutually exclusive.   They all make it possible to consider leadership as a matter of degree rather than as a dichotomous distinction between leader and followers   According to any of these views, any (and every) member of the group can be considered as exhibiting leadership insofar as he exercises power effectively, performs various functions, promotes organization along functional lines, or has symbolic value

However, the ways in which power, functions, and so forth, are combined and assembled into any given leader role is a very complex matter, as we have noted earlier in this chapter   For example, the allocation of power and functions to such a role in any group will depend on such various factors as the nature of the formal or informal specifications for that role in the group, the nature of the external tasks confronting the group, the internal problems of maintenance that the group must solve, and the abilities of those eligible for the role

Thus in the study of leadership the investigator encounters the converging effects of virtually all the factors outlined in this book It is our opinion that leadership research will be most fruitful when it adopts an indirect and analytical approach to its task Rather than going directly into the complex phenomena and surplus-meaning-laden terminology encompassed by the term leadership, research must first be directed toward clarifying problems of power structures, norms and goals, task requirements, functional roles, etc, each of which is complex and challenging enough in its own right In short, an understanding of leadership must rest on a more basic understanding of the structure and functioning of groups

## SUMMARY

An analysis of functionally requisite roles in a group is begun by distinguishing two broad functions which must provide outcomes above each member's $CL_{alt}$ if the group is to survive. *Task functions* are those which (provide rewards to the members by virtue of the group's ability to operate successfully on its environment) that is, by virtue of the group's usable power over its environment. However, all members may not be adequately or continuously rewarded even if the group's usable power is high For example, schemes for allocating rewards within the group may be inequitable, or long delays may occur before rewards are paid out *Maintenance functions* are those which, in viable groups, add (compensations to keep all of the members above $CL_{alt}$)

More specifically, task functions would include such activities as (diagnosing the problem) posed by the environmental task (preparing the task for group action) and (training the various members to perform task assignments Maintenance functions include such activities as assessing the outcomes being obtained by the various members, allocating rewards, and creating new rewards for the members, particularly affiliative ones

As these specific activities are performed with regularity by specific individuals, expectations begin to form to regularize these performances, and role differentiation begins to emerge. At this stage we inquire whether there are any principles which suggest the most effective ways for organizing these functional activities into roles Suggestions are made about the optimal ways in which abilities might be allocated among members and organized within member-roles Further recommendations are made about the grouping of activities to reduce both mutual interference and communication or synchronization costs

From a variety of research evidence it seems likely that task and maintenance functions should not be performed by the same persons (although an important exception to this may occur when there are clear-cut norms that specify task activities of group members) However, other evidence suggests that the task and maintenance roles, although differentiated, should be in a mutually supportive coalition if the group is to be effective

As far as *leadership* functions are concerned (e g , planning, making decisions, coordinating member activities), research evidence seems to indicate the desirability of centralizing some of these functions in the *leader* role and distributing or delegating others throughout the membership

The discussion then turns from the ways functional roles *should be* organized to the factors that affect their *actual* organization    Roles are often imported more or less intact from other important or salient groups, for example, the family    Further, sheer group size may affect the degree of differentiation between roles, especially between leader and follower    Role differentiation may also be dictated by the social environment. the communication network imposed on a group appears to determine in part its degree of role differentiation.

The chapter concludes with a brief discussion of leadership and suggests that this topic can best be investigated by giving first priority to an improved understanding of the basic processes of group functioning.

# Bibliography

Adams, S   Status congruency as a variable in small group performance   *Soc Forces*, 1953, 32, 16–22

Allport, F. H.   *Social psychology*   Boston   Houghton-Mifflin, 1924

Allport, G W   The historical background of modern social psychology. In G. Lindzey (Ed ), *Handbook of social psychology*   Cambridge, Mass · Addison-Wesley, 1954   Pp 3–56

———   *The nature of prejudice*   Cambridge, Mass   Addison-Wesley, 1954

Alper, Thelma G   Memory for completed and incompleted tasks as a function of personality   Correlation between experimental and personality data   *J Pers*, 1948, 17, 104–137

———   The interrupted task method in studies of selective recall   A reevaluation of some recent experiments   *Psychol Rev*, 1952, 59, 71–88

———   Predicting the direction of selective recall. Its relation to ego strength and *n* achievement   *J abnorm soc Psychol*, 1957, 55, 149–165

Arsenian Jean M   Young children in an insecure situation. *J abnorm soc Psychol*, 1943, 38, 225–249

Asch, S E   Forming impressions of personality   *J abnorm soc Psychol*, 1946, 41, 258–290

———   *Social psychology*   New York   Prentice-Hall, 1952

Atkinson, J W   The achievement motive and recall of interrupted and completed tasks   *J exp Psychol*, 1953, 46, 381–390

Attneave, F.   Some informational aspects of visual perception   *Psychol Rev*, 1954, 61, 183–193

Azrin, N, and O. R Lindsley. The reinforcement of cooperation between children   *J abnorm soc Psychol*, 1956, 52, 100–102

Back, K W   Influence through social communication   *J abnorm soc Psychol*, 1951, 46, 9–23

Bales, R F. *Interaction process analysis*   Cambridge, Mass   Addison-Wesley, 1950.

———, and P E Slater   Role differentiation in small decision-making groups   In T Parsons, R F Bales, and others, *Family, socialization and interaction process*   Glencoe, Ill   Free Press, 1955   Pp 259–306

Bales, R F, F L Strodtbeck, T. M Mills, and Mary E Roseborough   Channels of communication in small groups   *Amer. sociol. Rev*, 1951, 16, 461–468

Bass, B M, and Fay-Tyler M Norton   Group size and leaderless discussions   *J appl Psychol*, 1951, 35, 397–400

Bass, B M   and C R Wurster   Effects of company rank on LGD performance of oil refinery supervisors   *J appl Psychol*, 1953, 37, 100–104.

Bates, F L   Position, role, and status   A reformulation of concepts   *Soc. Forces*, 1956, 34, 313–321.

Bavelas, A   A mathematical model for group structures   *Appl Anthrop*, 1948, 7, 16–30

————   Communication patterns in task-oriented groups   *J. acoust Soc Amer*, 1950, 22, 725–730

Benne, K D, and P Sheats.   Functional roles of group members   *J soc Issues*, 1948, 4, No 2, 41–49

Bennett, Edith B   Discussion, decision, commitment, and consensus in "group decision"   *Hum Relat*, 1955, 8, 251–273

Benoit-Smullyan, E   Status types and status interrelations   *Amer sociol Rev*, 1944, 9, 151–161

Berkowitz, L   Sharing leadership in small, decision-making groups.   *J abnorm soc Psychol*, 1953, 48, 231–238

————   Group standards, cohesiveness, and productivity   *Hum Relat*, 1954, 7, 509–519

————, and B I Levy   Pride in group performance and group-task motivation   *J abnorm soc Psychol*, 1956, 53 300–306

Berlyne, D E   Conflict and choice time   *Brit J Psychol*, 1957, 48, 106–118

Bettelheim, B   Individual and mass behavior in extreme situations   *J abnorm soc. Psychol*, 1943, 38, 417–452

Blau, P M   Patterns of interaction among a group of officials in a government agency   *Hum Relat*, 1954, 7, 337–348

Bondy, C   Problems of internment camps   *J abnorm soc Psychol*, 1943, 38, 453–475

Bonney, M E   Popular and unpopular children   A sociometric study   *Sociometry Monogr*, 1947, No 9

Bovard, E W, Jr.   Group structure and perception   *J abnorm soc Psychol*, 1951, 46, 398–405

————, and H Guetzkow   A validity study of rating scales as a device to distinguish participants in stable and temporary groups   University of Michigan *Conference Res Reports*, August 1950

Bowerman, C. E, and Barbara R Day.   A test of the theory of complementary needs as applied to couples during courtship   *Amer sociol Rev*, 1956, 21, 602–609

Bradney, Pamela   The joking relationship in industry   *Hum Relat*, 1957, 10, 179–187

Brehm, J   Post-decision changes in the desirability of alternatives   *J abnorm soc Psychol*, 1956, 52, 384–389

Brown, J S, and I E Farber   Emotions conceptualized as intervening variables —with suggestions toward a theory of frustration   *Psychol Bull*, 1951, 48, 465–495

Brown, R W   Mass phenomena   In G Lindzey (Ed), *Handbook of social psychology*   Cambridge, Mass. Addison-Wesley, 1954   Pp 833–876

Bruner, J S, Jacqueline J Goodnow, and G Austin   *A study of thinking*   New York Wiley, 1956

Bruner, J S, and R Tagiuri   The perception of people   In G Lindzey (Ed), *Handbook of social psychology*   Cambridge, Mass · Addison-Wesley, 1954   Pp. 634–654

Burgess, E W, and P. Wallin   *Engagement and marriage*   Philadelphia Lippincott, 1953

Cameron, N, and Ann Magaret   Experimental studies in thinking. I Scattered speech in the responses of normal subjects to incomplete sentences  *J exp Psychol*, 1949, 39, 617–627

Cantril, H, and G W Allport  *The psychology of radio*  New York. Harper, 1935

Caplow, T.  A theory of coalitions in the triad  *Amer sociol Rev*, 1956, 21, 489–493

Cartwright, D., and A Zander  *Group dynamics*  Evanston, Ill  Row, Peterson, 1953

Cason, H  The influence of attitude and distraction  *J exp Psychol*, 1938, 22, 532–546

Chapanis, A, W R Garner, and C T Morgan  *Applied experimental psychology Human factors in engineering design*  New York  Wiley, 1949

Chapman, D W, and J A Volkmann  A social determinant of the level of aspiration  *J abnorm soc Psychol*, 1939, 34, 225–238

Chowdhry, Kalma, and T M Newcomb  The relative abilities of leaders and non-leaders to estimate opinions of their own groups  *J abnorm soc Psychol*, 1952, 47, 51–57

Christie, R  An experimental study of modifications in factors influencing recruits' adjustment to the army  New York·  Research Center for Human Relations, New York University, 1954

Clark, K B, and Mamie P Clark  Racial identification and preference in Negro children  In G E Swanson, T M Newcomb, and E L Hartley (Eds ), *Readings in social psychology*  New York  Holt, 1952  Pp 551–560

Coch, L, and J R P French, Jr  Overcoming resistance to change  *Hum Relat*, 1948, 1, 512–532

Coffin, T E  Some conditions of suggestion and suggestibility  A study of certain attitudinal and situational factors influencing the process of suggestion  *Psychol Monogr*, 1941, 46, No 4  (Whole No 241)

Cohen, A R  Upward communication in experimentally created hierarchies  *Hum Relat*, 1958, 11, 41–53.

Cohen, E A  *Human behavior in the concentration camp*  New York  W W Norton, 1953

Cottrell, L S  The analysis of situational fields in social psychology.  *Amer sociol Rev*, 1942, 7, 370–382

Crockett, W H  Emergent leadership in small, decision-making groups  *J. abnorm soc Psychol*, 1955, 51, 378–383

Daniel, W J  Cooperative problem solving in rats  *J comp physiol Psychol*, 1942, 34, 361–368

———  Higher order cooperative problem solving in rats  *J comp physiol Psychol*, 1943, 35, 297–305

Dashiell, J F  Experimental studies of the influence of social situations on the behavior of individual human adults  In C Murchison (Ed ), *Handbook of social psychology*  Worcester  Clark University Press, 1935  Pp 1097–1158.

Davis, A, B B Gardner, and Mary R Gardner  The class system of the white caste  In G E. Swanson, T M Newcomb, and E L Hartley (Eds ), *Readings in social psychology*  New York  Holt, 1952  Pp 280–288

Davis, K  *Human society*  New York  Macmillan, 1949

Davis, T E  Some racial attitudes of Negro college and grade school students.  *J Negro Educ*, 1937, 6, 157–165

Davitz, J R   Social perception and sociometric choice of children.   *J abnorm soc Psychol* , 1955, 50, 173–176

Deutsch, M   A theory of cooperation and competition.   *Hum Relat* , 1949a, 2, 129–152

———   An experimental study of the effects of cooperation and competition upon group process   *Hum Relat* , 1949b, 2, 199–232

———   Task structure and group process.   *Amer Psychologist*, 1951, 6, 324–325   (Abstract)

———   Conditions affecting cooperation: Section I   Factors related to the initiation of cooperation   Section II   Trust and cooperation.   New York Research Center for Human Relations, New York University, February 1957

Dickinson, R L , and L Beam   *A thousand marriages*   Baltimore   Williams and Wilkins, 1931

Dittes, J E , and H H Kelley   Effects of different conditions of acceptance upon conformity to group norms   *J abnorm soc Psychol* , 1956, 53, 100–107

Dodd, S C   A social distance test in the Near East   *Amer J Sociol* , 1935, 41, 194–204

Dollard, J , L Doob, N E Miller, O H Mowrer, and R R Sears   *Frustration and aggression*   New Haven   Yale University Press, 1939

Emerson, R M   Deviation and rejection   An experimental replication   *Amer sociol Rev* , 1954, 19, 688–693.

Eng, E W   An approach to the prediction of sociometric choice   *Sociometry*, 1954, 17, 329–339

Estes, S. G   The judgment of personality on the basis of brief records of behavior   Unpublished doctoral dissertation, Harvard University, 1937   Cited in G W Allport, *Personality*   New York   Holt, 1937, 507–509

Farber, M L   Suffering and time perspective of the prisoner   *Univ Iowa Stud Child Welf* , 1944, 20, No 409, 153–227

Fenchel, G H , J H. Monderer, and E L Hartley   Subjective status and the equilibration hypothesis   *J abnorm soc Psychol* , 1951, 46, 476–479

Fendrick, P   The influence of music distraction upon reading efficiency   *J educ. Res* , 1937, 31, 264–271

Festinger, L   Wish, expectation and group performance as factors influencing level of aspiration   *J abnorm soc Psychol* , 1942, 37, 184–200

———   The role of group belongingness in a voting situation   *Hum Relat* , 1947, 1, 154–180

———   Informal social communication   *Psychol Rev* , 1950, 57, 271–282

———   A theory of social comparison processes   *Hum Relat* , 1954, 7, 117–140

———   *A theory of cognitive dissonance*   Evanston, Ill   Row, Peterson, 1957

———, S. Schachter, and K Back   *Social pressures in informal groups*   New York. Harper, 1950

Festinger, L , and J Thibaut   Interpersonal communication in small groups   *J abnorm soc Psychol* , 1951, 46, 92–99

Fiedler, F E   *Leader attitudes and group effectiveness*   Urbana, Ill   University of Illinois Press, 1958

Flemming, C   A factor analysis of the personality of high school leaders   *J. appl. Psychol* , 1935, 19, 597–605

Folsom, J K   *The family and democratic society*   New York   Wiley, 1943

Fouriezos, N T , M L Hutt, and H Guetzkow   Measurement of self-oriented needs in discussion groups.   *J abnorm soc Psychol* , 1950, 45, 682–690

Frank, J D  Experimental studies in personal pressure and resistance. II Methods of overcoming resistance.  *J gen Psychol*, 1944, 30, 43–56

French, Elizabeth G  Motivation as a variable in work-partner selection  *J abnorm soc Psychol*, 1956, 53, 96–99

French, J R P , Jr  Organized and unorganized groups under fear and frustration  *Univ Iowa Stud Child Welf*, 1944, 20, No 409, 299–308

Gibb, C A  Leadership  In G Lindzey (Ed ), *Handbook of social psychology* Cambridge, Mass  Addison-Wesley, 1954  Pp 877–920

Gibb, J R  The effects of group size and of threat reduction upon creativity in a problem-solving situation  *Amer Psychologist* 1951, 6, 324  (Abstract)

Gilchrist, J C  The formation of social groups under conditions of success and failure  *J abnorm soc Psychol*, 1952, 47, 174–187

——, M E Shaw, and L C Walker  Some effects of unequal distribution of information in a wheel group structure. *J. abnorm. soc Psychol*, 1954, 49, 554–556

Goldberg, S C  Influence and leadership as a function of group structure  *J abnorm. soc Psychol*, 1955, 51, 119–122

Collin, E S  Organizational characteristics of social judgment  A developmental investigation. *J. Pers*, 1958, 26, 139–154

Gouldner, A W  *Patterns of industrial bureaucracy*  Glencoe, Ill · Free Press, 1954

Graham, Frances K , Wanda A Charwat, Alice S Honig, and Paula C Weltz  Aggression as a function of the attack and attacker  *J abnorm. soc Psychol*, 1951, 46, 512–520

Green, A W  *Sociology An analysis of life in a modern society*  New York McGraw-Hill, 1956

Gross, E  Symbiosis and consensus as integrative factors in small groups  *Amer. sociol Rev*, 1956, 21, 174–179

Gullahorn, J  Distance and friendship as factors in the gross interaction matrix  *Sociometry*, 1952, 15, 123–134

Gurnee, H  Maze learning in the collective situation  *J Psychol*, 1937a, 3, 437–443

——  A comparison of collective and individual judgments of facts  *J exp. Psychol*, 1937b, 21, 106–112

Haire, M , and Willa F Grunes  Perceptual defences Processes protecting an organized perception of another personality  *Hum Relat*, 1950, 3, 403–412

Haie, A P  A study of interaction and consensus in different sized groups  *Amer sociol Rev*, 1952, 17, 261–267

Harvey, O J , H H Kelley, and M M Shapiro  Reactions to unfavorable evaluations of the self made by other persons  *J Pers*, 1957, 25, 393–411

Hayner, N S , and E Ash  The prison as a community  *Amer sociol Rev*, 1940, 5, 577–583

Hebb, D O , and W. R. Thompson  The social significance of animal studies  In G Lindzey (Ed ), *Handbook of social psychology*  Cambridge, Mass Addison-Wesley, 1954  Pp 532–561

Heider, F  Social perception and phenomenal causality  *Psychol Rev*, 1944, 51, 358–374

——  Attitudes and cognitive organization  *J Psychol*, 1946, 21, 107–112

——  *The psychology of interpersonal relations*  New York: Wiley, 1958

Heinecke, C, and R F Bales   Developmental trends in the structure of small groups   *Sociometry*, 1953, 16, 7–38

Helson, H   Adaptation-level as a basis for a quantitative theory of frames of reference   *Psychol Rev*, 1948, 55, 297–313

Hemphill, J  K   Relations between the size of the group and the behavior of "superior" leaders   *J soc Psychol*, 1950, 32, 11–22

Henderson, M  T, Anne Crews, and Joan Barlow   A study of the effect of music distraction on reading efficiency   *J appl Psychol*, 1945, 29, 313–317

Heron, W.   The pathology of boredom   *Scientific Amer*, 1957, 196, No  1, 52–56

Hersey, R   *Zest for work*   New York  Harper, 1955

Hilgard, E  R   *Theories of learning*   New York  Appleton-Century-Crofts, 1948, 246–247

Hiller, E  T   *Social relations and structures*   New York  Harper, 1947

Hites, R  W, and D. T  Campbell   A test of the ability of fraternity leaders to estimate group opinion   *J soc Psychol*, 1950, 32, 95–100

Hoffman, P  J, L  Festinger, and D  H  Lawrence   Tendencies toward group comparability in competitive bargaining   *Hum Relat*, 1954, 7, 141–159

Hogbin, H  I   *Law and order in Polynesia*   New York  Harcourt, Brace, 1934

Hollingshead, A  B   *Elmtown's youth*   New York  Wiley, 1949

Homans, G  C   *The human group*   New York  Harcourt, Brace, 1950

Horowitz, M  W, J  Lyons, and H  V  Perlmutter   Induction of forces in discussion groups   *Hum Relat.*, 1951, 4, 57–76.

Horwitz, M   The recall of interrupted group tasks   An experimental study of individual motivation in relation to group goals   *Hum Relat*, 1954, 7, 3–38

————   The veridicality of liking and disliking   In R  Tagiuri and L  Petrullo (Eds), *Person perception and interpersonal behavior*   Stanford·  Stanford University Press, 1958   Pp  191–209

Hughes, E  C   The knitting of racial groups in industry   *Amer sociol Rev*, 1946, 11, 512–519

Hurwitz, J  I, A  F  Zander, and B  Hymovitch   Some effects of power on the relations among group members   In D  Cartwright and A  Zander (Eds), *Group dynamics*   Evanston, Ill.  Row, Peterson, 1953   Pp  483–492

Husband, R  W   Cooperative versus solitary problem solution   *J soc Psychol*, 1940, 11, 405–409

Hyman, H  H   Psychology of status   *Arch Psychol*, 1942, No  269.

————   *Interviewing in social research*   Chicago  University of Chicago Press, 1954

Jackson, J  M, and H  D  Saltzstein   The effect of person-group relationships on conformity processes   *J abnorm soc Psychol*, 1958, 57, 17–24

Jenness, A   The role of discussion in changing opinion regarding a matter of fact   *J abnorm soc Psychol*, 1932, 27, 279–296

Jennings, Helen H   *Leadership and isolation*   New York  Longmans Green, 2nd edition, 1950

Jersild, A  T   Emotional development   In L  Carmichael (Ed), *Manual of child psychology*   New York  Wiley, 2nd edition, 1954   Pp  833–917

Jones, E  E   Authoritarianism as a determinant of first-impression formation   *J Pers*, 1954, 23, 107–127

————, and R  DeCharms   Changes in social perception as a function of the personal relevance of behavior   *Sociometry*, 1957, 20, 75–85

Kahn, R L , and D Katz   Leadership practices in relation to productivity and morale   In D Cartwright and A Zander (Eds ), *Group dynamics*   Evanston, Ill  Row, Peterson, 1953.  Pp 612–628

Kardiner, A   *Psychological frontiers of society*   New York  Columbia University Press, 1945

Katz, D , and R L Schanck   *Social psychology*.  New York. Wiley, 1938.

Kelley, H II   The warm-cold variable in first impressions of persons   *J Pers* , 1950, 18, 431–439

————   Communication in experimentally created hierarchies   *Hum Relat* , 1951, 4, 39–56

————, and T W Lamb.  Certainty of judgment and resistance to social influence   *J abnorm soc Psychol* , 1957, 55, 137–139

Kelley, H H , and M M Shapiro   An experiment on conformity to group norms where conformity is detrimental to group achievement   *Amer sociol Rev* , 1954, 19, 667–677

Kelley, H H , and J. W. Thibaut   Experimental studies of group problem solving and process   In G Lindzey (Ed ), *Handbook of social psychology*   Cambridge, Mass . Addison-Wesley, 1954   Pp 735–785

Kelley, H H., and E H Volkart   The resistance to change of group anchored attitudes   *Amer sociol Rev*   1952, 17, 453–465

Kelman, H C.  *Social influence and personal belief  A theoretical and experimental approach to the study of behavior change.*   Privately circulated monograph, 1956

Klein G S   Need and regulation   In M R Jones (Ed ), *Nebraska symposium on motivation*   Lincoln  University of Nebraska Press, 1954, Vol II   Pp 224–274.

Koch, Helen L   Attitudes of young children toward their peers as related to certain characteristics of their siblings.  *Psychol Monogr* , 1956, 70   (Whole No 426)

Koos, E L   *Families in trouble*   New York  King's Crown Press, 1946

Kounin J , N Polansky, B Biddle, H Coburn, and A Fenn   Experimental studies of clients' reactions to initial interviews   *Hum Relat* , 1956, 9, 265–293

Ktsanes, T   Mate selection on the basis of personality type  A study utilizing an empirical typology of personality   *Amer sociol Rev* , 1955, 20, 547–551

Lazarsfeld, P F , and R K Merton   Friendship as social process   In M Berger, T Abel, and C H Page (Eds ), *Freedom and control in modern society*   New York  Van Nostrand, 1954   Pp 18–66.

Lazarus, R S , J Deese, and Soma F Osler   The effects of psychological stress upon performance   *Psychol Bull* , 1952, 49, 293–317

Leavitt, H J   Some effects of certain communication patterns on group performance   *J abnorm soc Psychol* , 1951, 46, 38–50

Lewin, K   Analysis of the concepts whole, differentiation, and unity.  *Univ. Iowa Stud Child Welf* , 1941, 18, No 1, 226–261

————   Frontiers in group dynamics  I  Concept, method and reality in social science, social equilibria and social change   *Hum Relat* , 1947, 1, 2–38

————   Some social-psychological differences between the United States and Germany.   In Gertrud Lewin (Ed ), *Resolving social conflicts*   New York  Harper, 1948a   Pp 3–33

————.  Time perspective and morale.  In Gertrud Lewin (Ed ), *Resolving social conflicts*   New York  Harper, 1948b   Pp 103–124

———— Self-hatred among Jews  In Gertrud Lewin (Ed ), *Resolving social conflicts*  New York  Harper, 1948c  Pp 186–200

———— Group decision and social change  In G E Swanson, T M Newcomb, and E L Hartley (Eds ), *Readings in social psychology*  New York  Holt, 1952  Pp 459–473

————, Tamaia Dembo, L Festinger, and Pauline Sears  Level of aspiration  In J McV Hunt (Ed ), *Personality and the behavior disorders*  New York  Ronald Press, 1944  Pp 333–378

Lewis, Helen B  An experimental study of the role of the ego in work  I The role of the ego in cooperative work  *J exp Psychol* , 1944, 34, 113–127

————, and Muriel Franklin  An experimental study of the role of the ego in work  II The significance of task orientation in work  *J exp Psychol* , 1944, 34, 194–215

Lifton, R J  "Thought reform" of western civilians in Chinese Communist prisons  *Psychiatry*, 1956, 19, 173–196

Lindzey, G , and E. F Borgatta  Sociometric measurement  In G. Lindzey (Ed ), *Handbook of social psychology*  Cambridge, Mass  Addison-Wesley, 1954  Pp 405–448

Linton, R. *The cultural background of personality*  New York  Appleton-Century, 1945

Lippitt, R  A program of experimentation on group functioning and group productivity  In W Dennis (Ed ), *Current trends in social psychology*  Pittsburgh  University of Pittsburgh Press, 1951  Pp 14–49

————, N. Polansky, and S Rosen  The dynamics of power  *Hum Relat* , 1952, 5, 37–64

Lippitt, R , and R K White  An experimental study of leadership and group life  In G E Swanson, T M Newcomb, and E L Hartley (Eds ), *Readings in social psychology*  New York  Holt, 1952  Pp 340–354

Lipset, S M , M A Trow, and J S Coleman  *Union democracy*  Glencoe, Ill  Free Press, 1956.

Lorge, I , J Davitz, D Fox, and K Herrold  Evaluation of instruction in staff action and decision making  An Research and Development Command  Tech Rep No 16  Human Resources Research Institute, Maxwell Air Force Base, Alabama  1953

Lorge, I., J Tuckman, L Aikman, J Spiegel, and Gilda Moss  Solutions by teams and by individuals to a field problem at different levels of reality  *J educ Psychol* , 1955, 46, 17–24.

Luce, R D , and H Raiffa  *Games and decisions*  New York  Wiley, 1957

Luchins, A S  Experimental attempts to minimize the impact of first impressions  In C Hovland (Ed.), *The order of presentation in persuasion*  New Haven  Yale University Press, 1957  Pp 63–75

Lundberg, G A , and Mary Steele  Social attraction-patterns in a village  *Sociometry*, 1938, 1, 375–419

McClelland, D C , J W Atkinson, R Clark, and E Lowell  *The achievement motive*  New York  Appleton-Century-Crofts, 1953

Maccoby, Eleanor E , and N Maccoby  The interview  A tool of social science  In G Lindzey (Ed ), *Handbook of social psychology*  Cambridge, Mass  Addison-Wesley, 1954  Pp 449–487

McCurdy, H. G., and W E Lambert  The efficiency of small human groups in the solution of problems requiring genuine cooperation  *J Pers*, 1952, 20, 478–494

McDougall, W  *Introduction to social psychology*  London  Methuen, 1908.

McGregor, D  The staff function in human relations.  *J soc Issues*, 1948, 4, No 3, 5–22

MacIver, R M, and C H Page  *Society An introductory analysis*  New York· Rinehart, 1949

Maier, N R F  *Psychology in Industry*  Boston  Houghton-Mifflin, 1946

———, and A R Solem  The contribution of a discussion leader to the quality of group thinking  *Hum Relat*, 1952, 5, 277–288

Marquart, Dorothy I  Group problem solving  *J soc Psychol*, 1955, 41, 103–113

Marrow, A J, and J R P French, Jr  Changing a stereotype in industry  *J soc Issues*, 1945, 1, No 3, 33–37.

Martin, W E, J C Darley, and N Gross  Studies of group behavior II Methodological problems in the study of interrelations of group members  *Educ psychol Measmt*, 1952, 12, 533–553

Masling, J, F L Greer, and R Gilmore  Status, authoritarianism and sociometric choice  *J soc Psychol*, 1955, 41, 297–310

Mausner, B  Prestige and social interactions  *J abnorm soc Psychol*, 1954, 49, 557–560

Menzel, H  Public and private conformity under different conditions of acceptance in the group  *J abnorm soc Psychol*, 1957, 55, 398–402

Merei, F  Group leadership and institutionalization  *Hum Relat*, 1949, 2, 23–39

Merton, R K  Bureaucratic structure and personality.  *Soc Forces*, 1940, 18, 560–568

———  *Social theory and social structure*  Glencoe, Ill  Free Press, 1957

Michotte, A  *La perception de la causalité*  (2nd Ed )  Louvain  Publications universitaires de Louvain, 1954

Miller, N. E., and R Bugelski  Minor studies in aggression. II. The influence of frustrations imposed by the in-group on attitudes expressed towards out-groups  *J Psychol.*, 1948, 25, 437–442

Mills, T M  Power relations in three-person groups  *Amer sociol Rev*, 1953, 18, 351–357

Mintz, A  Non-adaptive group behavior  *J abnorm soc Psychol*, 1951, 46, 150–159

Moreno, J L  *Who shall survive?*  Washington, D C  *Nervous and Mental Disease Monogr*, No 58, 1934

Mouton, Jane S, R R Blake, and J A Olmstead  The relationship between frequency of yielding and disclosure of personal identity  *J Pers*, 1956, 24, 339–347

Muldoon, J F  The concentration of liked and disliked members in groups and the relationship of the concentrations to group cohesiveness  *Sociometry*, 1955, 18, 73–81

Murray, H A  The effect of fear upon estimates of maliciousness of other personalities  *J soc Psychol*, 1933, 4, 310–329

———  *Explorations in personality*  New York  Oxford University Press, 1938

Nash, D J, and A W Wolfe  The stranger in laboratory culture  *Amer sociol Rev*, 1957, 22, 400–405.

Newcomb, T M  *Personality and social change*  New York  Dryden, 1943.
——— Autistic hostility and social reality  *Hum Relat*, 1947, 1, 69–86
——— *Social psychology*  New York·  Dryden, 1950
——— An approach to the study of communicative acts  *Psychol Rev*, 1953, 60, 393–404
——— The prediction of interpersonal attraction  *Amer Psychologist,* 1956, 11, 575–586
Osborn, A F.  *Applied imagination*  New York  Scribner, 1957
Osgood, C E , and P H Tannenbaum  The principle of congruity in the prediction of attitude change  *Psychol Rev*, 1955, 62, 42–55
Parsons, T.  *Essays in sociological theory*  Glencoe, Ill  Free Press, 1949.
Pastore, N  The role of arbitrariness in the frustration-aggression hypothesis  *J abnorm soc Psychol*, 1952, 47, 728–731
Pepitone, A.  Motivational effects in social perception  *Hum Relat*, 1950, 3, 57–76
———, and G. Reichling  Group cohesiveness and the expression of hostility.  *Hum Relat*, 1955, 8, 327–338
Perlmutter, H V , and Germaine de Montmollin  Group learning of nonsense syllables  *J abnorm soc Psychol*, 1952, 47, 762–769
Pessin, J  The comparative effects of social and mechanical stimulation on memorizing.  *Amer J Psychol*, 1933, 45, 263–270
Philp, Alice J  Strangers and friends as competitors and cooperators  *J genet Psychol*, 1940, 57, 249–258
Polansky, N , and J Kounin.  Clients' reactions to initial interviews  *Hum Relat*, 1956, 9, 237–264
Potter, S  *The theory and practice of gamesmanship*  New York  Holt, 1948
——— *One-upmanship*  New York  Holt, 1951
Powell, R M  Sociometric analysis of informal groups—their structure and function in two contrasting communities  *Sociometry*, 1952, 15, 367–399
Rado, S  Emergency behavior, with an introduction to the dynamics of conscience  In P M Hoch and J Zubin (Eds ), *Anxiety*  New York  Grune and Stratton, 1950  Pp 150–175
Raven, B H , and J Rietsema  The effects of varied clarity of group goal and group path upon the individual and his relation to his group  *Hum Relat*, 1957, 10, 29–46
Riley, Matilda, R Cohn, J Toby, and J W Riley  Interpersonal orientations in small groups  A consideration of the questionnaire approach  *Amer sociol Rev*, 1954, 19, 715–724
Robinson, D , and Sylvia Rohde  Two experiments with an anti-Semitism poll  *J abnorm soc Psychol*, 1946, 41, 136–144
Rommetveit, R  *Social norms and roles*  Minneapolis  University of Minnesota Press, 1954
Rosenberg, S , and J Curtiss  The effect of stuttering on the behavior of the listener  *J abnorm soc. Psychol*, 1954, 49, 355–361.
Rosenthal, D , and C N Cofer  The effect on group performance of an indifferent and neglectful attitude shown by one group member  *J exp Psychol*, 1948, 38, 568–577
Ross, E A.  *Social psychology*  New York  Macmillan, 1908
——— *Principles of sociology*  New York  Century, 1921

Sarbin, T A   Role theory   In G Lindzey (Ed )   *Handbook of social psychology*  Cambridge  Mass  Addison-Wesley, 1954  Pp 223–258

Schachter, S   Deviation, rejection and communication   *J abnorm soc. Psychol*,  1951, 46, 190–207.

———, N Ellertson, Dorothy McBride, and Doris Gregory   An experimental study of cohesiveness and productivity.   *Hum. Relat*, 1951, 4, 229–238

Schanck, R L   A study of a community and its groups and institutions conceived of as behavior of individuals   *Psychol Monogr*, 1932, 43, No 2 (Whole No 195)

Schein, E H   The Chinese indoctrination program for prisoners of war   *Psychiatry*, 1956, 19, 149–172.

Scott, W H., J A Banks, A H Halsey, and T Lupton   *Technical change and industrial relations*   Liverpool  Liverpool University Press, 1956.

Sears. R R.   A theoretical framework for personality and social behavior   *Amer Psychologist*, 1951, 6, 476–483

Seashore, S E.   *Group cohesiveness in the industrial work group*   Ann Arbor, Mich  University of Michigan, Survey Research Center, Institute for Social Research, 1954

Sewall, Mabel   Two studies in sibling rivalry  I  Some causes of jealousy in young children   *Smith College Stud in Soc Work*, 1930, 1, 6–22

Shaw, Marjorie E   A comparison of individuals and small groups in the rational solution of complex problems   *Amer J Psychol*, 1932, 44, 491–504

Shaw, M E   Some effects of unequal distribution of information upon group performance in various communication nets   *J abnorm soc Psychol*, 1954, 49, 547–553

———, and J C Gilchrist   Repetitive task failure and sociometric choice   *J abnorm soc Psychol*, 1955 50, 29–32

Sherif, M   *The psychology of social norms*   New York  Harper, 1936

———  A preliminary study of inter-group relations   In J H Rohrer and M Sherif (Eds.), *Social psychology at the crossroads*   New York  Harper, 1951  Pp 388–424

———, and Carolyn W Sherif   *An outline of social psychology*   New York  Harper, 1956

Sidowski, J B, L B Wyckoff, and L Tabory   The influence of reinforcement and punishment in a minimal social situation   *J. abnorm soc Psychol*, 1956 52, 115–119

Siegel, P S, and J J. Brantley   The relationship of emotionality to the consummatory response of eating   *J exp Psychol*, 1951, 42, 304–306

Simmel, G   The number of members as determining the sociological form of the group   (Translated by A W Small )   *Amer J Sociol*, 1902, 8, 1–46 and 158–196

———   The social role of the stranger   In E A Schuler, D L Gibson, Maude L Fiero, and W. B Brookover (Eds ), *Outside readings in sociology*   New York Crowell, 1953   Pp 142–146

Simpson, G E, and J M Yinger   *Racial and cultural minorities  An analysis of prejudice and discrimination*   New York  Harper, 1953

Skinner, B F   *Science and human behavior*   New York  Macmillan, 1953

Smalley, Ruth E.   Two studies in sibling rivalry  II  The influence of differences in age, sex, and intelligence in determining the attitudes of siblings toward each other   *Smith College Stud in Soc Work*, 1930, 1, 23–40

Smith, K R Intermittent loud noise and mental performance *Science,* 1951, 114, 132–133

Smock, C D The relationship between test anxiety, "threat expectancy," and recognition thresholds for words *J Pers,* 1956, 25, 191–201

Solomon, L The influence of some types of power relationships and motivational treatments upon the development of inter-personal trust New York Research Center for Human Relations, New York University, January 1957

South, E B Some psychological aspects of committee work *J appl Psychol,* 1927, 11, 348–368

Spector, A J Expectations, fulfillment, and morale. *J abnorm soc Psychol,* 1956, 52, 51–56.

Stephan, F F, and E G Mishler The distribution of participation in small groups An exponential approximation *Amer sociol Rev,* 1952, 17, 598–608

Stern, E, and Suzanne Keller Spontaneous group reference in France *Pub Opin Quart,* 1953, 17, 208–217

Stouffer, S A An analysis of conflicting social norms *Amer sociol Rev,* 1949, 14, 707–717

———, E. A Suchman, L C DeVinney, Shirley A Star, and R. M. Williams. *The American soldier* Vol I *Adjustment during army life* Princeton Princeton University Press, 1949

Strickland, L H Surveillance and trust. *J Pers,* 1958, 26, 200–215

Sullivan, H S *The interpersonal theory of psychiatry* New York W W Norton, 1953

Sutherland, J D, and Isobel E Menzies. Two industrial projects *J soc Issues,* 1947, 3, No 2, 51–58

Tagiuri, R Relational analysis An extension of sociometric method with emphasis upon social perception *Sociometry,* 1952, 15, 91–104

Talland, G The assessment of group opinion by leaders and their influence on its formation *J abnorm soc Psychol,* 1954, 49, 431–434

Taylor, D W, P C Berry. and C. H Block Does group participation when using brainstorming facilitate or inhibit creative thinking? *Admin Sci Quart,* 1958, 3, 23–47

Taylor, D W, and W L Faust Twenty questions Efficiency in problem solving as a function of size of group *J exp Psychol,* 1952, 44, 360–368

Thibaut, J W An experimental study of the cohesiveness of underprivileged groups *Hum Relat,* 1950, 3, 251–278

———, and J Coules The role of communication in the reduction of interpersonal hostility *J abnorm soc Psychol,* 1952, 47, 770–777

Thibaut, J W, and H W Riecken Authoritarianism status, and the communication of aggression *Hum Relat,* 1955a, 8 95–120

———. Some determinants and consequences of the perception of social causality *J Pers,* 1955b, 24, 113–133

Thibaut, J W, and L Strickland Psychological set and social conformity *J Pers,* 1956, 25, 115–129

Thompson, Laura *Personality and government* Mexico, D F Ediciones del Instituto indigenista interamericano, 1951.

Thorndike, R L The effect of discussion upon the correctness of group decisions, when the factor of majority influence is allowed for *J. soc Psychol,* 1938a, 9, 343–362

——— On what type of task will a group do well? *J abnorm soc Psychol,* 1938b, 33, 409–413

Thornton, G R   The effect of wearing glasses upon judgments of personality traits of persons seen briefly. *J appl Psychol*, 1944, 28, 203–207

Timmons, W M   Can the product superiority of discussors be attributed to averaging or majority influences? *J soc Psychol*, 1942, 15, 23–32

Verplanck, W. S   The control of the content of conversation  Reinforcement of statements of opinion  *J abnorm soc Psychol*, 1955, 51, 668–676

Vinacke, W E, and A Arkoff   An experimental study of coalitions in the triad  *Amer sociol Rev*, 1957, 22, 406–414

Vreeland, F M   Social relations in the college fraternity. *Sociometry*, 1942, 5, 151–162.

Waller, W W, and R Hill   *The family, a dynamic interpretation*   New York  Dryden Press, 1951.

Whyte, W F.   *Street corner society  The social structure of an Italian slum*   Chicago  University of Chicago Press, 1943.

———   The social structure of the restaurant   *Amer J Sociol*, 1949, 54, 302–310

Wiehe, F   The behavior of the child in strange fields   In K Lewin, *A dynamic theory of personality*   New York  McGraw-Hill, 1935   Pp 261–264

Wilensky, H L   *Intellectuals in labor unions*   Glencoe, Ill   The Free Press, 1956

Willerman, B   Group decision and request as means of changing food habits. Washington  Committee on Food Habits, National Research Council, April 1943

Williams, R. M., Jr, and others   *Friendship and social values in a suburban community*   Eugene, Oreg   University of Oregon, 1956

Winch, R. F   *The modern family*   New York  Holt, 1952

———   The theory of complementary needs in mate-selection  A test of one kind of complementariness   *Amer sociol Rev*, 1955a, 20, 52–56

———   The theory of complementary needs in mate-selection  Final results on the test of the general hypothesis   *Amer sociol Rev*, 1955b, 20, 552–555

———, T Ktsanes, and Virginia Ktsanes   The theory of complementary needs in mate-selection  An analytic and descriptive study   *Amer sociol Rev*, 1954, 19, 241–249.

Wispe, L G, and K E Lloyd   Some situational and psychological determinants of the desire for structured interpersonal relations. *J. abnorm. soc Psychol*, 1955, 51, 57–60

Wood, H G   An analysis of social sensitivity. Unpublished doctoral dissertation, Yale University, 1948

Wright, H F   The influence of barriers upon strength of motivation   *Contr psychol. Theor.*, 1937, 1, No 3, 74–75

Wright, M E   The influence of frustration upon social relations of young children   *Charact Pers*, 1943, 12, 111–122

Young, K  *Social psychology*   New York  Crofts, 1944

Zelditch, M   Role differentiation in the nuclear family  A comparative study. In T Parsons, R F Bales, and others, *Family, socialization, and interaction process*   Glencoe, Ill   Free Press, 1955   Pp 307–351

Ziller, R C   Scales of judgement  A determinant of the accuracy of group decisions   *Hum Relat*, 1955, 8, 153–165

Zillig, Maria   Einstellung und Aussage   *Z Psychol*, 1928, 106, 58–106.

# *Name Index*

# Subject Index